# CAPITAL AND THE COMMON GOOD

# CAPITAL AND THE COMMON GOOD

*How Innovative Finance Is Tackling the
World's Most Urgent Problems*

## GEORGIA LEVENSON KEOHANE

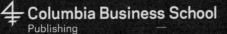
Columbia Business School
Publishing

Columbia University Press
*Publishers Since 1893*
New York    Chichester, West Sussex
cup.columbia.edu

Library of Congress Cataloging-in-Publication Data
Names: Keohane, Georgia Levenson, author.
Title: Capital and the common good : how innovative finance is tackling
the world's most urgent problems / Georgia Keohane.
Description: New York : Columbia University Press, [2016] | Series: Columbia
business school publishing | Includes bibliographical references and index.
Identifiers: LCCN 2016002655 | ISBN 9780231178020 (cloth : alk. paper)
Subjects: LCSH: Finance—Social aspects. | Finance—Moral and ethical
aspects. | Capitalism—Social aspects. | Social responsibility of
business. | Common good.
Classification: LCC HG101 .K46 2016 | DDC 174/.4—dc23
LC record available at http://lccn.loc.gov/2016002655

Columbia University Press books are printed on permanent
and durable acid-free paper.
Printed in the United States of America

c 10 9 8 7 6 5 4 3 2 1

Cover design: Noah Arlow

To my Family.

# CONTENTS

# ACKNOWLEDGMENTS

As with all things, I owe this book to the unwavering support of family, friends, and colleagues.

*Capital and the Common Good* began life as a series of discussions with Lorenzo Bernasconi and Saadia Madsbjerg at the Rockefeller Foundation, where they lead the organization's path breaking work in innovative finance, including its "zero gap" portfolio. Generous grant support from Rockefeller was only the beginning. I am grateful for all I learned from the innovative finance experts who participated in an early scoping session at the foundation's New York offices, including Concepcion Aisa-Otin, Beth Bafford, Mike Belinsky, Bulbul Gupta, Kirstin Hill, Eileen Neely, Mark Reed, Ommeed Sathe, Jason Scott, Abby Jo Sigal and Beth Sirull, and from those I would later meet at Rockefeller's glorious Bellagio center: Nick Ashburn, Shari Berenbach, David Bresch, Adam Connaker, Christopher "Edge" Egerton-Warburton, Robert Filipp, Brinda Ganguly, Abyd Karmali, Katherine Klein, Ken Lay, John McArthur, Sucharita Mukherjee, Jeremy Rogers, Lakshmi Venkatachalam, Richard Wilcox, David Wood and Glenn Yago. I am especially obliged to scholar and practitioner Jane Hughes, who was a vital thought partner in the formative stages of this project.

I can't think of a better home to have undertaken this work than New America. Thank you to Anne-Marie Slaughter, whose leadership and encouragement were essential to this venture, and to getting the larger Program on Profits and Purpose up and thriving. Thank you, as always, to Jonathan and Jennifer Allan Soros for their support and friendship in this and every endeavor. I'm also very appreciative of the goodwill and wishes of many New Americans, including Mark Schmitt, Reid Cramer, Fuzz Hogan, and Tomicah Tillemann in Washington, DC and Tyler Bugg, and Beth Dembitzer at New America NYC.

Further uptown, Columbia Business School and the Tamer Center for Social Enterprise continue to be a source of inspiration. No doubt I learn more from my students than they do from me. Invaluable, too, has been the counsel of Columbia colleagues Bruce Usher, Ray Fisman, Sandra Navalli, Sara Minard, and Sarah Holloway.

This research would never had made it to book form without the stellar team at Columbia University Press. I am very lucky for Myles Thompson's original vision for this enterprise, and I am indebted to Stephen Wesley for his patience and keen editorial eye. Thank you also to Meredith Howard, Ben Kolstad, and Christian Purdy for their arcane-to-accessible translations and perseverance.

At the intersection of finance and philanthropy, investment and public policy are some of the most creative and committed people I know. Risking numerous omissions, I owe special thanks to those whose time and insights shaped these pages: Frank Altman, Bindu Ananth, Tammi Arnold, Catherine Banat, Andrew Billo, Josh Cohen, Ronald Cohen, Cheryl Dorsey, Michael Faye, Paula Goldman, Jonathan Greenblatt, Matt Greenfield, Emily Gustafsson-Wright, Kippy Joseph, Matt Klein, Surya Kolluri, John MacIntosh, Jude O'Reilley, Edwin Ou, Andi Phillips, Jenn Pryce, Heike Reichelt, Kate Starr, Robynn Steffen, Lenora Suki, Joanna Syroka, Brian Trelstad, Darren Walker, Jeff Walker, Brian Walsh, Flory Wilson, Adam Wolfensohn, and Justine Zinkin. I am particularly grateful to Audrey Choi, Liz Luckett, Tracy Palandjian, and Sonal Shah for their humbling expertise and generous friendship.

Special thanks, as always, to Bill Drayton, Josh Gotbaum, Alan Jones, and Bill Meehan. Thank you, AJ and Noah Gottdiener, for wrestling with early manuscript drafts. Perhaps unwittingly, Bo Cutter's fingerprints are everywhere on this book. In recent years, our formal and informal discussions about the direction of the US and global economy have guided and improved my thinking about the role of innovative finance in tackling difficult problems.

Outside of my day job I am immensely fortunate to serve on the boards of a number of organizations at the forefront of innovative finance, including SeaChange Capital and Acelero Learning. Thank you as well to my fellow trustees on the boards of Bloomingdale Family Head Start Program and the Brearley School. I have learned so much from our work together, and from these organization's leaders, about operational excellence and tireless dedication.

And of course nothing is possible without the love, patience, humor and support of my family. To Nat, who has been by my side for the last twenty-five years, in this, and every other adventure. Thank you, Frances and Eleanor, for inspiring your parents. And thank you to our parents, Nan and Bob Keohane, Isabella Levenson and Bob Shapiro, and Conrad Levenson and Amy Singer, for all your help and wisdom—and for showing us how to get the job done.

Mom, as always, and especially, thank you.

# CAPITAL AND THE COMMON GOOD

# Introduction

## *Innovative Finance and the Visible Hand*

As Christopher ("Edge") Egerton-Warburton pedaled his bike along the Buckingham Palace Road in the summer of 2002, the gears began to shift. A Goldman Sachs banker by trade, Edge considered the investment challenge—and conundrum—posed to him by the Chancellor of the Exchequer: how to help the United Kingdom honor its commitment to the Millennium Development Goals (MDGs), an ambitious and global effort to tackle poverty and its many dimensions—among them hunger, child and maternal health, preventable disease, and education. Why, Edge wondered, if investments in social and economic development were so cost effective, did we fail to make them? And was it possible to borrow from his world of structured finance to turn future government aid pledges into money for social investment today—when it was most valuable?

This thinking would lead to the creation of the International Finance Facility for Immunization (IFFIm) and the world's first vaccine bonds, raising billions of dollars from the capital markets for lifesaving medicines and transforming the way we think about global health and development, public-private partnerships, and the potential of finance to help solve some of the world's most urgent problems.

First imagined that summer, IFFIm was formed when the UK Government, inspired to achieve the MDGs, but daunted by the shortfall of public funds to do so, approached Goldman Sachs for help. A new international financing facility (IFF) was subsequently designed by the UK Treasury and Edge's team at Goldman, who settled on immunization for their first IFF pilot. Vaccines, they believed, offered a particularly high rate of social and economic return and represented a massive market failure. Private capital doesn't automatically flow to cures for diseases that affect the world's poorest because of *demand risk*. Consumers who need the medicines cannot pay enough for pharmaceutical companies to recoup their investment. When it comes to this public need and public good, Adam Smith's invisible hand—the law of supply and demand—doesn't apply. To overcome this market failure, IFFIm turned to some time-tested strategies from the capital markets: bundle together *future* cash flows and promise to repay those to investors in exchange for cash *today*. In this case, that meant front loading, or converting long-term government aid pledges into bonds that could, in turn, fund vaccines. While IFFIm supplies the finance, it has partnered with the Global Alliance for Vaccines and Immunization (GAVI), a nonprofit at the forefront of global health, to take care of the immunizations.

IFFIm's bonds represent an innovative approach to finance—a kind of creative and "visible hand"—that corrects for market failure and provides for the public good, bringing greater resources to bear on some of our most pressing challenges: fighting poverty, improving global health, mitigating climate change, and building strong and inclusive communities.[1] Innovative finance has a particularly critical role to play when our aspirations are deeper than our pockets—when traditional public and philanthropic funding for these investments is not enough. Innovative finance is about *more* and *better*: attracting additional resources for investment in solutions to these problems, as in the case of IFFIm, and improving the efficiency of the funds we already have. In fact, as we will see in the pages that follow, innovative finance is as much about the incentives that encourage sound decision making as it is about money. Innovative finance is not the same as financial innovation; innovative finance intentionally looks to solve problems, to overcome market failure, and to meet the needs of the poor and underserved. What is new is not the engineering, but the application. As in the case of IFFIm, this involves thinking beyond borders, overcoming market failures in one context with solutions from another. This adaptive approach is a hallmark of innovative finance; capital for the common good in the twenty-first century.

∽

By any historical measure, we live in an era of remarkable progress. The first decades of this new century have seen unprecedented improvements in our collective well-being—most notably, advances against extreme poverty, gains in infant and maternal health, inroads against preventable diseases like malaria and tuberculosis,[2] and strides in what the development field calls *financial inclusion*—a greater number of people with access to basic banking and financial services. Although these advances tend to be concentrated—tremendous economic growth in places like India, Brazil, and China accounts for much of the aggregate and global reduction in poverty—substantial development benefits are taking hold in places long gripped by privation. For example, Africa's GDP has grown 5 percent per year over the last decade, across an increasingly diverse set of countries and industries.

Although economic growth underpins much of the improvement in welfare, it is important to remember that markets alone, guided by the so-called invisible hand, do not ineluctably deliver greater prosperity.[3] Markets are constructs, shaped by laws and customs. And when markets fail to produce a set of broad-based and sustainable public goods, we need a more visible hand: concerted efforts by governments, multilateral agencies, philanthropies, and, increasingly, socially minded investors to meet needs and solve problems. This does not necessarily mean direct government regulation or intervention. Often, as we will see, it takes the form of a new kind of partnership finance, of which IFFIm is a signature example. In this book, we will examine how creative configurations of nonprofit, commercial, and public-sector entities come together to harness market forces in the face of market failure. When these partnerships develop new or improved ways to pay for investments in public goods and social and economic development, we call it *innovative finance*.

The need for this kind of work across the public and private sectors has never been greater. Despite our progress, disease and poverty persist in many quarters, exacerbated by climate change and conflict: nearly 95 percent of the world's poorest live in places that are either environmentally or politically fragile, or both.[4] Many are forced to seek sanctuary in other countries, and half of the 60 million refugees in the world today are children. As these challenges compound one another, governments often lack the resources or capacity to manage short-term crises or to make longer-term investments in prevention and resilience. The human toll is staggering, and the cost to societies is evident in any number of ways, including lagging GDP growth. Poverty and environmental degradation remain the enemies of thriving societies, thwarting economic development and broad-based prosperity.

2015 marked an important milestone in government efforts to grapple with some of these challenges. The United Nations (UN) outlined its Sustainable Development Goals (SDGs), seventeen aspirations focused on ending extreme poverty and promoting shared economic well-being, social development, and environmental protection by 2030. These global goals build on the Millennium Development Goals, put forward at the beginning of the twenty-first century, but are even more ambitious.[5] In December 2015, in Paris at COP21, the countries of the world agreed for the first time to a global framework to reduce climate change. Yet momentum is not money. Our hopes for global, inclusive and sustainable economic development require significant investment, whether they are formally embedded in these multilateral commitments or comprise the even broader set of development objectives articulated by all countries around the world. For reference, the UN estimates that it would cost $3.9 trillion a year to achieve the SDGs; current levels of public and private funding cover only $1.4 trillion. Whether or not these particular goals and projections are the right ones, it is clear that government funds, in the form of domestic spending and foreign development assistance, aren't enough. Philanthropy, too, has an important role to play in the development agenda but represents only a small slice of overall funding. Total charitable giving in the United States is approximately $350 billion a year. The hope is that innovative finance can close the gap.

This shortfall was addressed most recently at the Third International Conference on Financing for Development in July 2015 in Addis Ababa, Ethiopia, but it has bedeviled the international community for decades.[6] In fact, the term *innovative finance* was first used in 2002 when it was apparent public funds were inadequate to achieve the Millennium Development Goals. The hope was that it would be possible to identify new sources of funds, particularly from the private sector, to bear on public challenges like climate change and global health—in the way partnerships like IFFIm would come to exemplify. In the years since, the term has come to focus both on increasing the funds available—from existing public and new private sources—and on improving the efficiency of these investments.[7]

We take this more expansive view: in the face of market failure, innovative finance can harness new sources of capital and improve the efficiency of existing funds to underwrite critical needs. In this book, we examine a number of recent visible hand experiments to better understand what works, what doesn't, and why. The intent is to illuminate the lessons of some of these new tools, providing a road map that allows us to replicate, adapt, or scale the successes; develop the next generation of innovative financing mechanisms; and inspire a new cadre of innovators. Over the long term, we hope to improve the ways finance can help achieve lasting change and build healthy, inclusive, stable, and resilient communities around the world.

## Building on the Past to Finance the Future

The notion that economic prosperity, social welfare, and political stability are mutually reinforcing is hardly new. The original Bretton Woods institutions—including the World Bank and the International Monetary Fund (IMF)—were founded in the last century on the premise that peace and cooperation would require the reconstruction of economies ravaged by war—most notably, Germany and Japan. In addition to these original entities (later expanded to include the International Development Association and the International Finance Corporation), a system of regional development finance institutions emerged to foster development in emerging economies across the globe.[8] At the sovereign level, development finance institutions (DFIs) such as the UK's CDC Group (the world's oldest DFI), Germany's KfW (formed in 1948 as part of the Marshall Plan), and the United States' Overseas Private Investment Corporation (founded in 1971 to mobilize private capital to address global development challenges), enlist the basic tools of finance—below-market-rate (concessionary) and market-rate loans, grants, guarantees, insurance, and equity investment—to bolster economic growth. China's recent proposal for a $100 billion, fifty-seven-member Asian Infrastructure Investment Bank, signaling substantial shifts in the geopolitical and economic landscape, is the latest incarnation of these kinds of DFIs.

### Evolutions in Development Assistance

Of course, not all money flows through development finance institutions. Bilateral development assistance agencies use grants and aid—money that does not need to be repaid—to fight poverty, end human suffering, and promote political stability. For decades, these institutions—including the U.S. Agency for International Development (USAID), the UK Department for International Development (DFID), and, more recently, the Norwegian

Agency for Development Cooperation (NORAD), Swedish International Development Cooperation Agency (SIDA), and Canadian International Development Agency (CIDA)—have been responsible for much of what we think of as international development through their official development assistance (ODA) budgets. In 2014, total ODA was approximately $135 billion, while the major multilateral development banks originated approximately $100 billion in new loans. It is worth noting that emergency humanitarian assistance, which will also be discussed in this book, differs, at least historically, from ODA. When countries around the globe are hit by disaster—either natural or man-made—the UN solicits donor support through an appeals process and coordinates relief through agencies like the World Food Program and the Office of the High Commissioner for Refugees. However, we will see that, as humanitarian emergencies become more protracted, the objectives of crisis response and long-term development assistance, both requiring investments in resilience, begin to fuse. So, too, perhaps, should the ways in which we finance them.

The debate about the appropriate size, scope, and efficacy of ODA has been raging for decades. Since the 1970s, the world's wealthiest countries have agreed, at least in principle, that an ODA commitment of 0.7 percent of GNP (generating hundreds of billions of additional dollars) could go a long way toward meeting poor countries' development needs.[9] Although there have been notable upticks from some countries in recent years—2013 and 2014 were record years, with $135 billion in aggregate ODA—most countries fall short of the 0.7 percent goal. (As the largest economy, the United States gives the most development assistance, even if its percentages are low.) Given long-term domestic fiscal constraints, wealthier countries are unlikely to increase their ODA budgets anytime soon. And even if they came closer to the 0.7 percent target, ODA would still fail to close the funding gap for our global development needs.

Whereas the dollar amounts of ODA haven't changed radically, the philosophy shaping how this money is spent has. The underpinnings of these shifts are many: a smaller appetite for overseas engagement generally and for generous aid budgets in particular; a concern about the ways in which aid dollars are used on the ground—the perception and reality that development assistance is often lost to mismanagement or corruption and does not reach the intended beneficiaries; a growing conviction that market models bring a discipline, efficiency, and accountability to development that traditional grants lack; and a recognition that developing countries want and need more autonomy in shaping their own development needs and destinies. Accordingly, the United States, among other countries, has in recent years embraced more market-based approaches to development assistance. These involve conditional aid payments made in exchange for certain activities or after these activities are undertaken and increased use of investments rather than just grants.[10] In short, ODA has come to look and feel more like development finance. As we will explore, there is a growing affection for market models in economic development within wealthier countries, too. In the United States, for example, a robust community-development finance industry—a mix of public credit and private dollars—has grown up to fund local enterprises, real estate, and affordable housing in communities across the country.

### The Innovative Finance Imperative

Whether we seek to close the funding gap or to encourage more efficient delivery, we need new sources of capital to support our development objectives. This means more finance. So what makes that finance innovative?

Finance is not new. Finance's most basic product, money, appeared as early as 9000 B.C.E. in the form of bartered livestock. The first metal coins date to the seventh century B.C.E., and the Chinese invented paper currency in the ninth century C.E. Some of the most basic functions of finance— facilitating exchange, reducing risk, and allowing for *intertemporal transfer*, in which people borrow, in essence, from their future selves—are equally ancient practices that, in turn, have given rise to some useful instruments, like equity, debt, and the first derivatives. A mortgage, for example, represents the power of *front loading*—the ability to bring forward from the future resources we need today, allowing us to pay back our debts in small, manageable increments over time and match assets and liabilities, making possible all kinds of investments and opportunities that would not be available otherwise. Mortgage payments lent themselves to some of the first securitizations—poolings of multiple and diverse revenue streams into one security—which can be used to raise more investment from the capital markets, as in the case of IFFIm. What makes the finance *innovative* is not so much the tools per se—innovative finance is not financial innovation— as it is the new application.

The concept, and the power, of markets, is also age old. Markets do a good job matching supply and demand for a large array of goods and services on which economies are built and thrive. However, markets do not inevitably provide for all of our needs, and when they do not, governments, particularly in developed countries, have stepped in to supply necessary goods and services. Today, however, those public resources are no longer adequate.

## Market Failure and Market Solutions

What happens when markets fail to provide optimal outcomes? Let's consider the case of air pollution, a classic market failure, in which the costs of the activity are not borne by those responsible. An individual can enjoy a cigarette, unaware or unconcerned that secondhand smoke is bothersome and hazardous. Similarly, driving may be the most convenient form of transportation for a family, but they pay only for gas and car maintenance of their own vehicle, not for their contribution to local smog. A factory may belch pollution into the sky, affecting the quality of life downwind and miles away, even across national borders. Carbon dioxide emitted in one location contributes to global climate change, a rise in temperatures that may well be cataclysmic for us all.[11] In each of these instances, the market has failed to assign the cost, or price, of pollution to the polluters. As we will see in chapter 1, this kind of *negative externality* is sometimes referred to as a "tragedy of the commons." To correct this market failure, we need better cost-sharing to align individual incentives with collective well-being.

Another way to think of externalities is in terms of public goods, like clean air. These are essentially *positive* externalities: benefits people enjoy for which they have not paid. National defense is the textbook example of a public good—all citizens living in a country benefit, and the security enjoyed by one does not diminish or detract from the security enjoyed by others—but they can take many other forms. Public goods are not fixed; we can and do decide what they should be. Public health and other basic human needs, from financial security to large-scale infrastructure investment, are public goods.

In the case of negative externalities and public goods, resources do not flow in ways that are socially or economically optimal. The capital markets, left to their own devices, overinvest in activities with negative consequences—such as carbon-intensive development that leads to global warming—and underinvest in activities with great societal benefits—such as vaccines or better nutrition for the poor, financial services to ensure broad economic participation, and disaster management.

Throughout this book we will see how innovative finance can help address market failure: how policy makers, investors, philanthropists, development banks, financial institutions, and their nonprofit allies can shape incentives so investment flows to solve problems. Sometimes this means overcoming market failure by alleviating risk for investment in the public good or by ensuring that the costs of negative externalities are priced. Often it means introducing a financing instrument or approach to a new market. Recall that IFFIm issued a vaccine bond, bundling and front loading the cash flows of future government aid pledges to sell to investors, and used the proceeds to fund GAVI's vaccination work. There the innovation comes from the application of financial instruments—those typically used for things like corporate debt or mortgages—to public health. Of course, market solutions are not always sufficient. Often we also need regulation, or government or philanthropic grant support. But when markets can be harnessed productively and responsibly, there is a role to play for innovative finance. In the coming pages, we will see the visible hand at work tackling some of the world's most intractable problems by creatively financing climate change mitigation, medicines for the poor, disaster response and relief, access to capital for unbanked households and small businesses, and the growth of resilient and inclusive communities.

## The Larger Innovation Landscape: Technology and Ideas

Innovative finance does not occur in a vacuum. It develops in tandem or interplay with shifts and breakthroughs in the larger world—particularly innovations in technology and in ideas or changing norms or values. Often a combination of transformative ideas, technology, and finance can create a perfect storm—a financial crisis, perhaps—but also a dramatic advance in how we address persistent social or environmental problems.

### The Role of Technology

There are moments when technological innovation changes the economics of markets sufficiently to disrupt and transform industries. We have seen this in media, communications, and medicine—we have seen it, too, in finance. Economist and former Federal Reserve Chair Paul Volcker famously said that the only worthwhile financial innovation was the ATM. Indeed, these machines have changed the economics of consumer finance, making banking services available to new groups of people and in new places. But we disagree with Volcker.

As we will explore in this book, Internet and mobile technologies have allowed not only for improved communication but also for the massive transformation of financial services. When mobile devices serve as digital wallets, people can store and transfer money and make and receive payments for everything from remittances to utility bills to school fees. Digital payments have, in turn, translated into a host of new financial product possibilities, including pay-as-you-go consumer finance models for solar energy, potable water, health insurance, and discounted fares on public transportation. In other ways, data mining (using information gleaned from payments) improves predictive analytics for things like credit scoring and other risk assessments, reducing transaction costs and making certain kinds of loans and insurance possible. The combination of technologies, like mobile with satellite imagery, has created the possibility for weather and agricultural insurance that was once too expensive to provide or purchase.

More broadly, online platforms can democratize finance, increasing participation in the financial system by improving access to capital for borrowers and opportunities for potential investors. What began as peer-to-peer finance, or crowdfunding, has evolved into a larger marketplace lending industry. Banks have begun to respond to *disintermediation* (borrowers and lenders connecting without banks and their fees) by offering online lending themselves. The technologies underpinning marketplace lending are reshaping the financial services sector, which is an entire book in itself. We are particularly concerned with innovation, in either technology or finance, that meets the needs of the poor and overcomes the market failures that prevented those needs from being met in the first place. That distinction between financial innovation—an array of new products and services, many created by technological disruption—and innovative finance—a way to harness market forces explicitly and intentionally to address social or environmental challenges—is a defining theme of this book.

Technology is only a starting point. Success in innovative finance often requires a good FITT—the combination of finance, technology, and trust. This involves the personal and human interactions that make new products or services seem less complicated, daunting, or suspect. We observe this kind of FITT in numerous sectors.

### Changing Ideas, Attitudes, and Norms

In finance, as in technology, we typically think of intellectual innovation as scientific breakthrough: a better method for determining present value; a more sophisticated pricing model; the quants behind hedge fund investments. However, when it comes to innovative finance, some of the most transformational ideas in recent years are those related to changing attitudes and values—resulting in a more normative view of the world and the role that finance can and should play in solving our most entrenched problems.

First, as we have seen, there has been a distinct embrace of market models in the development community. Some of this is driven by economic necessity and fiscal realities. Even before the Great Recession, developed countries like the United States had limited interest in overseas engagement or burgeoning aid budgets. Scarce are the resources or political will to invest sufficiently in social or physical infrastructure at home, much less abroad.

Yet the evolution from aid to investment isn't simply about doing more with less. The persistence of global poverty, despite decades and billions of dollars devoted to development assistance, raises legitimate concerns about how resources are spent on the ground. Throughout this book we will see new finance models that help improve what economists call *agency*, aligning incentives in ways that encourage people—individuals and government leaders—to make decisions that both are in their own self-interest and benefit the society. Often this involves new forms of ownership. In the case of companies, private equity investors require managers of their portfolio companies to have significant ownership stakes. Similarly, publicly traded firms often compensate executives with stock. The idea is that owning something changes behavior. (You don't wash a rental car, the saying goes.) We will see innovations in aid and investment fashioned on these principles: allowances that make pollution a tradable asset and that price greenhouse gases so as to discourage their consumption and spur investment in alternative energy; pay-for-success aid, debt relief, insurance, and investment, all conditioned on demonstrated outcomes, whether they are in health interventions, disaster planning, or reduced recidivism.

Often the incentives in these innovative finance approaches improve cost-benefit analysis and motivate early intervention. Providing vaccines is cheaper than treating full-blown disease, containing an outbreak costs less than combating an epidemic, job training beats incarceration, and abating pollution is much more manageable than the catastrophic effects of climate change. Inaction on any of these can be devastatingly expensive. An ounce of prevention is worth a pound of cure.

Improved decision making and agency is not simply about appeasing the governance concerns of donors and investors. Ownership is also about process. For years, countries in both the Global North and the Global South (i.e., rich and poor alike) have recognized the importance of autonomy in development—of emerging economies owning their own development destinies by identifying, designing, and, where possible, financing their own needs. Many of the innovative finance successes we examine, from climate change to global health and financial inclusion, are intended to give countries and local communities a greater voice in the development process. The locus of control in development—where decisions are made and resources come from—is also evolving amidst tectonic shifts in the geopolitical landscape. The rise of oil-rich countries on the Persian Gulf and the growing economic power of countries like Brazil, India, and China mean that developing countries are increasingly fueling their own, and each other's, growth.

Although these geopolitical realignments and uncertainties may seem daunting, they have also helped to move issues of global economic development beyond the world of traditional policy makers. Innovative finance has succeeded, and will continue to do so, because of the larger community of people and organizations that are literally invested in global prosperity. Perhaps the most pronounced shift in recent years has been the emergence of social or sustainable finance and economics, a fusion of value and values in the larger marketplace of investors, business leaders, and consumers who recognize their stake in our collective well-being. From entrepreneurial start-ups to large firms, a growing belief that companies have a central and positive role to play in social benefit and social change drives operational decision making.[12] This is true whether the core business is defined by social or environmental objectives or the managers embrace rigorous environmental, social, and governance (ESG) measures across a broad range of activities, understanding that long-term financial performance is linked to sustainable business practices. Often these decisions are driven by changes in firms' risk and cost-benefit analyses, perhaps based on a new valuation of the benefits of a healthy and prosperous customer base, of a thriving and satisfied workforce, or of long-term risks like climate change. So, too, are the new market dynamics driven by consumers eager to pay for goods and services manufactured or sourced responsibly, in ways they see as consistent with their personal values. When these consumers are investors, financial service firms respond with *impact* investment products and opportunities to satisfy this demand.[13] Although there are competing definitions as to just what constitutes *impact investing*—including the nature of the returns and the size and scale of the overall market—there is no doubt that a large and profound movement is gaining momentum and shaping the investment landscape. *Impact investing* is not synonymous with the larger innovative finance field, but it is an important piece of it.

## Innovative Finance Versus Financial Innovation: Can Finance Do Good?

Needless to say, finance is not a panacea for the world's problems. Most of the challenges we explore in these chapters have as much to do with political constraints as they do with market failure. And there are more than a few who are skeptical of the promise of finance to do good. This distrust, magnified by the catastrophic financial crisis of the last decade, is not just about finance's general fallibility. It is trained, in particular, on what economist and Nobel laureate Paul Krugman has called "the destructive creativity" of derivatives and other so-called financial innovations.[14] Indeed, the collapse of the market for mortgage-backed securities, credit default swaps, and other derivatives and structured investment vehicles led to a massive cataclysm in other markets. Even though subprime mortgages might have initially made credit (and homeownership) more widely available, the shocks and recession they produced ultimately diminished the availability of credit for households and small businesses. The question is whether inherent in this kind of finance is a kind of structural risk that necessarily brings implosion, or whether the kinds of failures we saw in the financial crisis were related to other shortcomings—a host of information and incentive problems. We explore many of these broader issues in the book and ask whether and when it is possible to use finance to achieve valuable social outcomes.

These concerns, which echo Volcker's musing on ATMs, again underscore the difference between financial innovation—engineering—and innovative finance—an approach that looks to solve problems, overcome market and political failure, and meet the needs of the poor with products and services that improve lives. Virtual currencies, marketplace lending, speed trading, subprime mortgages, and payday lending are all financial innovation. Microagriculture insurance for poor farmers and pay-as-you-go financing—for off-grid solar electricity in Kenya and for discounted MetroCards in New York City—are innovative finance.

Unfortunately, there is little middle ground between a suspicion of finance on the one hand—a concern that our economy and society have succumbed to "financialization"[15]—and market fundamentalism on the other. The truth, of course, lies in between: financial solutions to entrenched problems have a place alongside enlightened oversight to guard against their pitfalls. In some cases of market failure, market solutions and innovative finance can be harnessed to achieve larger social goals.

This book is not an apologia nor an attempt to redeem finance's good name. Rather, it is an examination of a small slice of our global development agenda through a select few case studies that illuminate important lessons, themes, tensions, and truths about what happens when finance is pressed into service for the greater good. I hope that it will inspire further creativity in solving some of our world's most challenging problems.

## An Innovative Finance Road Map

### Climate Change

This book begins with climate change because of the urgency of the problem and the inherent interconnection between global warming and every other social and economic challenge we address. Furthermore, the natural resources field is well developed when it comes to illustrating issues of market failure, public goods, and externalities and translating these concepts into innovative and effective market-based solutions, thus laying the groundwork for each subsequent chapter. We begin by investigating the power of price signals when it comes to pollution and the architecture and power of tradable emission schemes. We then examine two examples of innovation in climate finance that have evolved in spite of the delay in the development of a global market for carbon. Reduction in Emissions from Deforestation and Forest Degradation (REDD) shows the potential of pay-for-success partnerships to reduce the destruction of rain forests and carbon emissions, though it is still in need of scale. In contrast, green bonds have experienced tremendous growth but lack any tight *green* definitions, a quantity-versus-quality conundrum we revisit throughout the book.

### Health

The second chapter explores a broad range of innovations that have emerged in recent years to improve financing for global health objectives. We examine various approaches, including micro levies like UNITAID and UNITLIFE; an array of *market-shaping* initiatives like prizes and challenges and GAVI's advanced market commitments; a variety of innovations related to debt, including loan forgiveness and debt swaps administered through the Global Fund, the Pledge Guarantee for Health, and IFFIm's vaccine bonds; and equity investments—including *impact investment* vehicles like the Global Health Investment Fund—that blend philanthropic and commercial capital for drug research and development and for other health interventions.

### Financial Inclusion and Access to Capital

In the third chapter, we'll see why access to capital and financial services is a vital component of the development agenda: a way for families to climb out of poverty and for small- and medium-sized enterprises (SMEs) to provide goods, services, and employment in regions of the world that are lacking. Accordingly, we trace the evolution of microfinance from its nonprofit origins to a fully commercialized industry and from a field built primarily around credit to one that has begun to offer a wider variety of financial services, including savings and insurance. We use IFMR Trust, an Indian microfinance company, to illustrate these innovations.

We also probe the technology-finance nexus that is mobile money; the growth in payments and new consumer finance tools that in turn encourage greater investment in other goods and services for the poor—from solar electricity to e-books. We investigate whether and how innovative finance can meet the needs of the particularly underserved, including women and farmers. Finally, we spotlight a handful of initiatives that are strengthening the capacity of local capital markets to invest in their own SMEs: MFX, for example, provides derivatives and other hedging strategies to emerging-market finance institutions; the African Loan Currency Bond Fund allows African SMEs to borrow and issue bonds in their own currencies; and the Ascending Markets Financial Guarantee Corporation insures bond issuances in local currency.

### Disaster Response, Relief, and Rebuilding

Our investigation into financing for disasters in chapter 4 begins where financial inclusion leaves off: in the realm of insurance. We distinguish between natural and man-made disasters, recognizing that they are connected and related to the issues addressed in previous chapters—climate change, health, and poverty and economic inclusion. We consider how extreme weather events can be modeled and priced and their risks *transferred*. At the macro level, we see how the African Risk Capacity (ARC) pools risk across countries to provide insurance against drought and how this innovative finance mechanism solves a number of governance challenges. We also explore how ARC and others use catastrophe bonds to unlock more private capital to insure against a range of hazards like hurricanes and epidemics. A pressing question in development is whether and how this kind of insurance, and the security it provides, can be brought to the household level. To answer, we delve into a number of innovative microinsurance case studies.

This chapter also takes a hard look at complex man-made disasters—thornier in some ways than natural disasters because they do not readily lend themselves to risk transfer. Displacement and dislocation—of, for example, refugees fleeing conflict—are political and not market failures. Nevertheless, we ask whether we can improve the way in which donor funds are raised and spent in humanitarian relief, particularly as protracted human emergencies become long-term development challenges. The chapter's concluding observations, with examples from investment-for-peace initiatives in the Middle East, return us to the original Bretton Woods theme: that economic development and political stability are necessarily intertwined.

## U.S. Community and Economic Development

On its face, the book's last chapter seems a departure from the others, as it focuses on a set of investment challenges facing the United States rather than on the needs of the world's poorest. These differences are important—but not unrelated. Fiscal and political constraints in developed countries limit their ability to invest in public goods abroad or at home, which only underscores the imperative for innovative finance in communities across the United States. This chapter is not meant to be a comprehensive domestic-investment agenda. Instead, we illuminate a number of innovative finance successes in the field of community economic development to help us understand how they might inform the next generation of public finance challenges and opportunities.

Specifically, we examine whether some of the *place*-based investment strategies, like the Community Reinvestment Act (CRA) and the Low Income Housing Tax Credit—which have unlocked billions of dollars in private capital for real estate, affordable housing, and enterprise development—lend themselves to more *people*-centric services. We look at innovations in financial inclusion and asset building, approaches intended to create wealth for the poor, often by simply connecting them to resources they are already eligible for, like the Earned Income Tax Credit. We also assess the U.S. experience to date with social impact bonds (SIBs), pay-for-success contracts among local governments, nonprofit service providers, and private investors, whose capital underwrites preventive services. The idea is that, if the interventions succeed, the investors will be repaid out of the social savings. The SIB industry is still new in the United States, and the track record is mixed. However, the larger lessons about good governance, evidence-based policy making, and *blended capital* are relevant for innovative finance in U.S. communities for a growing set of capital investments that fuse the *place* and *people* lenses—such as development projects that link affordable housing with community health centers, retail commerce, and public transportation. In this paradigm, mobility is critical to economic opportunity, and investments in physical and social infrastructure are mutually reinforcing.

### Financing the Future

The book concludes with a review of the lessons we have learned about innovative finance; a glimpse into promising areas for new exploration, including education and infrastructure; and a road map for the ways in which we can all advance the field, using our individual and collective contributions to forge a shared and prosperous future.

### Impact Investing

Impact investments—those made in companies, organizations, and funds with the intention of generating social and environmental impact alongside a financial return—are the subject of much discussion and enthusiasm. Although very much related to and a part of the larger field of innovative finance, they are not synonymous. Our expansive view of innovative finance includes both private and public dollars and (re)configurations of partnerships among governments, commercial investors, philanthropies, nonprofit and for-profit intermediaries, and others that seek more and better capital. Impact investments are an important subset of innovative finance.

Impact investors vary widely in terms of who they are—philanthropies, high-net-worth individuals, family offices, community-development institutions, donor-advised funds, and commercial investors large and small, for starters—and the nature of the of returns they seek, from concessionary (below-market-rate) to risk-adjusted market-rate returns. Some impact investors identify as such; others employ an impact thesis but describe their work in the language and terms of mainstream investment. Given these definitional ambiguities, it is hard to quantify the size and scope of the impact-investing market, but we do know it is a global and growing one. In 2015 JPMorgan and the Global Impact Investing Network, two organizations that have been tracking and shaping the field for the last several years, put the market at $60 billion, with roughly half of those investments going into developed markets like the United States and half into emerging economies. This is up from their $45 billion estimate a year prior. Impact investments are made across sectors, from health care to affordable housing, alternative energy to financial services—and everything in between.

The debates in the impact-investing field are many and go beyond the scope of this book. What is not disputed is that there are a growing number of socially minded investors seeking ways to fuse value and values, a burgeoning set of social purpose entrepreneurs and enterprises seeking this kind of capital, and a proliferation of intermediaries seeking to match impact resources with impact opportunities.

First coined in 2007, the term *impact investing* has come to describe a broad range of activities—including assessing and managing investments on the basis of their financial, social, and environmental performance—that use a broad range of tools, including grants, debt, and equity. Most in the field regard impact investing as an active investment, which means mobilizing assets into firms that intentionally create social value either directly through the goods and services they produce or, in some cases, through socially or environmentally responsible practices. This is different than the much larger field of socially responsible investing (by some estimates $3 trillion), which screens for companies that meet basic ESG standards or against those that are engaged in any undesirable activities (e.g., tobacco or firearm production) or places (e.g., Darfur).

Many suggest that impact investing isn't new; all entities comprise a blend of social, environmental, and financial value—it is simply a matter of degree and proportion. Philanthropies, through grants and investments, have long and intentionally pursued impact investments. As early as the 1960s, the Ford, Rockefeller, and MacArthur Foundations in the United States made program-related investments (PRIs) with a portion of their grant budgets. Although these are typically low-interest loans, as we will see in this book, the growth in volume and creativity of PRI use has meant loan guarantees or even equity investments. (From this perspective, community-development intermediaries like LISC, Enterprise, Living Cities, the Calvert Foundation, the Community Reinvestment Fund, Boston Community Capital, Reinvestment Fund, and others have been in the impact-investing business for a long time.) Foundations were responsible for $54 billion of the total $358 billion given by U.S. philanthropies in 2014, but foundations are required to spend only 5 percent of their total assets each year. This means that they sit on a much larger corpus of assets—close to $800 billion in the United States, by some estimates. Many advocates of impact investing believe this money should be unlocked for more impact investments. In the United States, the Heron Foundation—a leader in philanthropic impact investing—is committed to spending 100 percent of its assets on mission-related investing, and others are taking note. Similarly, in the last several years, we have seen a trend as some foundations—such as Bill and Melinda Gates, Skoll, Sorenson, Pershing Square, and the Omidyar Network, among others—begin to invest in social purpose, for-profit companies, often alongside mainstream investors. (This is why the new Zuckerberg Chan Initiative has incorporated as an LLC.) We will see examples of this kind of impact investing in the chapters on health and financial services.

Once philanthropy paved the way, the lion's share of the growth in impact investing has come from the private sector, from family offices, boutique investment funds, and larger commercial banks. Although some of the large investment banks entered the field relatively early with community-development and microfinance investments, nearly all mainstream financial service institutions—Morgan Stanley, Goldman Sachs, Citi, JPMorgan, Prudential, HSBC, Deutsche Bank, UBS, Bank of America, Barclays, Black Rock, and Bain Capital, for starters—now have dedicated social or sustainable finance units. This list is growing rapidly. In some cases, these remain within or include the firm's community reinvestment arm; in others, they are lodged squarely within asset management, in response to client demand for impact products.

There is also increasing specialization in the field—by both sector and geography. Some investors—such as the Soros Enterprise Development Fund, Triodos, Okio, Elevar Equity, The Social Entrepreneurs Fund, and Lion's Head Capital—think broadly about SME development. Others focus on particular industries; for example, firms such as Gray Ghost Ventures, Unitus, BlueOrchard, Omidyar Network, and LeapFrog, which once specialized in microcredit, have now branched out into other kinds of financial services and technology. Some, like the Global Health Investment Fund, focus on health R&D; Rethink Education focuses on education; and firms like Generation Investment Management, Encourage Capital, Equilibrium, and SJF Ventures embrace alternative energies and environmental sustainability in different ways. A growing number of funds, portfolios, and dedicated firms, like Pax Ellevate, employ a gender lens for impact investing and focus on women. Some funds—such as City Light Capital, the Impact America Fund, and Bridges Ventures U.S.—are squarely focused on the United States. In addition, a host of nonprofit and for-profit intermediaries—for example, merchant banks, advisories, and capacity-building entities—have emerged to facilitate these transactions.

Whereas much of the impact-investing industry focuses on institutions and high-net-worth individuals, others are looking to harness a much broader, retail interest in blending values and value. For example, the Calvert Foundation Community Investment Note, first created in 1995, allows people to invest as little as $20, and earn interest, on various development projects in the United States and developing countries. Recently, the foundation passed the cumulative $1 billion mark in notes issued to 15,000 investors. In 2015, Calvert had $229 million invested in 250 community organizations across all 50 U.S. states and more than 100 countries. Ours to Own is Calvert's most recent initiative to allow people to direct investment into their own communities. The rise of crowdfunding and peer-to-peer lending has increased retail opportunities for impact investing.

Whereas Calvert focuses on Main Street, there are numerous efforts to move impact investing further into the mainstream by unlocking a small fraction of the $200 trillion in the global capital markets, with a particular eye on institutional assets: endowments, pension funds, and insurance companies, which can take longer horizons with their investments. Some of this work has focused on creating better data—shared metrics and standards—that can lead to a common vocabulary and evaluation framework for social and environmental impact or a kind of social return on investment. The Impact Reporting and Investment Standards (IRIS) and Global

Impact Investing Rating System (GIIRS) were among the first-generation systems designed to assess impact. The most recent, which comes from the Sustainability Accounting Standards Board (SASB), may soon be used for public companies on the Bloomberg terminal, where ESG data are already widely available.

Other efforts focus on relevant policy levers. In 2013, the G8 Social Impact Investment Task Force was created and chaired by Sir Ronald Cohen, considered by many to be the father of impact investing, first in the UK and later as a kind of global movement. The task force's 2014 report, *Impact Investment: The Invisible Heart of Markets*, contained detailed recommendations about how to advance the field in each participating country and around the world.[16] In August 2015, the task force became the Global Social Investment Steering Group and will expand to include thirteen countries plus the European Union.

In these pages, we explore some of the policy reforms addressed in a 2014 report by the G8 task force's U.S. National Advisory Board, including enhancing and extending the CRA and other valuable tax credit programs, pay-for-success financing, and the investment capacity of agencies like OPIC and USAID. The report also emphasizes reform of the Employee Retirement Income Security Act (ERISA) and of the larger investment conventions that guide—but do not legally codify—norms around fiduciary responsibility. Recent and important gains have been made in areas of ERISA reform.

Impact investing and innovative finance share the same ultimate goal: a more equitable world in which we all have a role and a stake. For the most part, impact investing is about private capital invested in social enterprise activity. Innovative finance is about a more expansive set of resources and possibilities and the channeling of more of those resources in better ways to solve our most entrenched problems.

## Crowdfunding and Peer-to-Peer and Marketplace Lending

In recent years, crowdfunding has emerged as a financing model that allows small funders to invest in organizations in their early stages, particularly those that would otherwise struggle to obtain capital. Peer-to-peer (P2P) funding experiments first emerged in the nonprofit sector, but in the wake of the financial crisis, when credit markets tightened substantially for small and start-up businesses, crowd-investing models—debt and equity—made their way to for-profit ventures.[17] Advocates of crowdfunding call it a way to democratize finance, not only for entrepreneurs seeking capital but also for potential investors seeking access to investment opportunities.[18] Critics argue that once crowdfunding moves, as it has, from philanthropy to a large, profitable industry, the pitfalls for borrowers and lenders are many— what financial journalist Felix Salmon calls "a whole new world of opportunity when it comes to separating fools from their money."[19]

In fact, P2P is now a misnomer for what has become a multibillion-dollar *marketplace lending* industry. In 2014, approximately $16.2 billion was raised in marketplace lending, up 167 percent from 2013 and was expected to double again in 2015 to more than $34 billion.[20] Many expect $1 trillion in transactions over the next decade as Internet and mobile technologies make inroads into the $840 billion consumer-lending industry.[21] In this landscape, investors are no longer *peers*; platforms like Lending-Club and Prosper that started life matching borrowers and lenders directly now primarily match people seeking consumer or small business loans with large institutional investors. Social causes comprise less than 20 percent of the marketplace. The result of marketplace lending's popularity is nothing short of wholesale disruption and transformation of traditional banks as we know them.[22] Once companies like LendingClub, Prosper, and OnDeck discovered there were profits to be made by disintermediating (going around banks to make loans directly), banks began to respond with their own online and digital offerings. For example, in 2015, Goldman Sachs announced it was creating an online consumer-lending unit and product, to be available through an app.[23]

As we have seen, innovative finance is not financial innovation. In this book, we are chiefly concerned with innovations that address market failure with the intention of meeting unmet needs, particularly the needs of the poor. Access to capital, for households and small businesses, is a public good, as we explore in chapters 3 and 5. In the case of crowdfunding, we need to consider if and when these broader marketplaces are making vulnerable households and communities better off.

The industry began with that intention. For example, Kiva was founded in 2005 as a nonprofit microlending platform and has facilitated $742 million in loans (as of August 2015) through microfinance intermediaries in eighty-three countries. These are low-interest loans or, in the case of the new Kiva Zip, interest-free loans. When loans are repaid, donor-lenders can decide whether to have the funds returned to their accounts or to allow Kiva to reloan, which is what most do. Kiva and others paved the way for the growth of a larger crowdfunding industry, with market makers like Kickstarter and Indiegogo. Although these are for-profit companies—they keep a percentage of the funds raised—they remain in the donation- or reward-based camp. Donors do not receive financial returns for their investments. In recent years, a growing number of non-governmental organizations in health,[24] microfinance, and other areas of community and economic development have tried to tap into crowdfunding mechanisms to channel donations to individuals and projects. These efforts also include civic crowdfunding platforms like Citizinvestor, Spacehive, IOB, Y, and Neighborly, through which communities fund local infrastructure projects from new playgrounds and libraries to city-wide free Wi-Fi.[25] For the most part, this has not been investment capital proper, the kind of business needed to fund start-up, growth, and ongoing operations, but philanthropy for specific projects.

Recent industry growth has occurred where the lines separating traditional banking, crowdfunding, digital wallets, and consumer finance blur. Although debt or lending remains the largest marketplace category, equity investing is also possible (see, e.g., AngeList, Crowdcube, Seedrs, Crowdfunder, and Fundable). However, per SEC rules, equity crowd-investing remains limited to accredited investors, as regulators aim to balance the need and demand for capital on the SME side with consumer (in this case, small investor) protections. Not surprisingly, industry maturation has also led to specialization, including crowd-investing sites and companies dedicated to technology, health, real estate, insurance, and higher education finance and refinance (e.g., Pace, Upstart, Sofi, and CommonBond) in the form of loans and equity-like human capital contracts.[26] The emergence of e-commerce consumer finance and social media digital-payment systems collapse industry borders further.[27]

The question is whether this is financial innovation or innovative finance. Do these new products and services meet the needs of the poor or underserved in a new or improved way? In chapter 3, we explore at length the digital-payment and finance revolution taking place across the developing world. In the United States, we are gradually beginning to see the development of fin tech, or financial technology, companies and services targeting the needs of the underserved and vulnerable. For example, LendUp is a kind of socially responsible payday lender, offering customers short-term loans at low rates and helping them rebuild credit scores. Transferwise is a low-cost transparent way to send payments. In 2015, Citi joined with LendingClub and Veradero Capital to extend its CRA lending online—offering affordable credit to underserved borrowers and communities.[28]

As we discuss in chapter 5, traditional community-development lenders are concerned that their industry, which targets the capital needs of enterprises in underserved communities, has been caught flatfooted when it comes to the online marketplace. They worry less for investors than for unsophisticated borrowers who might be using some of the new lending platforms in injudicious and expensive ways.

Although crowdfunding and marketplace lending remain primarily developed-world phenomena, there is growing interest in emerging economies in using P2P financing to capitalize nonprofits and SMEs. In 2013, the World Bank issued a set of sanguine projections, estimating that crowdfunding could reach $96 billion by 2025 as a source of early-stage venture capital for the developing world (for reference, that is twice today's venture capital market).[29] This optimism is not built around global philanthropy or even wealthy investors finding opportunity in emerging markets; rather, it is based on the potential of the emerging consumer and middle classes in developing countries to become a source of capital for their own enterprises and markets.[30] In a word, *autonomy* in development finance.

# 1

# REDD Forests, Green Bonds, and the Price of Carbon

A picture is worth a thousand words—and sometimes a billion dollars. So thought Norway when satellite images of rain forests in the Brazilian Amazon confirmed the dramatic decline of deforestation, a major source of carbon emissions—and therefore climate change. In 2008, in an unusual pledge, the oil-rich Norwegian government promised to pay up to $1 billion for verified evidence that Brazil was reducing tropical deforestation—even while continuing to produce commodities like soy and beef. The hope was that this incentive—known as pay-for-success funding—would encourage sustainable development: more crops, less carbon. At the end of 2015, verdant photos in hand, Norway paid the final installment of its $1 billion in green for green. Was this aid? Bribery? A case of innovative finance? And what does it mean for climate change and our common future?

Although the consequences of rising global temperatures are challenging to quantify, we know that, if unmitigated, they will be catastrophic: higher sea levels that flood coastal and low-lying communities; warmed water systems and altered ocean chemistry that threaten marine life and the lives of those who depend on it; extreme weather events including wildfires, hurricanes, flooding and droughts, which, in turn, disrupt agricultural production, create famine and health crises, and exacerbate migration challenges. Because poverty and resilience are so intricately connected—the vast majority of the world's population lives in regions that are either environmentally or politically unstable, or both—climate change imperils the prosperity and stability that are the hard-won gains of development. As Pope Francis wrote in "Laudato Si," the first papal encyclical on stewardship, "We are not faced with two separate crises, one environmental and the other social, but rather one complex crisis that is both social and environmental."[1]

And yet, because climate change is man-made, mitigation and adaptation are possible. The primary drivers of global warming are gases like carbon dioxide ($CO_2$), methane, and nitrous oxide, which are the by-products of industrial production. These gases block heat radiating from the earth, preventing it from escaping the atmosphere and creating a greenhouse effect (this phenomenon is what makes earth habitable to begin with; the problems come when we increase the concentrations of theses gases in the atmosphere and magnify the greenhouse effect).[2] Moreover, there is general agreement about how much the emissions of these greenhouse gases need to be reduced to hold the increase in global warming to below 2 degrees Celsius (3.6 degrees Fahrenheit)—the level many scientists believe necessary to avoid the most disastrous effects of climate change.

Yet the economics are more challenging than the science. Can we put a price tag on the massive disruptions that will result from unchecked climate change? What does it cost to stem them, whether through reduced greenhouse gas emissions or other means? How do we continue to develop in ways that lift people out of poverty without further damaging the environment—or our collective well-being? How do we begin to produce and consume goods and services that require less energy? How do we encourage the development of robust and affordable sources of alternative energy—a process we know requires trillions of dollars in investment?[3]

Although the changes necessary to transition to a lower-carbon economy are daunting in dollar and political terms, there is ample evidence that the costs of inaction, of doing nothing but waiting for irreversible devastation—rising oceans, extreme weather, and exacerbated agriculture, health, and migration crises—far outweigh those of cutting greenhouse gas emissions now.[4] In fact, uncertainty only makes the case for action stronger when we consider the potential for the truly catastrophic—the "tail" risks of extreme weather and temperature rise—which are not adequately captured in our current models.[5] In finance terms, some have likened these events to black swans: the environmental equivalents of the unexpected but highly destructive cataclysms that led to the 2008 financial crisis.[6] In that sense, climate change intervention serves as a kind of insurance policy against the risky business of infinitely larger and more disastrous social and economic consequences.[7]

But how do we pay for all this?

In recent years, we have seen the emergence of climate finance: innovative and creative ways to unlock new resources to foster lower-carbon development and investment in alternative energies and approaches to sustainable growth. The first generation of innovative finance in natural resources management has been largely policy driven, often created or shaped by governments to internalize externalities and improve the way we spend dollars—as in the case of Norway and Brazil—to catalyze broader marketplace activity. Pay-for-success programs, whether in the form of pollution or development credits (e.g., payment not to pollute or not to develop) or contingent aid (e.g., payment, after the fact, for proof that deforestation has not occurred), are prime examples. As we will see, newer instruments and configurations—green debt, green equity, and other hybrid arrangements and investments—while still visible hand—are increasingly being created and shaped by the capital markets. Have they been effective? And if so, why?

## Market Solutions to the Problem of Negative Externalities

To understand how these new instruments work in practice, we need a little theory. Man-made climate change—and, in particular, unfettered emissions of pollutants like $CO_2$—is arguably the world's largest *negative externality*. That means the costs of the activity are not borne by those responsible. Negative externalities are a kind of market failure—a problem of incentives and resource allocation. The question becomes how we correct incentives to reduce carbon emissions and direct investment into lower-carbon technologies. This involves getting the costs right, which, in turn, involves getting the prices right. In the absence of a price on carbon, people, firms, and countries continue to pump carbon into the atmosphere, even though we know this is the primary anthropogenic cause of climate change, because it costs them nothing. How do we solve this? Let's begin with some Economics 101.

In 1968, ecologist Garrett Hardin's *tragedy of the commons* introduced the imagery and allegory of negative externalities in a metaphor that has animated both theory and practice in the environmental movement ever since. In Hardin's pastoral "commons," in which sheep are grazing, each shepherd benefits from allowing more of his sheep to graze, even when the pasture as a whole withers from overgrazing, diminishing overall productivity. Each shepherd would be better off if he restricted his flock, but no one has an individual incentive to do so. The problem is one of *collective action*, as the incentives of the individual are at odds with those of the larger, common good. "Therein lies the tragedy," writes Hardin. "Each man is locked into a system that compels him to increase his herd without limit—in a world that is limited. Ruin is the destination towards which all men rush, each pursuing his own interest in a society that believes in the freedom of the commons. Freedom in a commons brings ruin to all."[8] It turns out that this tragedy-of-the-commons construct is an important one for many, but not all, natural resource problems and the ways we have intervened to solve them. While dismal, economics isn't always tragic—especially when we consider the range of policy and innovative finance solutions that can defy or surmount Hardin's conundrum.

For the first part of the twentieth century, solutions considered for natural resource problems hinged on the work of Arthur Pigou, an economist who showed that government intervention of some kind, typically in the form of a tax, was necessary to correct for negative externalities along the lines Hardin describes.[9] This view was later challenged by Ronald Coase, who would go on to win the Nobel Prize in Economics[10] for demonstrating that the clear assignment of private property rights, an alternative to government-imposed taxes, could resolve some negative externalities.

These insights about property rights would lay the groundwork for the design of policy instruments like cap-and-trade regimes: when rights to a resource are well defined, all market actors have an incentive to avoid the degradation of that resource. By establishing "property rights" over clean air, for example, individuals or residents can be compensated if firms pollute their "property."[11] Broadly speaking, and as we will see in the chapters that follow, ownership creates and aligns incentives for proactive, productive agency.

Property rights also create what economists call *price signals*. By making property rights transferable—that is, by giving them a monetary value—policy makers can create a market that encourages environmentally friendly decision making. If pollution has a price, everyone is motivated to pollute less. For example, prices spur consumers to cut back on the use of carbon-intensive energy (i.e., fossil fuels) and purchase goods and services that require less of this kind of energy to produce. Companies, in turn, work to reduce their emissions or invest in alternative energy sources and technologies. This kind of pricing mechanism lies at the heart of market-based solutions not just for environmental problems but also for many of the massive social and economic problems we will encounter in this book. This is the economics-to-finance nexus and reminds us of the important role of policy in innovative finance.

## A Little Practice: Property Rights, Price, and Pollution

One of the most successful case studies in pricing externalities comes from the creation of a market for sulfur dioxide ($SO_2$) emission allowances.

In the 1960s and 1970s, acid rain caused significant harm to forests and aquatic life and was of great concern to communities across the United States. Although the culprit in much of the acidification was well known—coal-fired power plants emitting $SO_2$ into the air—there was significant debate about how best to curb these emissions. In 1990, with the urging and support of a handful of innovative environmental groups like the Environmental Defense Fund, a cap-and-trade scheme was written into Title IV of the Clean Air Act Amendments of 1990, passed by Congress and signed into law by George H. W. Bush. The idea was that property rights—in allowances or *credits* to pollute, which could be used or traded—would enable coal producers to reduce emissions more cheaply and more efficiently than would regulations prescribing specific reduction amounts. The hope was to cap annual and aggregate $SO_2$ emissions to 8.95 million tons at the country's 3,200 coal plants; this represented a reduction of 50 percent from 1980 levels, or nearly 9 million tons annually.

To make this work, the cap-and-trade program issued pollution allowances to each coal-fired power plant, representing the tonnage of $SO_2$ it could emit. The utility was then free to determine how best to make $SO_2$ cuts. If it reduced emissions and did not use all its allowances, the utility could sell them to others who hadn't successfully reduced emissions (or bank them for future use). The ability to sell (trade) excess allowances encouraged power plants to get below their own caps as cost-effectively as possible.

Thus, a commodities market for $SO_2$, and the first large-scale cap-and-trade regime, was born. As the commodity is standardized, trading in the marketplace reveals a "price," and the emergence of trading "infrastructure"—exchanges, brokerages, and so on—lowers the transaction costs even more.[12]

The SO$_2$ allowance market is widely viewed as a success of policy and innovative finance. The benefits of the cap-and-trade regime have outweighed the implementation and enforcement costs. On the finance side, the SO$_2$ program catalyzed the emergence of the kind of infrastructure—brokerages and other intermediaries—that can accommodate large trading volumes, as well as a variety of SO$_2$ derivative products, including forwards and swaps. Studies show the cap-and-trade scheme has indeed stimulated the development and adoption of new pollution abatement technologies. These hallmarks of success—product standardization, decreasing cost, and ongoing innovation—that have brought additional private capital into this public marketplace, make it a useful template for other interventions, including, as we will observe, the case of carbon.[13]

Seen another way, cap-and-trade represents an early kind of pay-for-success financing. The price puts a monetary value on a reduction in pollution, and firms are paid for that reduction with an allowance they can then sell. As in the Norway-Brazil example, it's a payment not to pollute. We'll examine many examples of pay-for-success finance under different names and guises in the coming pages of this book.

One of the more interesting outcomes of the SO$_2$ story is one of unintended consequences. In 1990, the primary concern about acid rain was its damage to the environment. It turned out, however, that the cleaner air from lower SO$_2$ emissions substantially reduced sickness and mortality, particularly in urban areas. In fact, the greatest gains from SO$_2$ reductions have come in public health.[14] This, too, is a significant lesson for how we think about—and finance—our larger sustainable development goals, as issues of environment, health, and poverty are necessarily intertwined.


## Property Rights and Sustainable Development: Air, Land, and Sea

We've walked through the mechanics of SO$_2$ reduction in order to understand the theory and practice of property rights in innovative finance: how we can use policy to shape market solutions to market problems. Once we know how and why this works, we can see the imprint elsewhere and start to imagine even broader applications.

Indeed, air pollution is not the only sphere where cap-and-trade schemes complement traditional "command and control" regulations. Those of us who live in or visit cities like New York will recognize cap-and-trade in the buildings around us.

Policy makers attempting to balance development and zoning objectives—and using familiar efficiency and cost-benefit rationales—have created transferable development right (TDR) schemes. Accordingly, buildings that have not reached their height limits under zoning regulations can sell their air rights to developers to build buildings that exceed those limits. In Times Square, the proximity of low-lying, landmarked theaters and enormous new skyscrapers is no coincidence; often the latter have purchased the air rights of the former. The same is true in Chelsea, where owners of land beneath and to the west of the High Line are compensated for the fact they cannot build vertically by their ability to sell their air rights to developers who can and do. In midtown in particular, but across Manhattan, petite and soaring buildings side by side often reveal an air rights trade.

Most recently, the Hines real estate development company began construction in August 2015 on 53W53, a luxury skyscraper formerly known as Tower Verre. Perched on West Fifty-Third Street next to the Museum of Modern Art (MoMA), the project is also known as MoMA Tower and will rival the Empire State Building in height, well in excess of local zoning prescriptions. To do this, Hines has been amassing air rights for a decade, paying $85 million for the unused airspace of neighbors St. Thomas Episcopal Church, the University Club, and MoMA. The project only recently lost the distinction of becoming the city's largest residential tower (that will now go to 432 Park, another air rights vortex).[15] These projects are not uncontroversial. Both these and similar developments have raised concerns about the altered skyline, the shadows they will cast on Central Park, and the ways in which they have perhaps skewed New York's development priorities.

Developers also seek out TDRs when looking to build over wetlands—marshes, swamps, or bogs that are covered in water for at least some of the year. Developers typically like wetlands because they are cheap, as the environmental services or benefits wetlands provide—water purification, groundwater recharge, flood control, and habitat for many species of fish, birds, and mammals—are not reflected in the property price.[16] Here, again, in an effort to stem wetland loss, policy makers have created markets where there were none for these environmental services or benefits.[17] Cap-and-trade for wetlands, known as *mitigation banking*, requires developers to offset the wetlands they "convert" (build on) by purchasing a credit to create or preserve wetlands somewhere else. Not surprisingly, there is a growing market and healthy appetite for wetland restoration credits, which can be purchased through brokers. Today there are approximately 2,000 wetland banks in the United States, transacting several billion dollars in credit sales a year.[18] The most famous wetland developer in history might be Walt Disney, who, in the 1960s, amassed nearly 30,000 acres (40 square miles) of Florida swamp for his Orlando theme park. Today, as Disney's company continues to expand, it is involved in large-scale wetland credit purchases and other preservation projects with partners like the Nature Conservancy. Similar conservation markets are evolving for endangered species—a kind of biodiversity banking—and for high-quality drinking water through state revolving loan funds.

Some of the most innovative cap-and-trade advances have occurred offshore. As long as there have been human communities, people have relied on the oceans for food. And for most of human existence, the seas' bounty has seemed to be boundless. Even today fish are the primary source of protein for more than 1 billion people, and the fishing industry is the engine of coastal economies worldwide. And yet the oceans are a tragedy of the commons writ large. Negative externalities abound, and as we have depleted the oceans, diminishing returns have set in, particularly where population pressures and the industrialization of the fishing industry are most pronounced. More than 80 percent of fisheries worldwide operate at or beyond sustainable levels.[19]

Fishing, it is often said, is like a bank account: you must leave the principal (in this case, fish stocks) intact and live off the interest. But globally the seas are overfished, drawing down the principal, the regenerative stocks of fish. Traditional government interventions and restrictions have only exacerbated the problem in many places. Restrictions on fishermen—time limits for fishing or boat limits for fleets—can instigate a competitive "rush to fish," further depleting the fishing stocks.[20] Even without government intervention, many fishery managers set a maximum total catch, and individual fishermen and boats are motivated to bring in as many fish as they can before the fishery hits its limit.

As early as the 1970s, places like New Zealand, Australia, and Iceland put in place cap-and-trade–like fishing arrangements that have come to be known as *catch-share management*. Under a catch-share program, scientists determine an optimal number of fish that can be harvested annually—not unlike a total amount of $SO_2$—called the *total allowable catch* (TAC). Commercial fisheries are then allocated permits for their share of the TAC, and individual fishermen can trade or lease shares through *individual fishing quotas* (IFQs) or *individual transferable quotas* (ITQs). As Coase would have predicted, a market is created by property rights—in this case, in the form of access permits to a certain amount of fish.

Formally created in 1986, New Zealand's market for IFQs has stemmed overfishing, restored fish stocks, and improved revenue per boat (in some cases by as much as 80 percent) and is credited with stabilizing that country's local fishing communities.[21] In recent years, similar *limited access privilege programs* (LAPPs) have been put in place worldwide, including at about fifteen major fisheries in the United States, and innovative public-private initiatives related to financing and valuing future catches are gaining traction with partnerships of philanthropies, nonprofits, and impact investors.[22] Fisheries continue to be a promising area of exploration for innovative finance.

Whereas air pollution cap-and-trade schemes like that for $SO_2$ require government intervention at least for the initial allocation of allowances, many fishery LAPPs are community designed and managed. This is an important distinction. In 2009, political scientist Elinor Ostrom won the Nobel Prize in Economics for her work on these kinds of shared resources, demonstrating how farmers and fishermen—communities that understand deeply how their livelihoods depend on the health of their resources—often generated their own innovative schemes to collectively harvest resources. These collaborations are frequently successful because they are based both on well-defined property rights *and* on trust and long-term community assessments of the productivity and value of a collective resource.[23] Among the insights from Ostrom's work: there is nothing inevitably tragic about natural resource management. Tragedy can be, and often is, averted by local community solutions to collective action problems. In the case of fish, local communities understand better than any federal policy makers or outside investors the importance of that resource to their livelihood. The significance of local agency and ownership in economic development is a theme we will revisit throughout this book.

## Climate Change Re-price: The Case for Carbon

It is not surprising, given the successes of various cap-and-trade regimes, that economists and policy makers alike have looked to price as the most promising means of tackling carbon emissions and climate change. Some argue for a Pigouvian tax—the kind already in use in Europe, the UK, and parts of Canada—to price carbon, discourage carbon-intensive consumption, lower emissions, and generate billions in revenue in the process. Advocates for cap-and-trade suggest that, as in the case of $SO_2$, tradable allowance regimes are more flexible than taxes and harness market forces (and companies) to direct emission reductions to where they can be achieved at the lowest costs. Still others have suggested that it is possible to have some kind of cap-and-trade–tax hybrid. Although the debate regarding the relative efficiency of a carbon tax versus cap-and-trade is beyond the scope of this book, it is generally agreed that a price on carbon is necessary to reduce carbon consumption and unlock the investment necessary to realize a lower-carbon economy.

The politics of that price signal are a different story. As is well known and documented,[24] the road to a national carbon cap-and-trade regime along the lines of that for $SO_2$ has been rocky in the United States. In 2009, the country came its closest when the Waxman-Markey climate change bill, which contained the architecture for a tradable emissions scheme, passed in the U.S. House of Representatives but not in the Senate. In anticipation of that national legislation, companies and investors mobilized billions of dollars in capital so they could develop and adopt technologies and other goods and services that would abate carbon emissions, mitigate further climate change, and build more resilient systems. Despite the failure to create a national cap-and-trade program in 2009, there is evidence that many enterprises and investors now include carbon in their business decisions, effectively putting a price on carbon in expectation of and preparation for further market development (and in response to the existence of other carbon markets around the globe). This is important because it tells us a fair amount about risk management—about how corporate leaders view climate change and their role in its mitigation. Microsoft, for example, charges its business units an internal tax for their carbon use; the proceeds go into a common fund that the company uses to invest in things like alternative energy. It is estimated that more than a thousand major corporations now price their carbon emissions, and at least 450 companies—including Disney, Walmart, and big oil companies like Chevron and BP—do so with some kind of internal fee or tax. That number is expected to double in the coming year.[25] For these firms, price provides an easy-to-use common denominator to internalize the externalities. According to Tamara DiCaprio, Microsoft's senior director of sustainability, "When we started talking about carbon emissions not in metric tons, but in terms of dollar amount, the business people could understand it. We're all speaking the same language now: What is the cost to my group?"[26]

Today approximately forty countries and more than twenty cities, states, and provinces are now using or planning to use a price on carbon to reduce greenhouse gas emissions.[27] In 2005, the European Union (EU) created its own emissions trading system (EU ETS), the world's first and largest cap-and-trade system for carbon. By most measures, the EU ETS has been successful in building a market, generating an accepted price for tradable carbon credits and the kind of market infrastructure—things like brokerages and trading desks—necessary to facilitate significant trading volume. China, the world's largest emitter, has seven local markets and in September 2015 announced that it would introduce a national emissions trading system as early as 2017.[28] Regional efforts are also emerging in the United States. California's emission trading market, in place since 2013, covers emissions from power plants, factories and the transport sector, making it the most comprehensive in the world in terms of coverage. In the Northeast, nine states have established a cap-and-trade program for their power sectors via the Regional Greenhouse Gas Initiative. Under the Clean Power Plan promulgated by the U.S. Environmental Protection Agency in 2015, many states are expected to elect to use trading programs to help meet required emissions reductions.

The fact remains that the larger and more robust the market and the louder and clearer the price signal, the more capital moves toward lower-carbon activity, technology, and investment. Recent momentum, such as the agreements reached in Paris at COP21, suggest that countries around the world, including the two largest carbon emitters, the United States and China, are focused on making climate change policy a national and global priority, with an eye toward innovative finance solutions to the problem.

Of course, cap-and-trade is not without risks and critics. For one thing, market solutions, even those that correct for market failure, still depend on some degree of functioning market dynamics. There are times when demand, and therefore price, collapses. If prices are too low, firms will not switch from high-carbon fuels like coal to gas or other alternatives, which is the desired effect. This happened in the case of the EU ETS when the recession drove down production and therefore demand for energy (and carbon). Reforms to the EU ETS are expected to improve price by restricting supply (i.e., by taking some of the allowances off the market).[29] There have also long been equity concerns about cap-and-trade specifically and about market-based solutions generally, particularly those that depend on property rights. For a time, the criticism within developed countries was trained on the notion that companies could effectively pay to pollute, buying their way out of reducing emissions. Intracountry concerns have largely been assuaged, as the cases of $SO_2$ and other cap-and-trade examples have demonstrated cost-effective success in reducing pollution and improving ecosystems and public health. However, the same tensions arise between developed and developing countries in any system where wealth can purchase the prerogative to continue polluting, even if the recipient country benefits in monetary terms.

## From Green to REDD, and Back to Brazil

While policy makers advance in their efforts to create robust markets—and pricing signals—other innovative finance approaches to tackling climate change have emerged that rely less on direct policy intervention and more on a kind of transition between the public and private marketplaces.

To understand better, let's return to the Brazilian rain forests.

It is not hard to imagine how the destruction of rain forests hurts biodiversity. Second only to coral reefs in terms of biodiversity, rain-forest ecosystems also support the 70 million people who live in them. Perhaps less intuitive, deforestation is a major source of climate change, accounting for roughly 15 percent of global $CO_2$ emissions. This is as much as the combined output of all cars, trucks, buses and trains. The lion's share of these deforestation-related emissions comes from two places: the Amazon and Indonesia. Rain forests serve as "sinks" for $CO_2$—absorbing and storing it so it cannot enter the atmosphere. Reducing deforestation is critical to climate change mitigation and is one of the more cost-effective approaches to the problem.

Pay-for-success programs to reduce verified emissions from deforestation go by the acronym REDD, which stands for Reducing Emissions from Deforestation and Forest Degradation.[30] The Norway-Brazil case exemplifies REDD in action: Norway pledged up to $1 billion to Brazil for verifiable proof that deforestation had decreased—that's the success piece. The intent is for payments to make it more economically feasible and attractive for countries and farmers, ranchers and forest communities to conserve forests than to cut them down.

The motivation behind REDD is as much long-term sustainable development as it is forest protection or emissions reduction. To date, the primary driver of growth in countries like Brazil has been the development of commodities like palm oil, soy, and beef, often through deforestation—clearing trees to raise crops and cattle. REDD's pay-for-success design is meant to motivate less carbon-intensive production; in a place like Brazil, that means improving economic output while decreasing emissions.

REDD schemes were originally premised on the idea that that forest conservation could attract significant financial resources through carbon-pricing mechanisms, such as credits or TDR-like offsets, that, in turn, could be traded on the carbon markets. Over time, the delayed development of these compliance markets in places like the United States has meant that, to date, the REDD framework has evolved as a kind of innovative finance development assistance, relying primarily on public sources of funds; the private capital markets have yet to be fully harnessed.

Pay-for-success is indeed an innovation in finance, even if that finance is in the form of aid. As we have seen, payments are intended to make emission mitigation cost effective for Brazil and Brazilian producers: leaving forests standing is often cheaper than investing in renewable energy (and much cheaper than carbon capture technologies)—and of course cheaper still than adapting to the catastrophic effects of climate change. An ounce of prevention is worth a pound of cure. "To put a complex political, economic, and scientific argument in its simplest terms," says Mark Tercek of the Nature Conservancy, "if you can prevent pollution in the first place, then you won't have to spend huge sums of money to clean it up later."[31] REDD therefore differs from traditional grant-based development assistance, which historically has not been contingent upon verifiable performance objectives. REDD is not unique in this shift in development aid; it is part and parcel of a shift in the way donors think about how to most efficiently use their official development assistance (ODA) budgets.

Rather than a uniform approach, the REDD movement has stimulated a number of "demonstration activities"—various voluntary programs and projects undertaken by consortia of governmental and nongovernmental organizations to test ways in which countries and local landholders could be motivated to protect forests. To date, many countries have prepared REDD plans and schemes with assistance from the World Bank's Forest Carbon Partnership Facility (FCPF), the UN-REDD Program, the Global Canopy Program, and others.[32]

Perhaps most interesting are the bi- and multilateral activities emerging outside of these formal institutions, often between countries in the Amazon like Brazil, and wealthy donor nations like Germany, the United Kingdom and the United States. The most well known REDD initiatives have emanated from Norway, a country that has become extremely wealthy in recent decades from its North Sea oil and has used some of this wealth for innovative development aid generally (the country spends more than 1 percent of its GDP on ODA, the highest percentage of any country) and for climate change initiatives in particular. In 2008, Norway created its own International Climate and Forest Initiative to support REDD activities in countries willing to make substantial improvements in their rates of deforestation. It promised to provide up to $1 billion for demonstrated reductions in deforestation in both Brazil and Indonesia, countries with large, valuable, and disappearing rain forests. The different experiences in Brazil and Indonesia tell us a lot about the success of pay-for-success.

In 2008, Norway pledged $1 billion for Brazil through the creation of the Brazilian Amazon Fund, payable if Brazil brought its annual rate of deforestation down below its 1996–2005 average of approximately 19,508 square kilometers per year. The Amazon Fund was to be administered through BNDES (Banco Nacional de Desenvolvimento Econômico e Social) to finance projects that would reduce deforestation and promote sustainable development more broadly in the Amazon. Brazil was a promising partner for Norway not simply because the rates of deforestation of the Amazon canopy were alarming but also because Brazil had recognized deforestation as an impediment to long-term economic development and was already hard at work addressing the problem, aiming to reduce its deforestation rate 80 percent by 2020 (versus the previous decade's average) as a matter of national law and policy. Accordingly, Brazil has cut its deforestation rate over 75 percent since 2005 (relative to the 1995-2004 baseline), years ahead of schedule (see figure 1.1). What is notable is that Brazil's economy grew 7.5 percent per year in this period, with agricultural production and profitability increasing substantially in many legally protected regions. In other words, production increased while emissions decreased. It is estimated that this reduction in deforestation reduced Brazil's global warming pollution by nearly 1 billion tons.[33] As a result of the demonstrated reductions in deforestation—the verification comes through satellite photos of the Amazon, backed by sophisticated remote-sensing techniques and on-the-ground surveys —Norway has allocated the full $1 billion to the Amazon Fund, and Germany and Petrobras are now also supporters. The Norway-Brazil agreement has been extended to 2021.

The Brazilian REDD agreements with Norway are largely considered a success, though not without qualification. The various pieces of the innovative pay-for-success structure warrant further consideration. Nancy Birdsall, William Savedoff, and Frances Seymour at the Center for Global

Figure 1.1
Yearly Rate of Deforestation in the Brazilian Amazon, 1988–2013
*Source*: All figures are derived from official National Institute of Space Research (INPE) data.
*Note*: The figures refer only to the Brazilian Amazon, which accounts for roughly 60 percent of the Amazon rain forest.

Development have studied REDD extensively and conclude that, on balance, the Brazilian government's efforts, supported by Norway, enhanced the legitimacy and strength of local conservation advocates, pushing the government toward greater action on deforestation and changing incentives for commodity producers when it comes to deforestation.[34] Similarly, Norway's role as a champion and larger player in elevating deforestation and innovative ways to finance it through pay-for-success development assistance is important to the field.

Interestingly, the fact that the Norway-Brazil deal did not ultimately hinge on market-based tradable offsets, as originally envisioned, may have been important to its early success. Brazil, like other developing countries, has opposed the idea of offsets, as they seemed to let wealthier countries off the hook—allowing them to purchase the right to pollute from developing countries rather than reducing their own emissions. This tension between more developed and developing nations has simmered for decades, in a number of spheres, as emerging countries both challenge the double standard—that wealthier countries industrialized in ways that were not sustainable, whereas developing countries are discouraged from doing so—and seek more autonomy in their own development today. In the realm of climate change, this issue was addressed most recently at the 2015 UN Climate Change Conference in Paris but, as we will see, remains an ongoing issue and priority for developed and developing countries alike.[35]

In the case of the REDD arrangement with Norway, Brazil has been able to design and, in effect, own its own low-carbon development, an important step toward "sovereignty," (agency) in the development process.[36] To that end, BNDES has served an important role as credible third-party broker. As a Brazilian bank, it has decision-making and implementation capacity beyond Norway's influence. It is also independent of the Brazilian government, which gives some assurances to Norway and other donors that, as much as possible, spending decisions are less politicized than they often are with traditional direct-to-government aid. Although there have been criticisms of BNDES—in particular for its slow start in soliciting, evaluating, and developing a pipeline of projects consistent with the Amazon Fund mission—by and large it brought trust and credibility to the innovative finance arrangement on all sides.[37]

The REDD agreements are not without challenges or concerns. For starters, monitoring and assessing reductions in deforestation and $CO_2$ emissions is difficult. It requires the establishment of the right baseline or reference level and accurate verification with satellites of progress toward measurable and predetermined objectives. The success of the program, in fact, hinges on precise and reliable data evaluation. This is easier proscribed than done.

Critics of Brazil's REDD agreements suggest that causality is hard to prove. Indeed, Brazil's rate of deforestation had begun to decline prior to 2008; the country was already on the path to lower-carbon development. It is difficult to determine whether and exactly how much REDD motivated further reductions in deforestation. This is important because REDD funding is meant to be additional—to spur improvements in forest management and a more sustainable development than would have occurred otherwise. This is the function of all innovative finance.

There is also concern over what economists call *leakage*: conserving forests in one place only to shift deforestation to another. Brazil might pursue REDD projects in one region that would go a long way toward reducing deforestation while at the same time in other regions undertaking major development initiatives—hydropower dams, roads, and other infrastructure projects, often with BNDES as a lender—that could be destructive to forests and indigenous people. (REDD efforts are typically national in scale in an effort to prevent leakage). The question is where REDD fits into a larger, national development strategy. This, too, must be asked of all innovative finance efforts.

Finally, REDD raises questions about how pay-for-success works in practice and what its advantages and limitations are. One of the virtues of pay-for-success is that it is hands-off—it lets local governments and communities design policies and practices that they believe will best achieve results. The autonomy that pay-for-success fosters is a hallmark of innovative finance. However, this arm's-length arrangement means there is little way to determine whether local governments are acting in good faith—for example, whether they are working equitably with forest-dependent communities that lack sufficient land, resources, or other rights. Although pay-for-success is meant to align incentives to improve governance, it is no guarantee.

This brings us to Indonesia. In 2009, Indonesia became one of the first developing countries to set targets for reducing its greenhouse gas emissions—much of which came from deforestation.[38] The country's leading export commodities, like palm oil and timber for pulp and paper, are produced by burning down large swaths of forestland. The thick haze these forest fires produce poses a significant health hazard to Indonesians.[39] In 2010, Indonesia and Norway entered into a REDD pay-for-success arrangement, in which Indonesia agreed to a broad set of policies to address deforestation problems, including a moratorium on new licenses for forest exploitation.

Yet despite these commitments, Indonesia's deforestation—both legal and illegal—and related emissions increased through 2012. Accordingly, Norway did not release any payments. (There is some recent evidence that Indonesia's deforestation and greenhouse gas emissions have improved slightly, but they are still far short of the country's goal to reduce emissions by 26 to 41 percent by 2020.[40]) The new government in Indonesia, elected in late 2014, will have the option to revisit negotiations with Norway regarding forest management funding.[41] Critics of REDD cite the lack of enforcement—the flip side of laissez-faire autonomy—as a shortcoming of pay-for-success. There is no payment for noncompliance, but neither are there proactive fines or penalties. Some argue that this amounts to "nonpayment for nonperformance" or, worse still, "sitting back and waiting for what's left of Indonesia's forests to go up in smoke."[42]

## Continuous Innovation: New Capital for REDD

Despite these real governance shortcomings, REDD is largely considered a promising way to give countries committed to sustainable development more resources. And yet, even if we consider the case of REDD in Brazil as an encouraging and successful model of development assistance, Norway's $1 billion is not enough. In some ways, this proves REDD's success: the total projected "supply" of potential emissions reductions from REDD (there is a significant pipeline of countries readying REDD programs) and similar initiatives could be as much as thirty-nine times larger than the total projected "demand," meaning Norway-like funding for these kinds of programs.[43]

Where will we find the capital to bring REDD to scale?

Norway and the Scandinavian countries in general (and northern Europe even more broadly) have been leaders in both ODA and climate change mitigation. Yet the particular circumstances of a country like Norway—with great wealth created through the oil riches of the North Sea and a small, homogeneous population that supports government use of some of that wealth to fight climate change and poverty beyond its own borders—are not readily replicated. The World Bank and UN estimate that investments needed for climate change mitigation and adaptation far exceed all the ODA, well designed and other, available. This suggests a need for broader carbon markets, which was the original premise for REDD. Although some developing countries did not initially embrace offsets and tradable emission credits, many now see direct access to the capital markets as a relatively autonomous way to harness funds for climate change mitigation and adaptation,[44] certainly a path to scale. It is also a promising area of exploration for innovative finance, as a number of nascent initiatives are looking to connect REDD to the broader capital markets.

One such proposal considers how an endowment—which countries like Brazil and Indonesia could initially capitalize in various ways—could create a kind of global sovereign wealth fund to stem deforestation. The annual payout or returns from the endowment would go to REDD efforts.

Another idea is to link REDD efforts in Brazil and elsewhere to cap-and-trade programs in other jurisdictions such as California. Solutions to global warming, the thinking goes, require global reductions in $CO_2$; they needn't come only from California but could be achieved in places like

Brazil by stemming deforestation.[45] The promise of using California's cap-and-trade market for carbon to drive more capital to REDD initiatives has led to a number of innovative alliances. For example, the Environmental Defense Fund and Encourage Capital, an investment firm focused on financial, social, and environmental returns, are developing a REDD Acceleration Fund (RAF) to channel private capital for compliance grade REDD+ credits.[46] One promising source of these kinds of credits is Acre, a state in Brazil that has slowed its rate of deforestation by 70 percent since 2005 but that hopes to protect the forest still covering 87 percent of its surface—an area the size of New York State.[47] The RAF facility would be capitalized initially through an innovative "blend" of sources: corporations seeking compliance offsets, philanthropies providing grants and first-loss guarantees, and impact investors. RAF also hopes to catalyze further marketplace development—e.g., a decision by California to allow REDD+ credits into its market—by signaling to policy makers that there are both investors ready to purchase offset credits (the demand) and projects that lend themselves to carbon reduction (the supply).

## Green Bonds and the Search for Scale

As we see with REDD, when it comes to crowding in additional private capital for sustainable development, the hope for scale rests largely on a price on carbon and on the development of markets for carbon reduction. We are getting there piecemeal. In the meantime, however, signs of scale are appearing where they often do in finance—in fixed-income instruments. The current bond market stands at $100 trillion. Accordingly, banks, governments, multilaterals, and companies have begun to use *green bonds* to raise capital for investment in environmentally friendly projects. Just what does this new asset class tell us about innovative finance? Can we use it to solve market failure at scale?

Green bonds are indeed the most-talked-about fixed-income newcomer. They had a record year in 2014, with over $35 billion in issuances, up more than threefold from the year before (see figure 1.2).[48] Although some had expected that growth to continue through the next year—perhaps hitting $100 billion—2015 looked more like the prior year, with $41 billion in new issuances. "In markets, momentum is everything," says Sean Kidney, CEO of the Climate Bonds Initiative, a nonprofit that tracks growth in that market.[49]

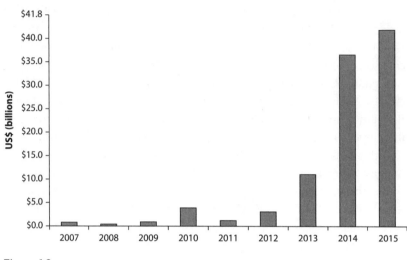

Figure 1.2
Total Value of Green Bonds Issued, 2007–2015
*Source*: Climate Bonds Initiative.

Just which way are green bonds headed? And why? We will look for answers to these questions, but first we need to consider some definitions.

Bonds, green or otherwise, are simply a kind of debt, or loan, but with multiple owners or lenders—they are IOUs issued by a government or company that entitle lenders to get their money (principal) back in addition to a (fixed) interest payment. From the investor perspective, bonds are considered safer than equity, an ownership stake that shares in both a company's upsides and its downsides. The relative safety of debt and the fact that bonds are tradable and liquid mean far more money flows each year to bonds than equity shares. The amount of corporate debt issued in the United States in 2014 was over $1.4 trillion; the amount of equity issued through initial public offerings was approximately $100 billion (though the total would be higher if the secondary market was included).

Green bonds, also known as climate bonds, are bonds that governments or companies issue to raise funds for climate mitigation, climate adaptation, or, it turns out, just about any other kind of environment-friendly project. Bondholders are repaid from revenues from the projects financed.

In 2007, to accommodate the investment preferences and environmental concerns of a handful of European pension fund investors, the World Bank created a new security that would ringfence or direct funds to development projects that satisfied their environmental criteria. Thus was born, almost by accident, the first green bond. Since then, the World Bank has issued more than $8.2 billion in green bonds in eighteen currencies—including its largest, to date, for $600 million in January 2015—and the International Finance Corporation (IFC) has issued $3.7 billion in green bonds. Together they pioneered the market, using their balance sheets and AAA credit to channel capital to a variety of green priorities.

In fact, the uses of the proceeds from these green bonds vary widely. The World Bank's first green bonds were issued to fund geothermal energy in Indonesia, rural solar power in Peru, free compact fluorescent bulbs in Mexico, and irrigation efficiency in Tunisia. In recent years, the bank has become more creative about the types of bonds it issues. In January 2015, for example, in conjunction with BNP Paribas, it closed its first Green Growth Bond—a green bond for European retail investors—raising $91 million for climate-friendly projects with an innovative equity-linked green bond.[50]

Today green bonds are being issued in countries around the world; in the United States, they have been issued by Massachusetts, Hawaii, New York, and California and by city governments, including Spokane, Washington; Washington, D.C.; and Asheville, North Carolina. In New York City Comptroller Scott Stringer is encouraging green bonds.[51] Across the Atlantic in Sweden, Gothenburg and Stockholm have issued green bonds, and in 2014, Johannesburg issued Africa's first municipal green bond to finance solar power, sustainable transportation, and biogas projects. In April 2015, Yes Bank sold India's first green bond (what the *Financial Times* has called the first green "masala bond"),[52] and it is anticipated that China—which plans to open its debt capital markets and cut pollution—could radically change the green bond landscape.

In June 2013, when Massachusetts became the first U.S. state or city to issue a green bond, the $100 million sale was oversubscribed and included many new institutional and individual investors, broadening and diversifying the state's investor base, which was one of the state's goals. Indeed, many of the state's thousand orders came from individual investors interested in supporting their local government's investment in the environment. In that sense, green bonds may be emerging as a way for individual investors to participate in "mission" investing that generates social or environmental effects. The bond has already been used for Superfund remediation projects, river revitalization, habitation preservation and restoration, energy efficiency and conservation in public buildings, and clean drinking water and water supplies.[53]

In 2014, cumulative municipal and corporate issuances of green bonds overtook issuances by development banks like the World Bank and IFC. Bank of America issued the first corporate green bond for $500 million in November 2013 to finance renewable energy projects including wind, solar, and geothermal and energy efficiency projects like lighting retrofits, cogeneration, and building insulation in residential, commercial, and public properties. That first green bond was used to finance projects like a $40 million LED streetlight project for the City of Los Angeles (the largest LED streetlight retrofit in the world) and retrofits for Oakland. In May 2015, Bank of America issued its second green bond for $600 million to fund renewable energy and energy efficiency projects as part of the company's $70 billion multiyear commitment to advance low-carbon economic solutions through "lending, investing and facilitating capital, providing advice and developing solutions for clients around the world." For each project financed, Bank of America tracks the estimated annual benefits as measured by things like global warming (metric tons of $CO_2$ avoided), water use avoided, energy saved, and energy produced. In June 2015, Morgan Stanley issued its own $500 million green bond. Although the company had underwritten numerous green bonds for multilateral development banks, corporations, and municipalities (having completed twenty-seven green bonds transactions as of June 2015), this was its inaugural offering. The bond will fund LED lighting enhancements, among other energy efficiency investments.[54] Outside of financial service firms, energy companies like France's EDF have also issued green bonds to finance renewable energy projects, including wind farms, solar, and biogas.[55] In 2014, Toyota issued what it called the auto industry's first consumer-finance green bond, with the $1.75 billion in proceeds to be used to fund consumer loans and leases for green vehicles like the hybrid Toyota Prius.[56] Other companies have grown even more innovative with their green bonds. SolarCity, for example, the largest installer of residential solar electricity in the United States, was the first U.S. company to "securitize" solar; to issue green asset-backed securities.

Just what does all this activity tell us about innovative finance? Are green bonds helping to close the finance gap when it comes to renewable energy investment? Are they attracting additional capital to the sector? Are they helping to bring down the cost of capital for riskier green investments? Are they addressing a fundamental market failure?

For starters, it is worth noting that there is no discount for green bonds. They are not cheaper than conventional bonds, and investors do not forfeit any yield or returns. To these investors, the pull of green bonds over, say, conventional bonds is primarily environmental.[57] Those who purchase green bonds often believe that they are less risky over the long term because they hedge against the risks of climate change or future regulation—offering a way to "decarbonize" their portfolios. For the most part, however, demand has been growing from institutional investors looking to satisfy corporate environmental objectives, driven by voluntary or compliance motivations to demonstrate the social and environmental effects of their overall holdings, while ensuring the financial returns remain "investment grade" (equal the market rate). As the World Bank learned with its first issuances and as Massachusetts discovered when its green bond was oversubscribed more and more investors want a green label. Offering or owning green bonds is therefore and in some ways akin to being a signatory to conventions like the aspirational UN Principles for Responsible Investment. These are voluntary commitments that do not require or enforce specific action. This is because there is no clear definition of what makes something "green."

Standard bond ratings that pertain to risk—AAA and Aaa, for example—are clear, but there is no definition, and no rating, for a bond's "greenness." To date, green bonds have been issued to underwrite a large range of infrastructure and energy projects, but green is in the eye of the beholder. (Take the case of hydropower, for example. At the World Bank, small hydro is considered renewable, and therefore green, but large hydro is not.) Companies, banks, and governments report on their bonds' environmental impact, but this is varied and voluntary. While some call for tighter definitions or gradations of environmental impact or value—a pale green or a deeper green—or green scoring to match the credit ratings, others counter that this kind of evaluation would slow or restrict supply; in the terms of the industry, it would reduce liquidity. It is precisely the simplicity of the bonds—which are "plain vanilla" and, for the most part, investment grade—that makes them easy to sell in the market.

Advocates for tighter definitions of *green* contend that standardization, and therefore credibility, is key to further market expansion (for all their growth, green bonds still represent only 2 percent of the bond market) and that the absence of clearer green ratings has led to investor confusion and the recent market slowdown.[58] A number of different industry groups are at work on this. The Climate Bonds Initiative has developed standards for renewable energy, buildings, land use, biofuels, and transportation. In 2014 and 2015, a consortium of investment banks—including JPMorgan Chase, Bank of America, Merrill Lynch, Citi, Crédit Agricole, Goldman Sachs, HSBC, and SEB—in conjunction with the investor group Ceres, developed voluntary guidelines in the form of Green Bond Principles to "encourage transparency, disclosure and integrity."[59] These principles, not unlike the UN Principles for Responsible Investment, identify categories of eligible projects intended for broad use by the market, provide issuers guidance, and aid investors with evaluative tools. However, they do not explicitly prescribe or rule out any categories. (In 2016, Moody's proposed a new methodology and scorecard for issuers to manage and report on their green bonds). For the most part, the banks take the view that individual issuers will determine what they believe is green and let the market decide just how green the bond is and whether to buy it.

Accordingly, most issuers voluntarily report on the impact of their green bonds, citing things like megawatts of renewable energy generated, tons of $CO_2$ emissions avoided, or hectares of land reforested. Bank of America, for example, publishes information on all the projects funded by its first green bond. These included, among others, the above-mentioned City of Los Angeles Streetlights Project, where new lights reduced energy use by 63 percent and reduced carbon emissions by 47,538 metric tons a year. The green bond also provided financing for the Antioch Unified School District in California to purchase solar panels for twenty-four schools, install energy-efficient lighting, and carry out HVAC upgrades. These investments were designed to produce electricity, generating both additional revenue and energy savings, and were anticipated to save the district $34.4 million over the twenty-five-year useful life of the project. Environmental benefits were estimated to include 7,700 metric tons of $CO_2$ avoided, 206,000 liters of water use avoided, 103 metric tons of non-hazardous waste avoided, 1,700 megawatt hours (MWh) of energy saved through energy efficiency, and 8,700 MWh of energy produced from the solar project.[60]

In addition to questions about future market growth, the lack of strict green definitions and the voluntary nature of reporting and impact evaluation raise the issue of *additionality*: Are green bonds bringing new capital to the sector to fund projects that would not happen otherwise? Are they lowering the cost of capital for investment in risky or alternative low-carbon technologies in a way that, as their champions had hoped, might "bankroll a clean energy revolution"?[61] Or are they simply marketing dollars for important infrastructure investments—not unlike war bonds in the past or other thematic issuances—but not fundamentally solving negative externality problems, the market failures underlying problems like climate change.

Critics point to a number of issuances that suggest the latter. For example, in 2014, the Massachusetts Institute of Technology refinanced bonds that were originally used to build energy-efficient buildings and designated $370 million of the refinancing as green—even though these new funds were fungible and used to support work with no new environmental benefits.[62] A similar debate took place when Massachusetts announced that a portion of its green bond would be used to fund a 725-space parking garage at Salem South University, near Boston. The state argued that the garage would house electric car–charging stations, provide parking for people traveling in carpools, and lead to reduced pollution from the cars of students who currently circled the campus looking for parking spots; dubious environmental advocates suggest the garage still encouraged people to drive, a major source of greenhouse gas emissions.[63]

We have defined innovative finance to mean resources that solve problems in new or different ways. Often this means lowering the cost of capital for projects that require additional investment, a visible hand to nudge the market in a different direction. We will see numerous examples of this throughout the book, including the case of the International Finance Facility for Immunization's vaccine bonds described in the opening pages. When it comes to climate change, we would hope a lower cost of capital would, in turn, drive investment into low-carbon technological innovation. To date, and the market is still young, we have not yet seen evidence of this occurring. Toyota's green bond, for example, has not led the car company to invest in the production of more hybrids or in the next generation of low-emissions technology.

Critics rightly contend that, if green bonds do not start to attract additional capital or address fundamental market failures and negative externalities, they may turn out to be a multibillion-dollar exercise in "greenwashing"—a public relations effort for companies that want to signal a commitment to mitigating climate change without taking any real action. Or, less cynically, green bonds may simply be the latest incarnation of the war or other themed bond—a marketing strategy long used by governments and companies to raise debt financing. Advocates counter that green bonds are an important step in improving awareness about the importance of sustainable growth and about the role of low-carbon investment, and portfolio management, in that process.

In many ways, the green bonds debate is about a "quantity" versus "quality" trade, a theme we will revisit in the pages that follow. The enormous social and environmental challenges we face require a commensurate

Although we focus here on green bonds, when it comes to climate change and the capital markets, the area of equity—public and private—is a particularly promising one for innovative finance.

For years, when we considered socially responsible investing (SRI), what we meant, in essence, was a "screen": a way to exclude the stocks of publicly traded companies engaged in undesirable activities—typically related to things like tobacco, gambling, or firearms—from our portfolios. Over time, basic environmental, social, and governance (ESG) indicators emerged that allow companies to measure their performance and investors to benchmark and assess accordingly: to screen out companies that score poorly on these dimensions or to actively select for others that score favorably. In turn, more robust ESG measures, entire indices and sustainability ratings, and accounting standards have grown up to bring even better data to investors, often via new and improved platforms, including the ubiquitous Bloomberg terminal. All told, SRI assets in the United States are approximately $3 trillion.

Yet SRI is only part of the picture. In recent years, many investors have begun to proactively put capital to work in companies and funds that intentionally advance environmental objectives and produce environmental goods and services focused on long-term sustainable development. Leaders in this field have included Generation Investment Management, Encourage Capital (formerly EKO), Equilibrium Capital Partners, SJF Ventures, and Capricorn—as well as a large number of other clean-tech and energy investors and major philanthropies worldwide.

For the most part, and regardless of the particular industries these investors focus on—energy, water, agriculture, fisheries, and pollution markets, among others—each subscribes to a version of a "sustainable capitalism" investment thesis: that is, a long-term view of costs and benefits that internalizes externalities and values social and environmental goods. This means different thinking about risk: the real exposure today, that real estate developers, insurers, agriculture, and other industries face from things like rising seas and extreme weather; the regulatory risks that will come with a price on carbon, making it expensive to own "stranded" assets like coal or petroleum reserves or to maintain energy-inefficient operations; and the reputational risk associated with pollution as public opinion—and investor preference—changes. This sustainable calculation has emboldened calls for endowments, pension funds, and other large institutional investors to decarbonize their portfolios. For example, the twelve-member Portfolio Decarbonization Coalition, led by the

UN Environment Program's Finance Initiative and the Swedish pension fund AP4, is hoping to soon double the $45 billion it represents in decarbonized assets. Others, including coalitions of investors, are looking to intermediaries to help them identify promising opportunities and companies in clean energy and tech to advance low-carbon alternatives.* In 2015, Generation Investment Management released its much-anticipated ten-year performance results, earning on average 12.1 percent a year, 500 basis points above the widely benchmarked MSCI World Index (7 percent per year). In other words, the sustainability thesis won the day. This kind of performance data can only advance the activist investor movement further as equity and debt expand the innovative finance tool kit.

* See, for example, "Fact Sheet: Obama Administration Announces More than $4 Billion in Private Sector Commitments and Executive Actions to Scale Up Investment in Clean Energy Innovation," The White House, Office of the Press Secretary, June 16, 2015, https://www.whitehouse.gov/the-press-office/2015/06/16/fact-sheet-obama-administration-announces-more-4-billion-private-sector.

level of investment, exceeding the scope of government and philanthropic resources. Yet private capital that flows at scale does not always correct the market failures we are looking to address: in this case, more investment into truly low-carbon technologies or other kinds of climate change mitigation and adaptation. We began this chapter by grappling with the sheer size of the climate change problem—rising sea levels and extreme weather, inter alia—and the implications for global agriculture, health, and migration that will affect us all. Despite the massive costs associated with mitigating global warming—investments necessary to slow the rate of greenhouse gas emissions—we know that the costs of *inaction* are far higher and more catastrophic; that is, an ounce of prevention is worth a pound of cure. Innovative finance makes it possible to buy that ounce.

We have examined the evolution of early policy-led innovative finance achievements: market-based solutions to market failures, largely built around pricing externalities and assigning a monetary value to a public good, such as clean air, wetlands, or a healthy fish stock. By aligning incentives and creating a property right and a payment mechanism for that right (e.g., a payment not to emit sulfur dioxide or carbon or a payment not to use crowded airspace), policy makers can create markets that balance development objectives with other social and environmental objectives that in the long term are mutually reinforcing. REDD showed us how a similar payment not to pollute—a payment not to cut down trees—could enhance sustainable development even in the absence of fully developed carbon markets.

REDD also exemplifies some of the larger advantages and limitations of pay-for-success financing: in the case of Brazil, it created the right financial incentives to stem deforestation, with payments conditioned on proof of performance. Moreover, it fostered a kind of autonomous development for Brazilians, who could determine how best to preserve their own forests. In the case of Indonesia, where deforestation continued, we saw the limits of this laissez-faire approach: pay-for-success can only encourage, not enforce, good governance. When it comes to climate change mitigation and adaptation, pay-for-success remains a promising area for innovative finance, and numerous nascent efforts (e.g., a methane pilot auction facility and a forest resilience impact bond) represent fruitful avenues for further exploration. Beyond climate, we will revisit the pay-for-success model in numerous incarnations in the chapters to come.

Yet as promising as pay-for-success has been in the case of REDD, it returns us full circle to the scale question, as even the most well-intentioned and well-designed development aid is not enough to support our broader sustainable development aspirations. Efforts to restart carbon market activity are vital to innovative finance, whether these are policy led or instead harness the broader capital markets. We have examined one "hot," and perhaps overheated, approach, green bonds, but there are numerous others—including those involving the equity markets—that can arm us in the fight against climate change. In the chapter that follows, we begin to unpack this much larger innovative finance tool kit as we examine the challenges of and solutions to global health problems.

# 2

# Health

## *Medicine for Market Failure*

If pricing carbon is hard, how do we put a price on a human life? This is the moral and economic question of global development. Do we value all lives equally? And if health is a public good, how do we pay for it?

In less than a generation, we have witnessed significant improvements in health across the globe: life expectancy has increased, particularly in poor countries, and the mortality rates for children, and women when they give birth to children, have been cut in half. We have made important gains against some of the world's most prevalent and preventable diseases: deaths from malaria have declined 45 percent globally and nearly 50 percent in Africa, tuberculosis deaths are down 40 percent since 1990, and new HIV/AIDS infections are down by one-third since 2001.[1] Yet there is nothing inevitable about these gains. Some are the result of GDP growth—increases in income and wealth have brought with them improvements in health, nutrition, and access to care. Economic growth alone, however, does not explain the progress we have made—that we owe to the hard work of local health workers, and to partnerships between government, philanthropy, and the private sector. In turn, as we explore in this chapter, many of these initiatives have been made possible by creative and visible hand investments in global health—what we call innovative finance.

## Why Do Health Investments Matter?

Like defense, education, or clean air, public health is a public good. Disease takes its toll on individual, household, community and national well-being. The benefits of preventing communicable diseases, of investing in cures, and of providing access to care are broadly shared—yet their high costs often discourage investment. Innovative finance has a role to play in improving the way government dollars are spent on public health, and in attracting new private capital to the task.

### Costs, Benefits, and Return on Investment

For lack of a better yardstick, we often translate preventable diseases and deaths into billions of dollars in diminished productivity and increased health-care costs for societies across the globe. For example, high malaria rates can cost more than 1 percent of GDP.[2] Ninety percent of global malaria deaths occur in Africa and account for at least $12 billion in lost productivity each year.[3] The economic weight of tuberculosis deaths on sub-Saharan Africa between 2006 and 2015 was approximately $519 billion.[4] And as massive as the macroeconomic drain is, it is nothing compared to what cannot be measured: generations lost.

These data remind us that despite the gains we have made toward our collective public health goals, we still have a long way to go. HIV/AIDS, tuberculosis, and malaria remain among the top health threats in sub-Saharan Africa. Approximately 207 million cases of malaria occur each year around the world, claiming the lives of 627,000 people,[5] and 2.1 million people were infected with HIV in 2013.[6] According to the World Health Organization (WHO), each day 18,000 children—more than 6 million a year—die before they reach their fifth birthday. The most common causes of these deaths are preventable: pneumonia, diarrhea, malaria, and birth complications. The majority of these children live in the poorest and most vulnerable communities without access to quality health care.

Almost no matter how we measure the cost, preventing disease is cheaper than treating it, and there are enormous costs to inaction. If this sounds familiar, it should. Sometimes the public good of prevention is truly global in nature. Communicable diseases, like climate change, do not respect borders. This is as true for high-profile pandemics like Ebola or

SARS as it is for commonplace killers like meningitis, and measles. These last two take the lives of hundreds of thousands of children each year.

It is precisely because the costs of these diseases are so high that the economic case for investing in health—the return on investment (ROI) for prevention—is strong. The data to support this at the disease- and health-system levels are abundant, for individuals, families, and communities, as investments in health allow people to pursue opportunities in education, employment, and other expressions of their human potential.[7] Exactly what the ROI is depends on what is measured. In the case of maternal and children's health, for example, evidence suggests a potential return of more than $20 for every dollar spent.[8] The Global Alliance for Vaccines and Immunization (GAVI) estimates that the vaccines it provides have an 18 percent ROI for the countries investing in them.[9] Every disease, every cure, has its own calculation. Bill Gates, the world's largest individual investor in global health, explains, "We invest in global health because we know that when health improves, life improves by every measure. . . . In global health, you save lives for $2,000 per life saved. I think that's a bargain. I'd like to buy more."[10]

## With Such High Returns, Why Don't We Invest?

Market failures abound in public health. We will address some of them here as we look at why we do not adequately invest in interventions and how innovative finance can solve investment conundrums.

Not surprisingly, many market failures occur in health technology and the development of drugs. Here the massive costs and long time horizons of R&D mean that pharmaceutical companies lack the incentive to invest in cures for diseases that disproportionately affect the world's poorest; there is no paying customer base for those medicines. For example, the total market, in dollar terms, for all vaccines in developing countries is estimated to be only $500 million annually,[11] which in part explains why we don't yet have an effective vaccine for a disease like malaria, which kills more than 1 million people each year, mostly children under five. This is true of cures for many diseases that kill people, ravage communities, and stunt economic growth. All told, 10 percent of global health R&D is devoted to diseases that affect 90 percent of the world's population. Solutions to global health challenges, however, require more than new technologies like drugs or vaccines. They often also involve addressing other barriers to opportunity and access, as poverty and well-being are so intricately tied.

## Why Innovative Finance?

Innovative finance matters because it can improve the ways we raise and spend existing resources and unlock new sources of capital by overcoming historical market failure. Many of the recent gains in public health have been achieved by an increased commitment in government spending, largely driven by support of the health agenda of the Millennium Development Goals (MDGs). In the last fifteen years, the world has invested more than $200 billion to improve health in lower-income countries.[12] Between 1990 and 2014, it is estimated that annual spending on health increased from less than $6 billion to more than $36 billion.[13] Since 2000, $228 billion (more than 60 percent of all development assistance) has funded solutions to maternal and child health issues, HIV/AIDS, tuberculosis, and malaria. Much of this funding has come from government official development assistance (ODA; figure 2.1)[14] and philanthropy. (The multibillion-dollar-a-year support of the Gates Foundation for health makes it not only the world's largest private funder but also a quasi-government player in

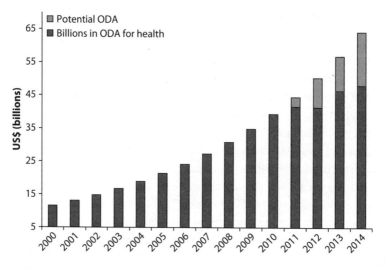

Figure 2.1
Actual Global ODA for Health Versus Potential ODA, 2000–2014
*Source*: IHME DAH Database, 2014.
*Note*: From 2000 to 2010, official development assistance increased an average of 11.3 percent per year with little variation. Starting in 2011, actual official development assistance was much lower than the 11.3 percent trend line, represented here as light gray.

development circles.[15]) However, it is worth noting that the lion's share of funding is provided by low- and middle-income countries themselves. For every $1 donors spent on global health, developing countries invest around $20. This is important to keep in mind because when it comes to health challenges, as in all development, many countries are, want and need to be financing their own solutions.[16] Nevertheless, whether the funds come from local government budgets or ODA, we know that public dollars and their philanthropic counterparts alone are insufficient to cover the health investment gap.

To that end, we explore the role of innovative finance experiments across geographies and asset classes—including taxes, levies, market-shaping initiatives, debt, and equity-like impact investing.

## The Global Fund

One of the first institutions created to address and finance the health objectives of the MDGs was the Global Fund to Fight AIDS, Tuberculosis, and Malaria. Launched in 2002, this Geneva-based public-private partnership was intended to be a war chest to prevent and treat these diseases, which together killed 6 million people a year. The Global Fund was founded on a relatively simple premise: communities and countries know what needs to be done to fight these scourges but are often too poor to start.

Since then, the Global Fund has received more than $41 billion in pledges: 95 percent of these have come from governments, and the remainder have come from philanthropic sources. This means it is not about market solutions or private capital. Its innovation is how it attracts, pools, and blends philanthropic and public capital, on the order of $4 billion a year, to support more than 600 local programs in 150 countries. On the operational side, its partnership model means that all stakeholders—government, civil society, technical and research partners, development agencies, philanthropic funders, and communities living with the diseases—share in the decision making. The Global Fund was designed around this commitment to local autonomy, allowing countries to tailor responses to what it calls "their own political, cultural, and epidemiological context."[17]

From the outset, the Global Fund built its funding criteria around performance-based assistance, not unlike Reducing Emissions from Deforestation and Forest Degradation (REDD). In practice, this means ensuing, rather than initial, funding is contingent on the results of previous investments.

For example, in the fall of 2015, the health ministers of Botswana, Namibia, South Africa, Swaziland, Angola, Mozambique, Zambia, and Zimbabwe, all of whom were working to eliminate malaria in their countries, devised a Global Fund–sponsored program, Elimination 8, which focuses on a coordinated regional approach to eliminating malaria. The Global Fund's $18 million grant will be used for a regional malaria surveillance system, a database, and a laboratory to improve the region's capacity to understand where malaria is occurring and how best to contain it. This grant is a follow-on to its previous grants of $275 million to these eight countries in support of their efforts to reduce the number of malaria cases.

Since its creation, the Global Fund has become the primary source of finance for programs to fight AIDS, tuberculosis, and malaria. It provides a quarter of all international financing for AIDS globally, two-thirds for tuberculosis, and three-quarters for malaria. As of 2014, programs it supports across 150 countries have treated 7.3 million people with antiretroviral therapy for AIDS, tested and treated 12.3 million people for tuberculosis, and distributed 450 million insecticide-treated nets to protect families against malaria. Global Fund–supported programs are on track to achieve their 2012–2016 goals: 10 million lives saved and 180 million infections averted.

Although the bulk of its financing comes from donor pledges, the Global Fund has explored creative ways to raise and pool additional funds. For example, in 2006 it created Product (RED), an initiative through which companies dedicate a portion of their sales on particular products to the fund. Although this has been high-profile , Product (RED)'s $295 million in revenues comprise less than 1 percent of total contributions to the fund.[18] In 2010, the Global Fund entered into a partnership with Dow Jones to create the Dow Jones Global Fund 50 Index$^{SM}$, designed to track publicly traded companies that support the fund's mission.

## Taxes and Levies

### UNITAID, UNITLIFE, and the Macroreach of Microlevies

In 2014, the Global Fund entered into a formal collaboration with UNITAID, another pioneer health organization, which was founded in 2006 by the governments of France, Norway, the UK, Brazil, and Chile. Like the Global Fund, UNITAID brings new funding for medicine, diagnostics, and the prevention of HIV/AIDS, malaria, and tuberculosis. Housed within the WHO, UNITAID began life as a drug purchase facility that negotiated lower prices for drugs and diagnostics and fast-tracked their development on behalf of poor countries. Today UNITAID looks for cost-effective ways to address prevention, treatment, and diagnosis of HIV/AIDS, tuberculosis, and malaria.[19]

UNITAID's own funding structure is unique, as the organization has raised 65 percent of its funds through an innovative airline ticket levy. The idea was to create a kind of solidarity levy to harness global funds in support of global public good. Initiated by France, the UNITAID levy ranges from $1 on economy-class tickets to $40 on business-class tickets. It is imposed on every airline ticket of every flight departing that country, although passengers in transit are exempt. The funds are collected by the French Civic Aviation Authority. Initially, there were concerns that this nominal levy might slow economic growth, but an independent evaluation found that it has not hurt airline revenue, air traffic, travel industry jobs, or tourism. Even during the financial crisis, revenues remained stable, at approximately 160 million euros per year.[20] The intent is that the levy should be small enough that passengers don't notice it or that it doesn't deter them from flying.

France has been joined by Cameroon, Chile, Congo, Madagascar, Mali, Mauritius, Niger, and the Republic of Congo in imposing the airline levy, which has generated approximately $2 billion. The UNITAID architects believe that by signing on, these countries are able to support their own and each other's health financing, allowing for a kind of "South-South cooperation in development."[21]

Many features of the design are worth exploring, should the levy be expanded or replicated. First, the levy is imposed on passengers, not on airlines, so as not to distort competition between airline companies. Second, many countries already rely on airline taxes to fund other initiatives, so the policy infrastructure is in place to layer on a new tax. Third, it is entirely optional, so participating countries determine what the amount of the levy is and how it is distributed. Although France charges a different amount for economy and businesses travelers, developing countries might choose to exclusively tax international or business-class passengers.[22]

Though comparatively small in the face of looming health finance needs, UNITAID is considered a success because the funds it generates for diseases like HIV/AIDS, malaria, and tuberculosis are truly additional to ODA. Of course, and as with any tax or funding source dependent on exogenous market forces, such as the price on carbon in a cap-and-trade system, a slowing of demand jeopardizes the reliability and predictability of funds. Although UNITAID claims revenue from the levy did not decline in the recession, significantly reduced airline travel would translate into less money.[23] It is also not clear how much more broadly the levy will be adopted. Many European countries already use airline taxes to support other initiatives; they may have limited interest in imposing an additional one.

The airline levy has inspired a new set of innovations on the theme. For example, in 2014 the Environmental Defense Fund facilitated a partnership in India between the Fair Climate Network (FCN) and IndiGo, the country's largest and fastest-growing airline. In this arrangement, airline passengers can make a voluntary contribution that IndiGo directs toward funding climate-friendly technologies, including biogas, alternative energy electrification, and water purification in rural India. There are also several creative design features. The partnership relies on IndiGo's purchasing carbon offsets that generated by FCN's and others carbon-mitigation efforts. This is a prime example of both the use of market-based credits and local ownership of development: development in rural India is financed by domestic Indian travel.[24]

### Reverse the Curse

The UNITAID example has opened a larger discussion about the role of solidarity levies in supporting global public goods, particularly when levies might be imposed on goods and services enjoyed by the world's wealthiest, like airline travel, to fund the unmet needs of the world's poorest. Such levies may offer an opportunity to reverse what is referred to in development as the "resource curse." Many countries with large stores of natural resource wealth, such as diamonds or oil, don't harness them for inclusive growth. Instead, many of these countries struggle with corruption, armed conflict, and deep poverty as different groups battle over control of the resources. Accordingly, economists and policy makers are exploring the possibility that countries could use a tax or levy to siphon off a small portion of the revenues from resource extraction and dedicate it to development goals. In other words, they could convert sovereign natural resource wealth, a kind of future sovereign wealth fund, into broader social wealth, to be spent today. For example, Botswana is the world's leading producer of diamonds, which account for a third of its GDP. It uses an extraction tax to fund a significant portion of its government services, allowing the country to spend substantially more on health per capita than many of its neighbors in sub-Saharan Africa.[25]

The allure of translating natural resource wealth into social investment motivated the creation in September 2015 of UNITLIFE, an initiative that uses a solidarity levy to address child malnutrition. Designed and championed by the UNITAID airline levy team, including Philippe Douste-Blazy, the UN's undersecretary general for innovative finance, and Robert Filipp, head of the Innovative Finance Foundation, UNITLIFE will impose a levy on extractive industries and is projected to generate as much as $300 million a year. In terms of resources, UNITLIFE will begin with oil, but there are plans to move on to gold, phosphate, and uranium from participants' state-owned companies. The Republic of Congo was the first country to sign on, committing 10 cents per barrel of oil.

---

The Cost of Child Malnutrition

Chronic child malnutrition has been connected to irreversible physical and cognitive development delays, tragic for the affected children and economically devastating for the countries and regions in which those children live. Consider the importance of nutrition and health services within the first 1,000 days, or 3 years, of a child's life. Their absence means the child's brain and body do not develop properly. Malnutrition is more pervasive than hunger, and its effects in these early years are often invisible until later in life. Further, because it affects brain development, its effects can be permanent. Malnutrition is responsible for nearly 3 million deaths each year, accounting for 45 percent of deaths of children under five.* The survivors, an estimated 40 percent of children in sub-Saharan Africa and South Asia, suffer stunted growth† and other grievous consequences. They often exhibit lower IQs and are more likely to drop out of school. As adults, they are one-third less likely to escape poverty. Undernourished mothers give birth to undernourished babies, perpetuating a devastating cycle of poverty.‡ For the poorest of the countries affected, it is estimated that the economic cost is approximately 6 percent of GDP. According to UNITLIFE, targeting child malnutrition in the thirty-six countries that account for more than 90 percent of all children whose growth has been stunted requires about $10.8 billion a year. However, the

ROI is extremely compelling: $100 for a "package" of interventions for children younger than two years of age is projected to return $3,000 in health-care savings and economic productivity.[§]

The problem of malnutrition, and the high rates of return from its prevention, have led to other recent innovative finance approaches. For example, a public-private partnership called the Power of Nutrition was launched in April 2015 with $200 million in commitments from the Children's Investment Fund Foundation, the UK Department for International Development, and the UBS Optimus Foundation. These resources will be channeled through a new World Bank trust fund and through a UNICEF six-to-one matched funding mechanism. The trust fund will leverage at least $100 million in financing from the International Development Association, the World Bank's fund for the poorest countries. This partnership aims to unlock $1 billion in public and private funds to tackle severe child malnutrition in some of these countries by supporting country-led programs at scale.[‖]

---

[*] Robert Black et al., "Maternal and Child Undernutrition and Overweight in Low-Income and Middle-Income Countries," *Lancet 382,* no. 9890 (June 2013): 427–51, http://www .thelancet.com/journals/lancet/article/PIIS0140-6736(13)60937-X/abstract.

[†] See "The State of the World's Children Report," UNICEF, 2015, http://www.data.unicef .org/resources/the-state-of-the-world-s-children-report-2015-statistical-tables. See also World Health Organization Global Database on Child Growth and Malnutrition, http://www .who.int/nutgrowthdb/en/.

[‡] Susan P. Walker et al., "Early Childhood Stunting Is Associated with Lower Developmental Levels in the Subsequent Generation of Children," *Journal of Nutrition 145* (April 2015): 823–28; "Improving Child Nutrition: The Achievable Imperative for Global Progress," UNICEF, April 2013, http://www.unicef.org/publications/index_68661.html.

[§] Tom Miles, "UN Entrepreneur Taps African Oil for Child Health," Reuters, September 19, 2014, http://www.reuters.com/article/2014/09/19/us-aid-innovation-idUSKBN0HE1YM20140919.

[‖] powerofnutrition.org; "The Power of Nutrition: New Fund Targets Billion Dollars for Children's Nutrition," Children's Investment Fund Foundation, April 16, 2015, https://ciff .org/news/power-of-nutrition/.

---

Over time, UNITLIFE hopes to enlist additional countries in its cause, particularly oil-rich nations like Nigeria and Angola or those on the Persian Gulf that have long been the "holy grail" of the development finance world. Filipp estimates a global rollout could generate at least $1.6 billion in oil revenue alone. As with UNITAID, Douste-Blazy sees this kind of innovative finance as a way to harness wealth for development. "The simple idea is to take a microscopic contribution of solidarity on economic activities that benefit most from globalization: mass tourism by plane, mobile phones, Internet, financial transactions, [and] extractive resources" and direct it to the needs of the poor.[26] Researchers at Oxford's Internet Institute are beginning to explore what an Internet levy might look like.

Critiques of UNITLIFE do not challenge the merits of the cause but question the efficacy of the financing strategy. For example, as in the case of REDD's pay-for-success, there is no compulsory enforcement mechanism. These kinds of voluntary contributions may not be stable or predictable if participating nations waver in their commitment. This is particularly true in countries that are not making the requisite social welfare investments in the first place. Critics of extraction taxes remind us that, by definition, mineral and oil deposits are exhaustible. In the more immediate term, a resource levy, like an oil or gold tax, depends on both the volume of extraction and the market price of the commodity, which can be volatile and unpredictable.

UNITLIFE's advocates counter that the levy can and will serve as an important additional source of funding for social investment. Different design features, including a 10-cents-per-barrel fee rather than a percentage fee, are meant to guard against oil price fluctuations. They also contend that, like UNITAID, UNITLIFE will be an effective source of South-South funding, offering countries a chance to finance their own development priorities. Although OECD countries do not participate in UNITLIFE's financing, they lend political support, which can act as an informal enforcement mechanism. It is important that the new organization be housed in an independent agency, as is UNITAID. In this case, UNITLIFE has an independent board that channels funds through UNICEF, which will manage the spending. This is important for governance concerns: the perception and reality that, in some developing countries, corruption and incompetence are severe obstacles to development, often the reason health investments aren't being made in the first place. "What's important to understand," says Douste-Blazy, "is that the money from UNITAID has never gone to a government or minister or head of state. The level of corruption is zero."[27]

It is worth noting the difference between microlevies along the lines of UNITAID and UNITLIFE and a larger set of taxes that are intended to discourage behavior while generating revenues. UNITAID and UNITLIFE are taxes that support public goods; they are not meant to price a social cost or correct a negative externality in the way a carbon tax does. Microlevies work because they are small enough to go unnoticed or at least not to diminish the activity—such as airline travel or resource extraction—on which their revenues depend. By design, they are progressive, meaning that they skim revenue from the activities of those who are already well-off or from resources that generate enormous wealth, like oil or minerals. The nature of the tax and the nature of the public good are unrelated. The tax could be levied on anything in order to generate revenue, and the decision about what to fund (ie malnutrition or malaria) is a separate one.

A number of new tax and levy schemes have been proposed or implemented along these lines. In 2009, the Taskforce on Innovative International Financing for Health Systems projected that the creation or expansion of taxes on things like airline travel could generate an additional $10 billion a year.[28]

Unlike UNITAID or UNITLIFE, many of these new levies are locally designed and administered. For example, in 1999, Zimbabwe became the first country to introduce an AIDS levy; the 3 percent it collects on gross monthly earnings of business- and formal-sector employees is managed by the National AIDS Trust Foundation (NATF). The levy was implemented to demonstrate the country's commitment to fighting HIV/AIDS and to alleviate reliance on external funding. Although it raises small sums relative to the larger national spending on the disease, NATF is a strong domestic organization for managing AIDS resources. This model is being closely examined by neighboring African countries.[29]

Whereas the Zimbabwe levy focused on income, value-added taxes (VATs) on goods and services can also be used to support public goods like health. In sub-Saharan Africa, VATs account for approximately one-quarter of all tax revenue and in some cases go directly to fund health.[30] For example, in 2004, Ghana, aiming to make health care more universally affordable, created its National Health Insurance Scheme (NHIS), half of which is funded through a VAT. Unlike microlevies or taxes on business earnings, VATs are typically regressive and therefore not historically good innovative finance candidates. However, Ghana's VAT deliberately excludes many goods and services the poor regularly need, like food, which suggests a different and promising path forward.[31]

Many countries have considered paying for local health initiatives by taxing remittances, funds sent to family members in home countries by members of the diaspora. Countries like Mexico already tax remittances for local development and infrastructure projects. The World Bank estimates that international migrants sent $583 billion in remittances to their home countries in 2014.[32] By some counts, remittances are three times the amount of ODA provided to many developing countries.[33] As appealing as the size and flow of these funds are, development economists warn that taxing remittances, often a critical source of income for the poor, may be counterproductive to long-term health and development objectives.[34]

Perhaps the most controversial of the levies proposed along these lines is a financial transaction tax, best known as a Tobin tax, which is an excise tax on currency exchange transactions. Originally proposed by Nobel laureate James Tobin as a way to reduce exchange rate volatility, slow speculative activity, and improve macroeconomic stability, the levy was later invoked as a way to tap wealth generated by currency speculators to fund public goods like the MDGs. Given the volume of currency transactions, it is estimated that this kind of tax could generate hundreds of billions of dollars in revenue each year. Within individual countries, broader financial transaction taxes are not uncommon; nearly forty countries already use this type of tax, often in the form of a VAT, to finance an array of local priorities. In the wake of the financial crisis, popular support for this kind of tax has grown. However, the financial services sector and others argue that these taxes will drive transactions and capital to tax-free locations, reducing economic activity (and tax revenue). France, which put into place its own financial transaction tax in 2014, has pressed for a European Union–wide tax, but this has been opposed by the UK, among others.[35] Although France pledged to allocate 15 percent of its financial transaction tax to development aid, particularly climate change and pandemics, most proceeds are used to finance other domestic priorities. While there have been calls for this type of levy in the United States there is no financial transaction tax, and it is unlikely, on both efficiency and political grounds, that this kind of tax will be put into place to fund public health anytime soon.[36]

## Sin Taxes and Public Health

In contrast to the taxes above, which look to harness additional revenue for public goods, other health taxes take direct aim at negative externalities. In other words, it is possible to use a health tax in the same way as a carbon tax: to discourage certain behaviors by putting a price on them and making them costly. The appeal of "sin" taxes on things like alcohol, tobacco, sugar, and gambling—which have harmful effects on public health—is that they can both discourage behavior and raise funds for programs that address the consequences of that behavior.

Sin taxes aren't particularly new. In the United States, Secretary of the Treasury Alexander Hamilton introduced the first federal tax on tobacco to pay down debt incurred during the Revolutionary War. Alcohol taxes in the United States also date to the eighteenth century, and in 1862, Abraham Lincoln imposed a tax on liquor to help finance the Civil War. In the modern era, developed countries have recognized that these products exact a substantial toll on public health and now use sin taxes, particularly on tobacco, to pay for treatments for chronic diseases like cardiovascular disease and diabetes, which often result from the use of these products. Sin taxes are becoming more prevalent in emerging economies, particularly where middle-income populations experience both infectious diseases and more chronic illnesses.[37]

Tobacco taxes, in particular, are what the WHO calls a "best buy" or a "win-win" for health, as they reduce usage, particularly among the poor, while also generating much-needed revenue.[38] Evidence from a growing number of studies shows that taxes that increase retail prices on tobacco by 10 percent can decrease consumption between 2 and 8 percent. In 2013, the Lancet Commission on Investing in Health estimated that a 50 percent price increase in cigarettes could prevent 20 million deaths in China and 4 million in India over 50 years.[39]

Countries vary in how they apply taxes on products like cigarettes—using either the total number of goods sold or the value of those goods. In wealthier countries, tobacco taxes on average account for 63 percent of the retail cost of cigarettes, though few countries meet or exceed the WHO-recommended 70 percent threshold. Countries also differ in how much of this revenue they actually allocate to health. For example, Rwanda, Guatemala, and Djibouti allocate tobacco taxes primarily for and directly to health, whereas Bulgaria, Mongolia, and Qatar dedicate small percentages, using most of the proceeds for other economic priorities.[40]

Given the vested corporate interests, it isn't always easy to implement a tobacco tax. In the United States, the tobacco industry spends millions of dollars a year to lobby against regulation and taxation. Furthermore, critics argue that tobacco taxes can lead to black market sales and that they are regressive, as the poor spend a disproportionately larger percentage of their income on tobacco. However, the data show that tobacco taxes have a positive macroeconomic effect on growth, given the tremendous health-care costs associated with tobacco-related diseases and the reductions in those costs that come when people quit smoking. In the United States, approximately $140 billion a year in health-care expenses is attributable to cigarettes.[41] It is estimated that a number of other developed countries experience GDP losses between 1 and 3.5 percent due to lost labor productivity and health-care expenditures caused by tobacco use.[42]

Tobacco taxes offer a promising innovative finance opportunity for low- and middle-income countries, and several are beginning to explore this option.[43] In 2013, the Philippines, which has high rates of tobacco and alcohol use and associated health costs, undertook significant reforms of its sin taxes in an effort to fund expansion of its universal health-care program. Although it is too early to assess the full efficacy of the program, in its first year it took in about $750 million. The country's government hopes that these taxes might allow it to expand its health budget for the poor by 43 percent.[44] The Philippines example is notable because other developing countries share the goals of universal health care and greater ownership of the financing their domestic health needs.

## Market Shaping: Shifting Risk and Paying for Success

In addition to creative levies to finance health, we have seen the emergence of a promising new class of *market shapers*—innovations that correct for market failure by recalibrating supply and demand. Unlike a tax, these approaches—prizes, challenges, and advanced market commitments, among others—aim to harness or stimulate market forces like competition to spur innovation, reduce costs, improve market information, and mitigate and shift risk. In the process, they can leverage new and additional funds to finance investment in public goods—in health and beyond.

### Prizes and Challenges

The proliferation of philanthropic and government prizes and challenges in recent years—what some have called both renaissance and revolution in public-goods finance—illustrates the enthusiasm for market shaping. Prizes are not new, of course. For centuries, they were a tool used to promote scientific breakthroughs, built around the basic market principle that competition fosters innovation.

Perhaps the most famous dates to 1714, when the UK Parliament's Longitudinal Prize led British clockmaker John Harrison to invent the chronometer, an instrument that determines latitude at sea (rather essential for naval dominance). Over the centuries, prizes have been responsible for a range of advances, in areas from food and agriculture to aviation (Charles Lindbergh's famous transatlantic flight earned him the Orteig Prize). Toward the end of the twentieth century, patents and grants became more common-place incentives tools, but the early twenty-first century has seen a rebirth of prizes and challenges in both the philanthropic and the public sectors.[45] In addition to those like the high-profile X Prizes in alternative energy, and space travel, genomics, and other fields, or the Breakthrough Prize in the life sciences, mathematics and physics, the Obama administration has pioneered prizes in traditional areas like defense and energy and in human service fields like education and health.[46] Prize sponsors employ them because they are pay for success: prizes are only awarded to proven breakthroughs and they shift risk onto the innovators. They are therefore cost effective as they leverage additional resources—the total value of invention and investment they generate significantly exceeds the cash value of the original prizes themselves. In this sense, prizes efficiently "pull" in innovators to work on problems, whereas grants "push" solutions through traditional grants .

When it comes to health, the most high-profile prizes are the Grand Challenges for Health. First sponsored by the Gates Foundation in 2003 (when $450 million was awarded to research projects involving scientists in thirty-three countries), these challenges have been taken up by a broad alliance of governments, philanthropy, development funders, and industry—visible hand partnerships—that develop demonstrable and measurable solutions to specific health challenges. Today a network of governments and funders—including Grand Challenges Canada and Grand Challenges for Development, administered by the U.S. Agency for International Development (USAID) in partnership with Sweden, Norway, the UK, Australia, the World Bank, and others—has made 1,741 awards in the areas of water, food, literacy, energy, agriculture, and health across eighty-one countries.[47] In 2015 alone, health challenges stimulated research breakthroughs across the world in malaria (with advances in mosquito population control and "outdoor" transmission), tuberculosis, malnutrition, newborn and infant health, pneumonia, and neglected tropical diseases.[48] These challenges have been successful in their own right, encouraging innovation and leveraging funds as an important innovative finance blueprint for new areas in global health.[49]

### Market Failure and the Orphan Problem

Another area where we have seen important market-shaping innovations is vaccine development and distribution. Vaccines are one of the most cost-effective interventions in public health—and also a tragic example of market failure.

In the developed world, we take the protections of immunization for granted. However, public health economics look different in poorer countries, where an estimated 22 million children are not inoculated against the most common diseases. Twenty percent of the 6 million children who die each year before the age of five lose their lives to vaccine-preventable diphtheria, pneumonia, diarrhea, and yellow fever.[50] Many others battle illness and disability that could be avoided: each year 90,000 children are born with severe birth defects due to rubella. In addition, 275,000 women die annually from cervical cancer, a disease that is 70 percent preventable with the HPV vaccine. Of these cervical cancer deaths, 85 percent are in the developing world, where women often do not have access to this protection.[51]

These conditions make the investment case for vaccines even more compelling, as development depends on health. Immunized children have greater cognitive abilities and are more likely to attend school and grow up to be productive members of their communities. Vaccines also significantly reduce costs for families and larger health systems by reducing illness and long-term disability. In 2010, it was estimated that the introduction and increased use of six vaccines (figure 2.2)—against pneumococcal

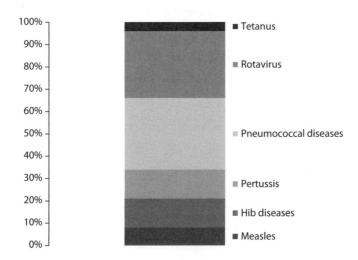

Figure 2.2
Distribution of 1.5 Million Preventable Child Deaths by Cause, 2010
*Source*: World Health Organization, 2010.

and *Haemophilus influenzae* type B pneumonia, meningitis, rotavirus, pertussis, measles, and malaria—in seventy-two of the world's poorest countries would save 6.4 million lives, avert 426 million cases of illness, and save $6.2 billion in treatment costs and $145 billion in productivity losses.[52] Even the current estimates of ROI for vaccine investments in poor countries, approximately 18 percent, do not fully capture a host of other and larger macroeconomic benefits.

And yet we fail to adequately invest in vaccines and other preventive medicines because of market failure. Drug development involves gargantuan costs, risks, and time. This is as true for innovation in medicines for developed markets as it is for innovation in those for poor countries. To move a drug from its early stage to market can take fifteen years, and each stage holds a new set of risks. In the developed world, investors and pharmaceutical companies make lottery-style bets on numerous molecules and drugs, knowing some will fail but anticipating that one in a diversified portfolio might prove different in terms of potential revenue and profitability. In developed countries, drugs that are proven but that lack market potential—often because they cure rare diseases that afflict small numbers—are known as orphans. Orphan drugs require subsidies for pharmaceutical companies to bring them to market; otherwise, they are abandoned. Drugs for poor people represent a related public-goods problem: demand is great, but ability to pay is small. The market size for all vaccines in developing countries—about $500 million annually—is not enough to spur investment from pharmaceutical companies.[53] This is in part why we don't yet have effective vaccines for diseases like AIDS or malaria which kill millions of people each year.

## GAVI's Advanced Market Commitment: Purchase and Power

Enter GAVI, an organization created in 2000 to address the vaccines-as-public-goods problem. Launched with support from the Gates Foundation at a time when vaccine distribution was faltering, GAVI brings together governments, nongovernmental organizations, philanthropies, multilateral institutions like the World Bank, and pharmaceutical companies to expand vaccination by improving access to new and underused vaccines. Countries that are eligible for GAVI support determine their immunization needs, apply for funding, cofinance the drug's production, and implement the vaccine program. The model was designed to leverage financial resources and expertise from private sources and make vaccines more affordable, available, and sustainable. The intent is to reach a point where developing countries can pay for these vaccines themselves. GAVI support is available to the seventy-three poorest countries in the world, and these countries have taken on an increasingly larger role in paying for their vaccines. In 2013, more than sixty countries cofinanced vaccines supplied by GAVI, and twenty-two of them are projected to graduate from GAVI's support by 2020.

GAVI's success has been remarkable. Since 2000, it has helped bring vaccines to 500 million children and prevent more than 7 million deaths from hepatitis B, *Haemophilus influenzae* type B (Hib), measles, meningitis A, pneumococcal disease, rotavirus diarrhea, and yellow fever.[54] It hopes to reach an additional 300 million children between 2016 and 2020, prevent 6 million more deaths, and save countries up to $100 billion by averting illness-related costs, including treatment and productivity loss.[55]

GAVI is a market shaper. It is perhaps best known for pioneering an *advanced market commitment* (AMC) for pneumococcal disease, an innovation that helped finance vaccinations for 11 million children. AMCs were first explored as an alternative way to address market failures in health R&D. Historically, governments and philanthropies have responded to the lack of investment in public-good drugs through grant funding, "pushing" them into the pipeline by underwriting R&D expenses or subsidizing production costs. In contrast, an AMC is intended to "pull" investment by focusing on demand rather than supply—by guaranteeing a paying market for the drug manufacturer. Like a prize and unlike a grant, the AMC is pay-for-success. Payment occurs only when the drug has been produced. This shifts risk to the manufacturer. It also leverages new and additional resources, allowing more private capital to flow, with price supports for the public good. AMCs were originally seen as a way to encourage companies to invest in R&D for new products and drugs; the GAVI pneumococcal case shows that they can also be used to increase production for an existing product at a lower price, accelerating its introduction into developing countries. Support for a proven product also means the funders are not "picking winners" in advance of production.

The pneumococcal AMC donors—including Canada, Italy, Norway, Russia, the UK, participating developing countries, and the Gates Foundation—pledged a total of $1.5 billion to fund the purchase of 2 billion doses of pneumococcal conjugate vaccine (PCV) at $3.50 per dose over ten years, beginning in 2009. This was 90 percent lower than the price of PCV in higher-income markets. Since its launch, two suppliers, GlaxoSmithKline (GSK) and Pfizer, have produced and distributed PCV to twenty-four low-income countries. Although precise returns data are unavailable, an independent evaluation estimated that these manufacturers have earned around 20 percent per year on their investment, consistent with historical industry performance.[56] In addition, the AMC has promoted ownership and autonomy in development. All of the developing countries receiving the vaccine have cofinanced its production.

As with all innovative finance, the question is whether we will see another AMC along these lines. The WHO, the Center for Global Development, and others have long advocated for an AMC to accelerate the development of a new vaccine for a disease like malaria, where there are currently ninety potential candidates, more than a dozen in clinical trials, and one now in the late stage.[57] Others are exploring whether AMCs can be used to encourage technological breakthroughs in sectors like alternative energy, involving similar public goods and market failure. In energy, as in health, high fixed costs and uncertain demand deter companies from making an adequate up-front investment. In both cases donors would like to encourage the entry of multiple providers, not just the production of one technology by one manufacturer.

This kind of market shaping—predicting the right prices, volumes, costs, and incentives—is challenging. AMCs are complex and time consuming to assemble. GAVI's pilot took a few years to get off the ground. Also, their funding is stable and predictable only as long as donors remain engaged. These are not investments that regenerate in a typical market sense.

Perhaps less complex than a full-fledged AMC, but equally important for financing global public health objectives, is the larger category of innovative *purchase agreements*. Through these kinds of negotiated arrangements, GAVI has helped to reduce prices on a range of vaccines, including the pentavalent vaccine (40 percent cheaper than the developed-market rate) and HPV (down by two-thirds from its price in developed markets). In 2012, GAVI—working through UNICEF, its supply partner—entered into a purchase arrangement for the rotavirus vaccine from two manufacturers, GSK and Merck, which included a volume guarantee and long-term supply agreement. By prepaying for a portion of the vaccine supply, GAVI allowed GSK and Merck to recoup their initial costs earlier and offer a substantially lower price (67 percent lower than the developed market rate, resulting in a savings of $650 million). GAVI hopes these purchase agreements will enlarge their vaccine-supplier base by sending strong and positive market signals to potential manufacturers, including companies in developing countries.[58] They may also lend themselves to replication in other markets. For example, GAVI's purchase agreements are not unlike (and could be a model for more) "take or pay" contracts in the energy sector, in which one side agrees to buy goods or services, typically electricity, at a given price or by a certain date, even if that buyer doesn't need or ultimately "take" it. In turn, this agreement provides guaranteed revenue for the seller or can be used as collateral for loans to finance investments in areas like plants or renewable energy.[59]

## The Role of Debt

Whereas market-shaping instruments offer a novel approach, health organizations have been unusually innovative with traditional financing instruments, particularly when it comes to debt.

Debt can be a powerful tool. It allows for what economists call *intertemporal transfer*, that is, borrowing against future earning for investment today. The ability to front-load—to bring forward future resources needed today—and to pay back debts in manageable increments over time, matching assets and liabilities, can provide all kinds of opportunities that would otherwise not be available. Yet debt comes at a price. The hope is that the returns on today's investment exceed what we must pay in interest for the loans. This is as true for individuals and households as it is for companies and countries. If the calculation is right, debt can empower. Equally powerful are the dangers of debt. As interest payments compound, debt becomes increasingly expensive and harder to repay. For these reasons, debt is also a fraught issue in our culture and finance.

### Debt Forgiveness

When it comes to health, some of the most innovative finance has less to do with creating new debt than with undoing old. The idea is that changing the terms of a loan agreement, either through debt conversion or forgiveness, can allow a country to focus on health spending rather than debt repayment.

For decades, development institutions and philanthropies have made low-interest loans to support development in low- and middle-income countries. Over time, many countries have accumulated debt that is unsustainable even at concessionary rates, and loan repayment crowds out social investment on health. In response, debt relief has evolved as a tool of development finance. In 1996, the World Bank and the IMF initiated the Heavily Indebted Poor Countries (HIPC) Initiative. The Jubilee 2000 Debt Relief Initiative—a high-profile global campaign supported by Bono, the Pope, and the G8 heads of state, among others—gave rise to the 2005 Multilateral Debt Relief Initiative (MDRI).

The MDRI provided a way for countries to work toward the MDGs in general and health priorities in particular. Economists, including Peter Henry, have demonstrated that debt relief does not necessarily improve development in the ways we expect or want to see. For example, it does not correlate with greater capital flows to some of the world's poorest places. For many countries struggling with governance problems, of which their poverty is both a symptom and a cause, removing *debt overhang* didn't make them more attractive to foreign investment or increase the amount of foreign aid given.[60] However, when it comes to improving the ways domestic funds are used—particularly by freeing resources to spend on health rather than on debt repayment—the HIPC Initiative and MDRI have been effective in many countries. For example, the IMF found that, prior to receiving debt relief through the HIPC Initiative, these countries were spending twice as much on debt payment as they were on health and education. After debt relief, they were spending only one-fifth as much.[61]

The power of debt relief is the animating design behind Debt2Health, an innovative loan-conversion initiative in which the Global Fund is partner and broker. For participating countries, the funds freed from debt payment are then invested in the Global Fund, which then helps to manage the health-sector program according to Global Fund standards and procedures. To date, Debt2Health has brokered five agreements involving Germany and emerging economies like Indonesia, Pakistan, Côte d'Ivoire, Egypt, and Ethiopia and one agreement between Australia and Indonesia. Debt2Health has successfully encouraged these countries to translate forgiven loan payments into health spending, particularly to fight tuberculosis, AIDS, and malaria.

Debt2Health has worked in part because it is a neutral third-party broker. One of the justifiable hesitations about debt forgiveness is related to governance. In those instances, donors need reassurance that the same problems that led to overindebtedness in the first place (mismanagement, or worse, malfeasance) will not interfere with the investment of freed resources in public goods like health. The emergence of brokers like Debt-2Health and the Global Fund, as we saw in UNITAID and UNITLIFE, can go a long way toward alleviating those concerns and circumventing problematic governance issues.

Given the scale of health needs and indebtedness, Debt2Health is small. To date, it has facilitated only about $200 million in transactions. Many believe that unless there is a significant mass of sovereign debt that can be managed through debt relief programs, the effects of debt forgiveness will remain modest.[62] However, Debt2Health has reignited interest in the promise of loan forgiveness. In recent years, new "buy-down" programs have emerged, in which a third party pays down a government's remaining debt obligations if that government successfully implements a specific project, often in the area of public health. For example, the Global Polio Eradication Initiative—a partnership among the WHO, Rotary International, the Centers for Disease Control, UNICEF, the Gates Foundation, and a series of development banks—makes low- or no-interest loans to countries like Nigeria and Pakistan to be used to purchase a polio vaccine or advance other polio eradication efforts. Following demonstrated reductions in polio, the philanthropies repay the loan for the vaccine.

### Trade Finance for Health: NetGuarantee and Pledge Guarantee for Health

Even though development assistance for health has increased noticeably in the last few decades, exactly *when* the funding will arrive and just *how much* it will be remain unpredictable. Even when funds are pledged, there are bottlenecks: it can take six to fourteen months for committed funds to be disbursed. In public health in poor countries, these delays can be the difference between life and death.

This kind of volatility presents grave challenges to countries that need aid and lack cash to bridge the timing gaps. Without financing options, governments and nonprofits that provide critical human services cannot properly forecast or budget. They also face stock-outs and higher costs for regular commodities and emergency goods. The Brookings Institution estimates that for every dollar of overseas development assistance, up to $0.28 in extra value could be captured through more predictable and readily accessible donor funding.[63] This means that, globally, as much as $2.8 billion could be gained each year through supply chain enhancements.

Better cash-flow management would go a long way toward meeting short- and long-term health needs. It turns out working capital is a public good.

This situation motivated Malaria No More in 2010 to create the innovative finance facility NetGuarantee. Capitalized with philanthropic funds, NetGuarantee was designed to accelerate the delivery of antimalarial bed nets by six to twelve months by issuing payment guarantees to bed net manufacturers in advance of aid disbursement. (NetGuarantee was originally the brainchild of an analyst at AIG well versed in commercial trade finance.) With NetGuarantee in place, Malaria No More arranged the delivery of 50,000 bed nets to Mozambique that prevented nearly 100,000 cases of malaria.

NetGuarantee would also offer proof of concept for the 2011 pilot launch of Pledge Guarantee for Health (PGH), a financing facility that would similarly apply the principles of trade finance to global health, procuring bed nets and medicines in a timely, affordable fashion. In the case of PGH, government donors act as guarantors to lending institutions, which then make short-term, low-cost commercial loans on the basis of pending aid commitments. In the PGH model, a participating commercial bank issues a letter of credit to a commodities supplier on behalf of a grant recipient. The supplier receives payment from the bank when its receivable is due, and the bank recoups its capital when the donor disburses its funding. PGH guarantees the bank loan and therefore enables the transaction. Although these are loans, not grants, they free up funds that would have been spent to pay higher prices for commodities or higher interest rates on commercial loans. They also allow countries to meet immediate health needs sooner.

PGH proved its efficacy with a number of highly successful initiatives, speeding the delivery of lifesaving goods. Like NetGuarantee and Malaria No More, one of PGH's earliest successes came in malaria prevention. In 2011, a PGH loan guarantee allowed the government of Zambia—working with the World Bank, UNICEF, the UN Special Envoy for Malaria, and Stanbic Bank Zambia—to distribute 1.6 million malaria-preventing bed nets before the rainy season rather than after. This reduced the procurement period from twenty-seven weeks to six, saving the lives of thousands of Zambian children.

In the Ukraine, PGH worked with Alliance Ukraine and Merck to improve the affordability of Peg-Intron, a drug that helped reduce the high hepatitis C infection rates in the HIV-positive population of Ukraine. The 50 percent price reduction then allowed the Global Fund to procure hepatitis C medicines for other countries with high hepatitis C/HIV coinfection rates.

In 2012, PGH worked with the UN Fund for Population Activities to speed the delivery of reproductive health supplies in Ethiopia and the Philippines. In the case of the Philippines, this meant bridging financial procurement that purchased contraceptives for the country's poorest, and marked the Philippines' first family-planning purchase in forty years. In Ethiopia, PGH, the World Bank, the UK's Department for International Development, and Merck accelerated the purchase of over 600,000 contraceptive implants—twice the amount that could be purchased without PGH—at a price that made reproductive health care accessible to 3 million more Ethiopian women, a 20 percent gain. The front-loading of this delivery resulted in a 40 percent enhancement in health outcomes, including reductions in maternal and child mortality.

In 2013, PGH moved to its new institutional home, Financing for Development (F4D), where it intends to bring the concept to scale. Through USAID's Development Credit Authority and the Swedish International Development Cooperation Agency (SIDA), PGH can leverage credit from commercial banks[64] and accommodate $1 billion of lending capacity each year. To date, twenty-six countries have used the facility. Its other partners now include suppliers like Merck, Bayer, Corporate Channels India, Cupid Ltd., Pregna International, and Vestergaard. In 2014, PGH joined with the Calvert Foundation to create a similar credit facility for nonprofit borrowers in 126 countries. With pan-African Ecobank, it will also provide financing to health and finance ministries for health supplies in thirty-six countries across sub-Saharan Africa.

As an alliance of business, nonprofits, government, and aid donors, PGH offers a number of innovative finance lessons. Chief among them is that timing matters. According to Ray Chambers, the UN special envoy for malaria and financing the MDGs, "funding is essential to hitting our targets. But the timing of that funding—the cash flow—can sometimes be as important as the absolute amount of money available. Timing often means the difference between life and death."

When it comes to replicating the PGH model, some point out that, although there is an enormous short-term financing need—perhaps as much as $100 billion on a cash-on-cash basis—PGH's transactions have been customized: hard to structure and hard to scale. However, PGH has identified a need and a market failure, demonstrated an innovative approach, and spurred related efforts. For example, UNICEF's Bridges Fund was recently launched to address the same bridge financing issues.[65]

## The International Finance Facility for
## Immunization: Health Securitized

We now return to our friend Edge, whose expertise in structured finance would help create the world's first vaccine bond. As we learned earlier, the International Financing Facility for Immunization (IFFIm) was formed in 2003 when the UK government approached Goldman Sachs for assistance and consultation about meeting the funding shortfalls for the MDGs. The other critical partner in this arrangement was GAVI, a leader not only in providing vaccinations but also in devising innovative ways to pay for them.[66] IFFIm would craft bonds by front-loading future donor commitments. The proceeds of these bonds have been used to fund GAVI's vaccination work.

Like PGH, IFFIm is all about timing. Front-loading here is important because money for global health is needed now, not just years in the future, when it is often pledged for. Furthermore, using that money to pay for interventions like vaccines today is substantially cheaper than remediating full-blown diseases in the future. The bonds allow us to monetize avoided costs (the business decision) and to raise money from the capital markets for that purpose (the financing decision).

The IFFIm innovation was not just issuing a bond; it was also securitizing long-term government pledges and converting them into immediate cash for GAVI to use to purchase and deliver vaccines. Once there are predictable revenue streams—in this case, aid pledges—it is possible to pool these streams and take advantage of their diversification for greater scale. This allows for *securitization*, a word that became tainted by the financial crisis—when the practice went disastrously awry in the case of bad housing loans—but that simply means pooling the promised cash flows of many income-generating assets into one income stream, bond, or security. The prospect of repayment from this stream serves as collateral to raise capital from investors.

The home mortgage markets, where the first securitizations developed, illustrate the point. An individual mortgage accomplishes intertemporal transfer: I can borrow from my future self to purchase a house today, repaying the loan, principal and interest, over time—in most cases, thirty years. The first securitizations looked to pool multiple mortgages and their predictable, but diverse, revenue streams to raise additional funds from the capital markets, making more mortgages possible. In 1970, Ginnie Mae, the U.S. government–backed housing lender, pioneered mortgage-backed securities (MBSs), which are also sometimes known as collateralized debt obligations (CDOs), by pooling individual mortgage loans and using this pool as collateral for the MBSs—which could be sold in the secondary capital markets. Although a toxic combination of MBSs and bad lending contributed to the financial crisis, the securitization process itself is sound in its most basic form.

More recently, innovative finance has applied securitization to pharmaceutical investment, which, as we have seen, has lagged in recent years on account of the cost, risk, and duration of the drug commercialization process. In developed countries, the diversified cash-flow stream of royalty payments flowing from pharmaceutical patents on established drugs can be used to structure pharma bonds, which can then be sold to investors. Diversification, created by using a large pool of uncorrelated risks, is the key to marketing these securities and thereby raising additional funds. The Bio-Pharma Royalty Trust and the Royalty Pharma Trust are some of the best-known pharma bond issuers. Others are exploring how these models might apply to other forms of intellectual property. For example, MIT's Andrew Lo has proposed a kind of drug development mega fund that would issue a research-backed debt obligation to fund the drug discovery process.[67]

But what about the health needs of the poor in developing countries? Can we use securitization to finance interventions for health where there are not typically monetizable intellectual property or blockbuster drugs? This is precisely what IFFIm seeks to do by pooling cash flow–generating assets—in this case future development assistance pledges from multiple sovereign governments—and repackaging this pool into discrete tranches that can be sold to investors.

In 2005, Italy, Spain, Sweden, and Norway joined the UK and France in committing their donor pledges to IFFIm. The following year IFFIm raised $1 billion through the inaugural issue of bonds to institutional investors. Since then, its list of donors has grown to include South Africa, the Netherlands, and Australia. Their pledges, in excess of $6.3 billion,[68] are used to repay IFFIm bondholders. The World Bank acts as IFFIm's treasury manager, which is important because it can issue AAA bonds in the capital marketplace. This high-quality credit keeps the cost of capital down. (This is an important difference from the green bond market. IFFIm bonds are supported or guaranteed by the World Bank and other sovereign credit, which subsidizes their cost.) From 2006 through 2013, IFFIm raised more than $4.55 billion from institutional and individual investors at an average interest cost of 0.83 percent. In November 2014, it issued its first *sukuk*—an Islamic equivalent of a bond, consistent with Sharia principles, which prohibit the charging or payment of interest. Unlike a conventional bond, which confers ownership of debt, a sukuk grants the investor a share of the asset, along with the commensurate cash flows and risks. The IFFIm sukuk raised $500 million for immunization,[69] marking the first social purpose–driven sukuk in the Islamic capital markets (and winning IFFIm the Financial Times award for Achievement in Transformational Finance). The IFFIm sukuk is innovative and important for a number of reasons, among them that it allows for more regional or local ownership of development finance. The sukuk investors participated because approximately 50 percent of the vaccinations IFFIm funds take place in the Islamic world.

Several independent evaluations have concluded that as a front-loading mechanism, IFFIm has been highly cost effective, generating strong financial returns for investors alongside large-scale immunization. For investors, vaccine bonds provide diversification, attractive risk-adjusted returns, and an opportunity for social-purpose capital deployment. For donors, IFFIm has exceeded expectations by achieving lower borrowing costs than a weighted composite of its donors would have provided, in addition to putting their long-term pledges to work now.[70] For GAVI, IFFIm's bond financing is both predictable and long term. Since 2006, IFFIm funding has allowed GAVI to double its expenditures in health programs to cover long-term planning, short-term needs, and advances in specific vaccines. For example, IFFIm financing made possible GAVI's purchase agreement for the pentavalent vaccine described above, providing $1 billion (more than 90 percent) of the guaranteed payment to UNICEF for initial doses. This particular vaccine immunizes against five infectious diseases: diphtheria, tetanus, pertussis, *Haemophilus influenzae* type B (Hib), and hepatitis B.[71]

### Future IFFIms?

As is always the question in innovative finance, we want to know whether these case studies are replicable. Like GAVI's AMC, IFFIm took years to put together under a specific set of circumstances, including significant political momentum behind the MDGs and strong leadership from Gordon Brown, the UK government, and support from the Bill and Melinda Gates Foundation. In that sense, IFFIm succeeded because it was donor driven. It also remains dependent on donor enthusiasm, commitments, and credit ratings. (Moody's and Fitch downgraded IFFIm's bond ratings when they also downgraded the credit of the UK and France, but this has not yet hurt fund-raising.[72]) Even if they are willing to fund, however, donors do not necessarily have the time or patience to put these deals together. Like the AMC, IFFIm does not offer a sustainable or regenerative source of funding. Front-loading better suits financing for one-time investments than for recurrent expenditures.

So will there ever be another IFFIm? Although complex (and not related specifically to vaccines), the long-awaited answer seems to be yes. In July 2015—at the Addis Ababa Third International Financing for Development Conference—the UN; the World Bank; the governments of Canada, Norway, Japan, and the United States; and the Gates Foundation announced the launch of a new, IFFIm-inspired financing facility: the Global Financing Facility (GFF) to support Every Woman Every Child. It is a five-year commitment for investment in reproductive, maternal, newborn, child, and adolescent health, where there is an estimated $33.3 billion annual funding gap.[73] The particulars of this financing facility are just taking shape.

## Equity and Impact Investing for Health

Beyond debt, innovative finance for global health R&D has made important strides through equity and forms of impact investing. Yet as the examples that follow will demonstrate, many of the successful and equity-like investments in health still require a blended capital mechanism—that is, funding from a range of investors with different social and financial return requirements. In some cases, this means philanthropic or concessionary capital in order to mitigate risk for commercial investors, whose capital is necessary, given the size of the finance gap.

Such is the design of the Global Health Investment Fund (GHIF), launched in 2013 as a partnership between the Gates Foundation and JPMorgan Chase, with seed funding from Grand Challenges Canada. To date, GHIF has mobilized $108 million from investors that include high-net-worth individuals, foundations (Gates Foundation, Children's Investment Fund Foundation), institutional investors (AXA Investment Managers, JPMorgan Chase, Storebrand), pharmaceutical partners (GlaxoSmithKline, Merck, Pfizer Foundation), government-backed funds (KfW Development Bank, SIDA), and the International Finance Corporation.

GHIF focuses on early-stage R&D—medical breakthroughs that bring the pipeline of interventions in development to those in need. In particular, GHIF seeks investments to eradicate preventable disease, save lives, and relieve pressures on health systems globally. By design, its investments are made in earlier stages of development than those we saw in GAVI and are therefore riskier—remember the lottery-ticket approach that equity investors take when it comes to R&D. To date, little development assistance or commercial investment has been willing to take this kind of "upstream risk" in emerging markets. GHIF effectively provides mezzanine funding to companies to complete projects they might not ordinarily take up, such as funding trials or bringing a drug or technology from the later stages of development to completion. Within five years, it hopes to achieve returns that would be acceptable to private equity or institutional investors and go on to raise more for the next fund. (GHIF estimates that this stage of R&D requires an additional $1 to $2 billion).

GHIF has a partial but substantial guarantee from the Gates Foundation and SIDA: the first loss of invested capital up to 20 percent is fully covered, with investors covering 50 percent of any subsequent losses. This guarantee works a bit like an insurance deductible, and has been an important lever to crowd in private investment and bring on other investors as limited partners in a typical private-equity sense. For some investors, the guarantee also helps align incentives, ensuring that everyone, including the Gates Foundation, has skin in the game—that is, a financial stake in the outcome and quality of the investments that goes beyond philanthropy.

GHIF's investment thesis is also innovative because it looks for dual-market applications and opportunities to make commercially viable the development of drugs for the world's poorest in ways that would not happen otherwise. This means finding drugs that can help the poorest but also have use, application, and market appeal to middle- and higher-income markets. As of July 2015, GHIF had made three investments along these lines, demonstrating in different ways the flexibility of private capital and its ability to do things that grants alone could not.

GHIF's first investment was $8 million in Epistem PLC, a biotech company that developed a technology that could diagnose both tuberculosis and antibiotic resistance to it *and* diseases like hepatitis C. The latter typically affects people in more-developed countries where there are higher-paying markets. Its second investment was $5 million in EuBiologics, a South Korean biopharmaceutical company that committed to manufacture an oral vaccine for cholera at a lower price for public-sector buyers.

GHIF's investment was in the machinery necessary to produce much larger quantities at a lower price, making it possible for GAVI to purchase the vaccine. If the vaccine had been funded by grants alone, philanthropies might have insisted on a price point too low to motivate the manufacturer to continue to produce at scale. Here the commercial equilibrium helped align incentives: the price was right for all parties, allowing GAVI to make the purchase, EuBiologics to make some profit, and GHIF to make a return.

GHIF's third investment was $10 million in the registration of Moxidectin, a medicine that was originally developed by Wyeth for animal health but that turned out to cure river blindness in humans. Although the drug passed Phase III trials, it languished in the lab when it was no longer profitable to take to the animal health market. When a research scientist in Australia discovered Moxidectin could treat scabies, a mite-caused skin condition common in wealthier countries, the FDA was willing to issue a priority review voucher, potentially worth enormous sums. Although the drug is not commercially viable as a treatment for river blindness, it likely will be for scabies. GHIF provided the capital to resurrect the trials and advance the development of the drug in exchange for a share in the value of the priority review.

GHIF is not alone in the growing world of impact investing. Its blended capital structure and dual-market investment thesis exemplify how equity can be used creatively in global health innovative finance. Others are similarly creative, even when their investments do not center, as GHIF's does, on R&D. For example, the African Health Markets for Equity (AHME) focuses on franchise health care, and the African Health Fund on a variety of health goods and services. Its portfolio includes investments in a Nairobi hospital dedicated to treating women and children, a private health-care provider in Ghana, and a syringe manufacturer in Kenya. Although these funds have mostly been in the $100 million range, Abraaj Capital is raising $1 billion to invest in health care in Africa, Asia, and Latin America.[74] These are but a few examples; it is estimated that perhaps 50 percent of the $60 billion in impact investing is directed to health.

Of course, these investments are not without their challenges. In their comprehensive assessment of private investment in global health in Africa and India, Sarah Gelfand and Beth Bafford confirm that, although there is a "robust private health marketplace" serving "low and middle income consumers," it has experienced numerous "growing pains." They note that this is particularly true for impact investors who seek "market or near market rate returns," but have not adequately accepted that in most cases they cannot accomplish their goals by solely serving the 'highest impact' bottom-of-the-pyramid populations." In short, they find the same misalignment of investor and enterprise expectations that characterizes the larger and emerging impact-investing industry.[75]

Although impact investing garners most of the attention in the discussions of innovative finance and health, the examples in this chapter show us that, in fact, there is a remarkably large and agile visible-hand tool kit. In fact, some of the most promising advances for financing health involve new and resourceful applications of time tested practices, whether they are taxes and levies, prizes and challenges, or plain old lending. UNITAID and UNITLIFE demonstrate the appeal of microlevies because they are small enough to go unnoticed but large enough to make a difference in public health. In contrast, sin taxes, like those on tobacco, are meant to discourage costly behavior while raising funds to treat the consequences of those behaviors. Health policy and regulation is easier to implement when vested interests are aligned, as when companies see the value of a healthy labor force and consumer base in their bottom lines. It's more challenging when public-good public policy runs counter to an industry's short-term business model, as is the case with tobacco and fossil fuels.

The Grand Challenges in health introduced us to a twenty-first-century incarnation of a centuries-old way to motivate innovators and encourage scientific breakthrough. These prizes are part of a new generation of market shapers that correct for market failure by recalibrating supply and demand: they pay for success and shift risk—and leverage new investment in the process. This is true, for example, of GAVI's AMC and smaller purchase agreements. Some of the most exciting new areas of innovative finance in health, such as an emerging health credit exchange modeled on natural resource cap-and-trade, undertake these kinds of market-shaping activities.

Perhaps the most fruitful area of innovative finance in health utilizes new or reconceived debt products. As we have seen, these include loan forgiveness and pay-downs, new forms of trade finance for health commodities, and IFFIm's unusually creative application of securitization, converting future donor aid pledges into cash for vaccines today. While these innovative finance mechanisms succeed because they harness new and additional sources of funding, they also improve incentives and allow us to make better investment decisions. IFFIm's front-loading is important—this intertemporal transfer is the role of Finance 101—because it allows GAVI to purchase vaccines, a profoundly preventive and therefore cost-effective health intervention. As in climate change, an ounce of prevention is worth a pound of cure. This also explains the power of NetGuarantee and PGH. The working capital they provide enables countries to buy medicines and bed nets months before traditional aid would allow. In poor countries, these months can be measured in lives.

We also saw numerous examples of ways in which innovative finance can improve governance, trust, and autonomy in development. To assuage donor concerns, UNITAID and UNITLIFE operate outside of the countries (in the WHO and UNICEF, respectively), minimizing the perception or reality that funds from the microlevies are misspent. Similarly, Debt2Health uses a third party, the Global Fund, to manage the way loan forgiveness is translated into health expenditures. Perhaps more importantly, many of these innovative finance approaches give countries the autonomy they want and need in the development process. From the outset, the Global Fund was designed to finance the needs identified and the projects designed and implemented by the countries themselves. GAVI, too, responds to requests from developing countries about their immunization needs and encourages them to cofinance the vaccine investments. This is a hallmark of innovative finance and will only become more important as countries pursue a different and larger set of health and development priorities related to access, health systems, and universal health coverage—that they will want and need to design and finance.

Of course, one of the reasons we see so many innovative finance experiments in health is that the need is so vast. Despite the conceptual breakthroughs and the important proof points, many of these advances remain small in scale. Debt2Health and PGH are two examples: each represents only a handful of bespoke deals, all of which complex to structure. The same is true for much larger transactions like GAVI's AMC and IFFIm's securitizations. For years, the development community has waited and hoped for the second iterations of these innovative finance all-stars. AMCs, like IFFIm's vaccine bonds, are challenging and time consuming to assemble. Both took a few years to get off the ground, and both had important political winds and champions at their backs. And of course, neither is regenerative: both need to raise new resources for each round of investment.

These factors explain the animating logic of the impact-investing movement: a search for scale and therefore returns that can replenish capital and attract commercial investment so that the world does not have to depend solely on the largess and preferences of donor ODA and philanthropy. As generous and well intentioned as both may be, we also know their resources are insufficient to meet our global health needs and aspirations.

Innovative finance is not an either/or. In this chapter, we saw how government or multilateral institution credit can be used to bring down the cost of capital and how philanthropic guarantees can crowd in private investment for risky, but potentially life-transforming, health investments. This is the role of the visible hand, shaping new arrangements in ways that bring more and better resources to bear on the most pressing global challenges.

---

Crowdfunding for Health

Crowdfunding may offer a promising channel of new and additional funding for health. As we have seen, crowdfunding, which began in the nonprofit sphere, has developed into a multibillion-dollar industry. The World Bank and others are optimistic that this trend might supply additional philanthropic or commercial capital for health. At present, funds remain relatively small and philanthropic. Not surprisingly, Kickstarter and other crowdfunding platforms have needed to tighten restrictions on the types of health products that can be funded—including those that are heavily regulated or make substantial treatment claims—for obvious liability and consumer protection reasons.

In recent years, health-specific online platforms have emerged, mostly in the developed world. These include MedStartr and Kangu, which are donation platforms for small health projects around the world that provide, for example, free surgeries, health facilities, and prenatal and childbirth assistance. In contrast, sites like Healthfundr connect health start-ups with for-profit, accredited investors. Relative to financial need, particularly for developing-country health, these channels remain small.

# 3

# Financial Inclusion and
# Access to Capital

We begin by considering the situation of a woman in her twenties who lives in a remote part of India. She is a client of a microfinance organization, and over the years, she has taken out a number of jewelry loans, using her gold as collateral—a common practice. One day, while walking to her job as an agricultural laborer, she is struck and killed by a passing automobile. In the wake of this tragedy, IFMR Trust, the parent company of the microfinance institution, learns that the woman was the breadwinner for five dependents. Her husband had left her, and she was working to support her two young children, a sibling, and her parents. "It was obvious that the financial intervention she needed most, much before the jewelry loan, was life insurance," laments Bindu Ananth, the chair of IFMR Trust.[1]

This insight not only transformed IFMR Trust into a leader in innovative finance but also is emblematic of a much larger set of changes taking place in the world of economic inclusion; efforts to improve access to an array of financial services for poor people, businesses, and communities across the globe.

Even though millions of families rise out of poverty each year, they often remain vulnerable to shocks like health emergencies, job loss, natural disasters, or other accidents with devastating consequences. Like life insurance, basic financial tools for saving, sending, or borrowing money can help people manage risk and absorb these shocks. Without them, hard-won economic gains can be readily eroded. Financial inclusion—ensuring all people, including the world's poorest, have access to basic financial services—is a public good. In recent years, we have made gains in expanding banking services to improve the resilience of households and the economic vibrancy of the communities in which they live.

The World Bank estimates that the number of people with a bank account grew by 700 million between 2011 and 2014. That means 62 percent of the world's adult population is now "banked," up from 51 percent. Much of this expansion, as we know and will explore, has been driven by mobile: hundreds of millions of people worldwide have gained access to electronic payment services by way of their cell phones. However, there are still 2 billion "unbanked" adults across the globe, and less than half of those in developing countries participate in the financial system (figure 3.1 shows the distribution of the unbanked across the world). For women in poverty, the numbers are even worse.[2]

Without access to basic financial services, most poor households operate in cash and depend on physical assets like livestock or jewelry or on money lenders to meet their short-term financing needs. These informal mechanisms are unreliable and costly. Not only does this take a toll on the household; exclusion from mainstream banking and financial services imposes

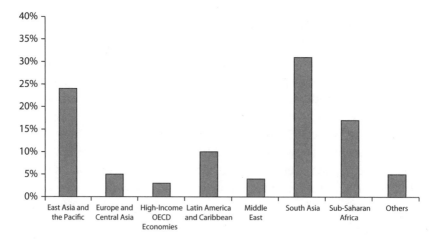

Figure 3.1
Global Distribution of 2 Billion Unbanked Adults, 2014
*Source*: 2014 Global Financial Inclusion (Global Findex) Database.
*Note*: As a result of rounding, percentages do not add up to 100 percent.

significant costs on society. When families cannot invest in health care or education, governments must pay for stronger social safety nets. Moreover, individual and household assets form the basis of any larger market system. Without deposits and savings, formal banks cannot make productive investments, including commercial loans. Without this credit, small businesses cannot expand and provide the goods, services, or employment that accelerates consumption, increases investments in human capital, and stimulates economic growth. In developing economies, only one-third of firms have bank loans, compared to half of those in developed countries. These underserved firms report that access to capital is a major constraint on their growth.[3] Therefore, for households and businesses, financial inclusion is a vital public good and a development priority for a growing number of countries.[4]

If there are so many social and economic benefits to financial inclusion, why is it so hard to achieve? What's the market failure? And where are the signs of progress?

## Microfinance 1.0

Microfinance is often considered the seminal case study of the power of innovative finance: an industry focused on the needs of the poor that has successfully scaled with private capital, grappled with the challenges of commercialization, and innovated in the face of new evidence and changing circumstances. But what is microfinance exactly, and what can we learn from it?

The early days of microfinance were about lending. For years, the terms *microfinance* and *microcredit* were effectively synonymous. Indeed access to capital in the form of loans is an important public good—but also a market failure. By definition, poor people and small businesses typically lack collateral and credit history. Because of this risk, lenders will make only small loans to them. As the costs of making these loans are steep (for due diligence, ongoing monitoring, and collection), banks either shy away from this lending in the first place or charge prohibitively high interest rates. Despite the large and unmet demand for credit, the economics make as little sense for commercial banks as they do for poor borrowers, who typically rely on informal lenders, often loan sharks, to meet their financial needs.

The intuitive appeal of microcredit has been its elegant simplicity: reverse market failure with market opportunity.[5] The original pioneers of microlending—people like Muhammad Yunus of the Grameen Bank and

Fazel Abed of the Bangladesh Rural Advancement Committee (BRAC)—demonstrated how small, affordable loans could be made to and repaid by poor people, unlocking a "virtuous cycle" of self-replenishing credit markets. In the case of Grameen, founded in 1976, Yunus showed how joint-liability loans to small groups of women translated into bankably high repayment rates, close to 99 percent.[6] Grameen is a for-profit bank—but one that is borrower owned—charging enough interest to be reinvested in the bank and recycled into new loans. Bangladesh was the testing ground, but it was not the only center of microcredit. Demonstration projects across the globe, from Brazil to Indonesia, proved that poor people could and would repay loans.

A tested model was necessary, but not sufficient, to expand the microcredit field. With philanthropic and public-sector support, an infrastructure emerged, including organizations and networks like Women's World Banking (WWB), committed to the financial inclusion of women, and the Consultative Group to Assist the Poor (CGAP). These organizations provide a range of supports for the growing number of microfinance institutions (MFIs) across the globe and for potential investors in the form of research, ratings systems, and advisory services. These developments are essential for scale, as they supply the data, information, proof points, and standardization necessary to attract commercial lenders to the industry. Today 100 million borrowers worldwide receive more than $80 billion in microloans annually, largely due to the infusion of private capital.

While the microlending model has been embraced and celebrated (among its recongitions, Yunus won the Nobel Peace Prize in 2006), the substantial growth of the industry has not come without challenges—and with them important lessons about commercialization and continuous innovation.

There is no doubt that scale requires private capital, but the question is whether scale and the profit motive pose a quantity-quality trade. Once there was proof of concept—the existence of a profitable market in which to lend—commercial lenders followed. Citigroup entered the microfinance business in 2005. The following year Morgan Stanley and Switzerland-based Blue Orchard placed the first rated microfinance bond offering with European institutional investors, raising $100 million for twenty-two MFIs across thirteen countries: Mongolia, Bosnia, Colombia, Peru, Bolivia, Mexico, Nicaragua, Ecuador, Azerbaijan, Albania, Georgia, Russia, and Cambodia. These Blue Orchard Loans for Development (BOLD) were the first collateralized debt obligations (CDOs) for microfinance.

Commercialization also brought about the conversion of MFIs from nonprofit to for-profit entities. In some cases, these for-profit companies turned to the public capital markets to fuel their expansion, as in the well-known cases of Compartamos in 2007 and SKS in 2010. Their initial public offerings proved controversial when they made their founders and investors rich, inviting an intense debate about the role of profits and purpose in the provision of public goods. Concerns about the quantity and quality of lending were exacerbated by repayment crises in countries like Nicaragua, Mexico, Morocco, and Pakistan in 2010 and 2011, when large numbers of indebted borrowers could not repay their loans. The most high-profile and political of the repayment crises, in the Andhra Pradesh region of India—a rash of farmer suicides, government backlash against microlenders, and a subsequent freeze on capital to the MFIs—rattled the microcredit industry around the world and prompted deeper soul searching about the commercialized model. It certainly brings scale, but did it also bring unintended perils?

The profit motive, Yunus and others long insisted, necessarily compromises the integrity of microcredit by privileging the needs of investors over those of the poor. Unchecked, the drive for quantity can compromise the quality of lending—a situation not dissimilar to the subprime crisis in the United States.[7] Defenders and advocates of the commercial microcredit model note that sharing profits with private investors is a prerequisite for reaching the billions of unbanked people worldwide. Both are true. Using private capital to bridge the finance gap requires care, productive government oversight, and a nuanced understanding of when and where market forces are effective—and when and where they are not. Research indicates that the first waves of commercialized microlending steered away from some of the most underserved populations, like the poorest of the poor. Furthermore, evidence suggests that some of the more profitable commercial models have not only moved upmarket by making larger loans to better-off clients but also turned away from women.

The scrutiny of microcredit has not been limited to the commercialization debates. Equally important have been investigations into the efficacy of microlending as a poverty-fighting tool. In recent years, a new wave of development economists[8] has used randomized control trials and other rigorous evaluations, including "financial diaries" of the poor, to answer these important questions: just how effective is microlending? And are there other financial products or services people need, and will use, to rise above and stay out of poverty?[9] Their findings, including those from a number of longitudinal studies, suggest that microloans alone may not be the cure-all we once believed or hoped they would be. Although often necessary, they are not sufficient to move the needle, at scale, on global poverty. As the World Bank concluded in 2014, the challenges of financial inclusion will not be solved "purely with an infusion of credit."[10] Instead, this research has helped fashion a much broader exploration of how other financial products and services, such as savings, pensions, and insurance, *can* advance the broader goals of poverty relief and financial inclusion. This is what we might call microfinance 2.0.

## Microfinance 2.0: Where We Are Headed

For many institutions focused on financial inclusion, the transition to a broader array of supports, products, and services beyond credit has been years in the making. This is particularly true with insurance, known in the development field as *microinsurance* when specifically designed to meet the needs of poor people.[11]

Take the case of MicroEnsure, which began life in 2002 when micro-lender Opportunity International decided to explore a broader range of products for its loan clients: first, it developed life and funeral insurance and then property and crop insurance to protect farmers against drought. In 2008, MicroEnsure became Opportunity's wholly owned insurance sub-sidiary, and today it serves 15 million people in seventeen countries around the world. The company continues to grow rapidly, reaching people who have never had any kind of insurance. In 2014, it added 8 million new cus-tomers in Africa alone.

MicroEnsure's growth relies on strong customer demand. Its product innovations are equally customer driven. Today it offers more than 200 microinsurance products across Africa and Asia, including life, health, accident, disability, unemployment, property, and agriculture insurance—and even political violence insurance. (The last covers the balance of a bor-rower's outstanding loan in the event his or her business is destroyed in uprisings or riots.)

MicroEnsure's health offerings exemplify how it tailors products to local market needs and conditions. As we saw in the previous chapter, the links between health and poverty are profound and complex. Poor fami-lies are less likely to get early, preventive and cost-effective treatment for an illness or other health needs because they lack the up-front cash or cannot take time off from work to see a doctor. Health emergencies often force families to dip into any savings or sell productive assets like livestock, equipment, or entire businesses, thus depriving them of the means to make money and break the cycle of poverty.

Although the economic case for health insurance is strong, there often are not affordable insurance options for those who need them most. As with credit, this is a market failure—and one not unique to developing countries. The social costs of a largely uninsured population are a problem the United States has only recently begun to address as a larger public good and public responsibility. In emerging economies, commercial insurers have not typically provided health coverage for a variety of reasons, including lack of reliable data and information for pricing, high acquisition costs (compared to the premiums they could charge), costly and complex administration, adverse selection (only sick people buy insurance, leading to an undiversified and expensive insurance pool), and lack of affordable reinsurance options. As with microcredit, this translates into no available insurance or insurance at rates the poor cannot afford. Historically, the development field has shied away from fully subsidizing premiums, even when it's possible, out of fear of *moral hazard*: insuring people who do not bear the cost of protection could lead to risky or unhealthy behavior.

When designing health insurance, MicroEnsure has worked to overcome these obstacles in innovative ways, primarily by focusing on reducing the costs of insurance for providers and consumers. Often this means taking on customer sales and acquisition, claims management, payment, and other back-office supports to remove the complexity for the health providers and their clients. Sometimes this means recognizing and paying for ongoing personal or business expenses that accrue during health emergencies or smoothing health payments. In India, for example, Micro-Ensure offers hospital insurance in the form of cashless access to hospitals for the poor. In the Philippines, its Hospicash pays customers a fixed amount of cash per day for each day of their hospitalization to cover health or nonhealth needs. In Ghana, it partners with microfinance banks to offer a cash derivative, Credit Health, which pays a borrower's loan installments while he or she is hospitalized. In Tanzania, it works with PharmAccess to provide comprehensive primary care for coffee farmers in a coffee cooperative there.

Although MicroEnsure is highly visible (winning the 2015 FT/IFC Transformational Business Award), it is only one of many financial service providers offering a broad range of financial services. For example, WWB works with a global network of thirty-eight MFIs to create "a broader safety net" of offerings in addition to credit, including savings and insurance. Its leaders believe that part of its mission is to advance microfinance 2.0 by showing "a broader range of financial institutions how to move beyond traditional microfinance to provide financial products that include savings and insurance."[12]

## New Investors

Perhaps following the trajectory of microcredit, we have seen a growing interest in microinsurance at commercial firms like Munich Re, Swiss Re, and Lloyd's of London. As the profit margins of their developed-market businesses tighten, these insurers have begun to explore other opportunities, including what they call emerging consumers: customers in developing countries that they believe are on their way to middle-class status and purchasing power. In 2010, Swiss Re estimated that the market for "commercially viable microinsurance products" was approximately 2.6 billion strong, in line with earlier assessments by Lloyd's of an attractive market size and growth trajectory.[13]

Are these insurers looking to provide a public good or simply seeking new and profitable market opportunities? Does that intentionality matter? What is evident is that the emerging impact-investing industry, consisting of investors who intentionally pursue profits with social or environmental purpose, shows a hearty appetite for microfinance 2.0. By some counts, financial services comprise nearly 30 percent of the impact-investing market.[14] For example, the private equity firm LeapFrog Investments, a self-described leader in "profit with purpose investing," closed a $400 million fund in September 2014, which was the largest to date specializing in low-income emerging-market financial services. The fund, which targeted investments in Africa and Asia, was oversubscribed—and three times the size of LeapFrog's first fund.[15]

LeapFrog has invested in companies providing insurance, savings, pensions, and payment services to customers earning less than $10 a day. According to the company, the current portfolio showed a 40 percent increase in operating revenue and a 39 percent rise in profitability in 2013, with investments of $10 to $50 million in companies in places like Ghana, Kenya, Nigeria, South Africa, India, Indonesia, the Philippines, and Sri Lanka. These include investments in companies like India's Mahindra & Mahindra Ltd. insurance brokerage business, which serves low-income consumers. LeapFrog has also invested in AFB, a financial tech platform in Africa; ArmLife, an insurance company in Nigeria; Bima, a mobile insurance company operating in emerging markets in Africa, Asia, and Latin America; Petra Trust, a Ghana-based pension company; Reliance, an Indonesian multi-insurer; Resolution, Kenya's fourth-largest health insurer; SMK, a Thai general insurer; Shriam, a provider of insurance, savings, and investment in India; and, recently, IFMR Trust, the Indian institution focused on financial inclusion mentioned in the beginning of this chapter and profiled more extensively below. In addition, LeapFrog invests in companies that others shy away from, including South Africa's All Life, an insurance company for HIV patients. Leapfrog estimates that, worldwide, the annual collective spending of "mass-market" consumers will grow from $2 to $5 trillion by 2022. It is worth reiterating that most institutions, including LeapFrog, define this demographic as those earning less than $10 a day. While this may the bottom of the pyramid, these investments are not targeted at the world's poorest.

### New Investments: The Case of IFMR Trust

How do these new microfinance companies offering an expanded array of products and services work in practice? Let's return to the case of IFMR Trust.

IFMR Capital, based in Chennai, is part of the larger IFMR group of companies created expressly to improve financial inclusion in India. One-third of India's 1.2 billion people live on less than $1.25 a day, and two-thirds live on less than $2 a day; half the country lacks a formal bank account (with millions trapped in debt to money lenders), and more than half lack any kind of insurance.

There are two pieces to the IFMR innovative finance model. The first relates to the story of the mother who lost her life to a passing automobile, leaving a large extended family without a source of income. In the years since, IFMR has devised an innovative approach to financial inclusion—a kind of holistic "wealth management"—designed to meet the broad set of financial needs of poor people in India's most rural regions, where only 5 percent of the population is served by either public or private banks. The second piece involves scale. IFMR has used structured finance to bring more capital to the local financial institutions it serves, allowing them to reach a broader set of clients.

Since its inception, IFMR has been at the forefront of microfinance. In some ways, this makes the story of the consequences of the young woman's death even more senseless. IFMR had already moved beyond credit and included life insurance in its product line. The fact that a jewelry loan, rather than life insurance, was sold to a woman with five dependents, either because the client was not convinced of the value of insurance or the person selling didn't fully understand her client's needs, is known in the industry as a *mis-sale*. In the case of IFMR, preventing mis-sales became part of a much larger overhaul of the business model.

In the years since this accident, IFMR has radically transformed its approach to microfinance. Because it uses local "wealth managers" to enroll clients, it can collect detailed household information—a data-rich financial snapshot—which allows for a customized range of products, including loan and credit services, deposit and savings accounts, remittance services, various types of insurance, pensions, and mutual funds, as well as many payment options. IFMR has found that there is high demand for noncredit products and services, particularly insurance and pensions.[16]

There are many innovative elements underlying this model, which is what IFMR calls its Kshetriya Gramin Financial Services (KGFS) approach. First, wealth managers are trained to understand and maximize the financial well-being of the client. Second, their decision making and accountability are radically simplified by technology. Wealth managers record information about a client's finances and circumstances on an electronic tablet that stores all the information and, using a series of algorithms, suggests appropriate financial products based on the client's profile and perceived risk.

Technology is the backbone, but the personal relationship that technology facilitates is the key. This means that wealth managers can be trusted members of local communities who put a human face on a large financial service firm. The product identification and recommendation is left to software and data. These tools also allow customers to see what effects products like insurance or savings can have on their lives. Customers are given a "single view" of the products and their assets. The complexity behind each product is not visible to the customers or the wealth managers. (IFMR's products are negotiated nationally with different insurers and regulated by different national entities. In contrast, the information facing wealth managers and clients is remarkably user friendly.)

Wealth managers are paid a fixed salary and evaluated on the overall "wealth maximization" and "well-being" of what they sell. They are not paid on commission, as many are in financial services; this means their compensation is not based on the volume of products sold or the sale of higher-margin products like debt. "The right analogy is health," says Ananth. "We believe our wealth managers should be more like doctors." It is their job to understand and educate the client, to earn their trust by delivering the right set of products. This means that, although the broad range of product and service offerings is valuable—and an important move beyond credit—the success of the model relies on customization, on matching the customer with the right products. Ananth says this means getting both the operations and the culture right.

Today IFMR is growing rapidly, with 600,000 clients in rural areas, and relies on a sophisticated branch model to support wealth management and product customization at the household level. IFMR Rural Channels, incorporated in 2011, operates the six KGFS units through 240 remote rural branches in three states (Uttarakhand, Orissa, and Tamil Nadu). These brick-and-mortar facilities are critical because they serve contiguous villages with high-speed connectivity. Deep penetration of villages makes IFMR a community institution and allows for what it calls "economies of scope," which reinforce the trust that allows for customized wealth management and advice. More than the operational model or the finance itself, the implementation of the model underlies the success.

The Tamil Nadu pilots show that, with sufficient penetration, the KGFS model is profitable.[17] Perhaps more pertinent to innovative finance, preliminary findings from the long-term evaluations of the KGFS model are positive in terms of financial inclusion. Enrollment is high and growing. There is strong demand for credit and noncredit services, particularly accident and life insurance and pensions. Those enrolled in KGFS services show much higher levels of formal (versus informal) borrowing than their control group peers.[18] To date, KGFS wealth management is improving the material well-being of enrolled households, moving the needle on financial inclusion and poverty alleviation.

And now to the issue of scale—how to reach more than 600,000 clients in order to meet the demand for financial services in India and beyond.

Like the clients they serve, MFIs such as IFMR are themselves capital constrained. This is in part because they have traditionally relied on banks and larger development-finance institutions for funding, which makes them vulnerable to a variety of risks. Take the repayment crisis in Andhra Pradesh, for instance, which halted bank funding to the larger sector on account of the political risk. Among the diversification lessons MFIs have learned, including the need to expand product and service offerings beyond credit, is the importance of broadening their own sources of capital to include mainstream capital-market investors. As we saw in the previous chapter, structuring a security out of a diverse portfolio of cash flows—in this case MFI microloans—offers a way to transfer risk and bring additional capital into the sector.

However, as we also see, securitization is a tricky business, and even more so since the financial crisis, when loan securitization took a particularly pernicious turn in the United States and across the globe. Historically, and even with the broad commercialization of microlending, there have been few direct securitizations of microfinance receivables. Nevertheless, as a nonbanking company, IFMR Capital has been able to structure a series of direct and rated securitization transactions: structured loan pools created by combining loans of small- and medium-sized originators (local MFIs) to create a portfolio diversified and large enough to take to the capital markets. In 2013, IFMR's Capital Mosec XXII was the first listed securitization in India.[19] In 2014, IFMR announced India's first collateralized bond obligation, which included eleven issuers.[20]

Through these transactions, IFMR pioneered a way to use the capital markets to grow, accessing a new class of debt investors, reducing dependence on traditional sources of funds, and spreading its risk over a larger range of financial institutions. This kind of risk transfer is critical for the KGFS model. Deep penetration within a village works well from a financial inclusion perspective. When it comes to exposure to risk, however, "small is not beautiful," says Ananth. Concentration leaves IFMR vulnerable to local risk, whether it is extreme weather or political upheaval. At a national level, IFMR can aggregate across nine districts in three disparate states in three different parts of the country. This creates an opportunity to pool and then transfer the risk out to the capital markets, mitigating some of the concentration risk. In its capacity as a structurer, arranger, and investor, IFMR Capital can bridge high-quality originators and the larger capital markets, working as a kind of wholesale financial intermediary that can increase the volume and lower the cost of borrowing for financially excluded families and businesses. The hope is to bring in more capital to drive financial inclusion to scale.

Of course, IFMR's drive for broader financial inclusion is not without its challenges. As it brings more capital into its work to expand services, it will have to be mindful of the expansion pressures and return requirements of this capital so as not to allow quantity to compromise the quality of its offerings. Furthermore, the model raises larger institutional questions about risk in places like India; although IFMR can transfer risk away from smaller, local institutions, who can ultimately transfer out risk for institutions like IFMR? Historically, lending to institutions in India, particularly those in rural areas, no matter how successful or creditworthy, has been limited by structural risk. As we will see in the next chapter, innovative finance is beginning to take on some of these larger structural challenges—such as regional- and country-level risk. This remains a nascent but promising and critical area for work in financial inclusion.

## The Role of Digital Technologies in Innovative Finance

Changes in the microfinance landscape have occured against the backdrop of massive technological change. Though not an innovation in finance itself, the advent of mobile has played a transformational role in fostering groundbreaking kinds of finance in developing countries, bringing capital, inclusion, and opportunity to the world's poor.

The rise of digital technologies—mobile, in particular—has revolutionized how many poor people use money: how they send and receive payments, whether these are remittances to family members, utility bills, health-care or education fees, or cash transfers from governments. There is growing evidence that digital wallets smooth consumption and encourage people to spend less, save more, and invest in their businesses and the human capital of their households. In short, by allowing people to participate in the larger economy, mobile money can improve financial inclusion and reduces poverty.[21] The data on women's economic participation and empowerment are particularly encouraging.[22]

Kenya leads the world in mobile money via M-Pesa, the digital payment platform created by Safaricom in 2007, when 75 percent of the country's population was unbanked. (*Pesa* means "money" in Swahili.) Today 80 percent of adult Kenyans own a mobile phone, 60–70 percent have mobile money accounts, and by some measures, more than 40 percent of the country's GDP flows through M-Pesa. Gains in financial inclusion are vast, encompassing people in both urban and rural areas. The majority of Kenyans living on less than $2 a day use M-Pesa. Across sub-Saharan Africa, where mobile technologies have filled the telephone, electricity, and larger infrastructure void, estimates place mobile money usage among adults between 12 and 25 percent, compared to the 2 percent worldwide average (figure 3.2).[23] These rates are higher than in Europe and the United

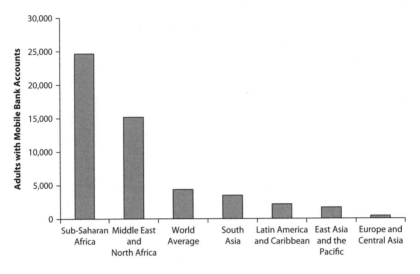

Figure 3.2
Mobile Bank Accounts per 100,000 Adults by Region, 2013
*Source*: Groupe Speciale Mobile Association, World Bank.

States, by most measures, and are expected to grow substantially in terms of both volume and market potential. McKinsey estimates that revenues from mobile financial services could rise from less than $1 billion in 2013 to $19 billion by 2025.[24]

For now, mobile money focuses on payments, but these are the entry points to a larger set of financial services. Although M-Pesa is not a bank, Safaricom has 80,000 agents who function like tellers. In recent years, other mobile money companies—including Paga, EcoCash, Splash Mobile Money, Tigo Cash, Airtel Money, Orange Money, and MTN Mobile Money—have followed M-Pesa, improving access across the continent.[25]

As mobile payment systems have become commonplace, banks themselves have begun to move in. Across Africa, mobile providers and more traditional financial service companies are working together to introduce more sophisticated financial services like insurance, consumer credit, or even investment options.[26] For example, Safaricom has partnered with the Commercial Bank of Africa to allow customers to transfer their M-Pesa money into interest-bearing savings accounts. The same is true with Econet wireless and EcoCash in Zimbabwe. Slowly, other health- or agriculture-related financial services are emerging. For example, Orange Mali

partners with MFS Africa to provide a health insurance program for preg-
nant women. CGAP estimates that in Kenya a large number of organizations (fifty-five, by last count) take advantage of M-Pesa's infrastructure to
make essential services and utilities (energy, health, education, and water)
more accessible to the poor. It calls this Digital Finance Plus. The existing
M-Pesa platform makes payments for these services easier for customers
and cheaper for providers.[27]

Development experts have long asked whether the M-Pesa experience
is replicable beyond Kenya—across the larger poor, unbanked world. The
growth of digital money and financial services depends on any number
of factors from the regulatory environment to a country's geography and
topography; an International Finance Corporation (IFC) study identified
fifty parameters that could determine whether or not mobile money takes
off in any given country.[28] For example, as early as 2001, the Philippines
became one of the first countries to have a basic mobile money transfer
system. However, a decade later, less than 10 percent of Filipino mobile
users without bank accounts actively used mobile money. In Kenya, initial growth of M-Pesa was driven by a large demand for domestic remittances—the ability to send money to relatives within the country. On the
banking and telecom side, Kenyan regulators were relatively lenient with
regard to Safaricom's buildup, viewing local vendors or agents as intermediaries rather than banking services. This has been called a "regulation to
follow innovation" approach.[29] These conditions do not hold everywhere.
In countries with stricter regulations, including South Africa and India,
Safaricom has experienced less rapid expansion when trying to introduce
M-Pesa.[30]

However, other countries offer more fertile ground. For example, in
Bangladesh, as in Kenya, mobile money is proving to be a valuable way to
send domestic remittances.[31] bKash has emerged as a popular, trusted way
for workers, who do not get time off to go to a bank, to send cash home to the
countryside. Launched in 2011, it is now used by over 17 million Bangladeshis
and handles more than 70 million transactions a day. It is backed by BRAC,
Bangladesh's largest nongovernmental organization and one of the world's
original pioneers of microfinance. Its success is attributed to the same
favorable conditions M-Pesa was met with: Bangladesh, like Kenya, has
a supportive regulatory environment that encourages over-the-counter
mobile money transfers through nonbank access points like stores.
Bangladeshis can use their phones like banks: depositing, withdrawing, and
transferring money; paying utility bills; and purchasing goods and services.

Today the number of registered mobile-money users in Bangladesh is approximately 23 million—15 percent of the total population—and they are moving an estimated $42 million through the mobile banking system daily. This is a significant development in a largely cash economy. It is also part of the central bank's strategy to expand financial access in a country where less than one-third of the population has a bank account. "All the money that people used to carry around or keep in their mattresses is now going into the banking system," says Kamal Quadir, CEO of bKash. "Mobile banking has become a digital mattress for Bangladeshis."[32]

Like Safaricom's M-Pesa, bKash grew rapidly when the company focused on the unbanked. "We're not competing in the traditional space occupied by commercial banks—we serve the small fry who is unbanked," Quadir says. Unlike M-Pesa, however, bKash is not delivered by a mobile phone company or bank. Instead, it takes advantage of a variety of digital platforms, including phones, kiosks, and local stores where users can send or receive money through known proprietors. bKash's CEO believes that, over time, it might be possible to use the data from mobile money transactions to form credit histories, particularly working with organizations like BRAC that have a deep experience with microlending. "In the future, people could apply for small loans on their phones and get approval and disbursement within minutes."[33]

As in Kenya, the growth of nonbanking companies like bKash has spurred interest from commercial banks that historically have been reluctant to open costly rural branches. Increasingly, however, these banks view mobile as a cost-effective way to reach the unbanked. As of 2015, nineteen Bangladeshi banks had obtained licenses to provide mobile money services. Bank models of mobile money tend to grow more slowly than their nonbanking counterparts, as the accounts the former offer are strictly regulated. Accordingly, Bangladesh's commercial banks contend that their products are more reliable, safe, and secure than bKash transactions, for which there is no insurance if something should go wrong. Banks can also offer additional products like savings and credit.

Of course, these questions of regulation and the disruption of traditional banking models by digital platforms are not unique to emerging economies. As discussed in the next chapter, Internet and mobile technologies are revolutionizing finance across the globe in ways that we are just beginning to understand.[34] To date, there has been little work on virtual currencies like Bitcoin and their role in fighting poverty, improving financial inclusion, or correcting for market failures to provide public goods.

## The Promise of Pay-As-You-Go

Digital payments offer flexibility and cost effectiveness, paving the way for new forms of consumer finance. This in turn expands access to an array of goods and services once unavailable to those in poverty.

Consider *pay-as-you-go* (PAYG) financing for clean energy in the developing world, where 2 billion people are not on an electricity grid. Instead, they rely on unhealthy and dangerous alternatives, purchased in small, expensive batches: kerosene and candles for lighting, disposable lead-acid batteries for flashlights, and diesel generators for various needs.[35] In homes, kerosene lighting burns and poisons, polluting the air and producing over 90 million tons of carbon dioxide emissions each year. Therefore, alternative energy sources are a public good. There have been many efforts to provide finance to clean-energy entrepreneurs that are delivering green technologies and services to the poor. In the last decade, many small companies have developed high-quality solar-powered solutions and distribution models, targeting the needs of energy-poor populations. But these products are too expensive for broad adoption, even if consumers know the investment will pay for itself. Poor people simply lack the upfront capital and financing options like loans, leasing, and other payment methods to make these purchases.

We return to Kenya, where nearly 80 percent of households rely on kerosene for lighting because they are entirely off the national electricity grid or they can't afford to link to it. (Connecting to that grid costs around $412, or 35,000 Kenyan shillings.) Because kerosene can cost families over $200 a year, a one-time investment of $199 in solar panels makes smart economic sense. However, the up-front costs make this impossible.

Enter the PAYG financing model—making solar power a little more possible. The Kenyan start-up M-Kopa (*kopa* means "borrow" in Swahili) installs solar panels and a wireless payment and monitoring device, which allows the household to pay the costs back in small installments—a kind of microleasing scheme.[36] As of May 2015, M-Kopa, the global leader in PAYG clean energy, had registered 200,000 customers across East Africa. However, it is not the only provider. Although Kenya (via the M-Pesa platform) is the largest market, there are an estimated twenty-five to fifty small companies in this space, across sub-Saharan Africa, Asia, and Latin America.[37] They have begun with solar energy but promise a variety of alternative energy products. For example, Angaza's SaaS (software as a service) product enables distributors of a variety of alternative energy products and services to offer PAYG pricing. By some estimates, PAYG is increasing alternative energy purchases to four times the rate at which they would be occurring otherwise. The World Bank, Bloomberg New Energy Finance, and the Global Off-Grid Lighting Association (GOGLA) estimate that off-grid solar is now a $300 million a year industry.[38]

Not surprisingly, there are innovative variations on the financing model. In some cases, the customer can eventually own the asset through a rent-to-own program, creating a first-time credit history in the process. We are also starting to see evidence that once a household owns an asset, such as solar lighting for their home, they might refinance, using the asset to generate additional money to live on. In the case of solar, some companies charge customers for days or weeks, whereas others charge for actual electricity usage (watt or kilowatt hours). The specific financing terms, like the size of the required down payment, also vary. In every case, the objective is to deliver energy that is affordable to customers at a price that is competitive with dirty or efficient options like kerosene.[39]

PAYG represents a positive synergy: the innovation in finance results from and unlocks further technological innovation. As in the computer industry, improvements in the reliability and functionality of certain technologies—solar or other alternative energy in this case—have reduced the size and cost of the product. The prospect of a paying market—one facilitated by digital payment—encourages innovators to invest in product enhancement.

Of course the potential of PAYG isn't solely related to energy. CGAP's Digital Finance Plus initiative has identified more than sixty start-up companies that harness digital finance to provide access to goods and services for the poor, in places like Kenya, Tanzania, and Uganda, with high mobile adoption rates. Water is a prime example. In Kenya, Grundfos Life-link allows customers to purchase water from smart card–operated water pumps (customers can load money onto smart cards through M-Pesa). Kickstart sells smaller water pumps to farmers through PAYG (the initial deposit on the pump is made through M-Pesa), as does Water.org. Although equipment finance is the most fertile ground today in developing countries, it is not impossible to imagine how PAYG and branchless banking can improve access to essentials in health, education, and beyond. For example, in Kenya, Kytabu offers a subscription service to textbooks. Customers can use mobile money to pay as they go, chapter by chapter, and read the content on their phones. And there is no reason these advances should remain in the developing world. Entrepreneurs in the United States are exploring how to make certain expensive monthly purchases, like cable television or discounted monthly passes for public transportation, available in affordable and smaller installments. This is innovative finance at work.

---

Is Cash Still King?

While much of this chapter focuses on the conversion of payments into finance, it is worth remembering that the digital money story is still very much about cash. The truth is that cash remains a critical staple of many developing economies, along with the basic safety nets governments provide in these economies. Therefore, improving the efficiency, transparency, and security of cash payments plays a critical role in improving the well-being of the world's poor. This is an important feature of innovative finance.

Although hard currency has been around for millennia, governments have only recently begun to deploy cash as a proven way to fight poverty. In 2015, it was estimated that governments worldwide made $550 billion worth of cash transfers to between 750 million and 1 billion people in emerging markets.* This is because, for better or for worse, cash transfers have become the safety nets through which governments in many poor countries address basic needs. Cash transfers, both conditional and unconditional, with some of the strongest and most rigorously tested evidence bases across Africa, Asia, and Latin America, have been shown to reduce poverty and improve lives. Although the outcomes vary across evaluations—by design and definition cash transfers allow people to determine and purchase what they need—numerous studies show that in the short term, cash transfers allow families to invest in the health and education of their children. Over the long term, they allow people to save and invest, generating increases in future income. Although cash seems an intuitive solution to poverty, governments and donors have long been reluctant to simply make cash "handouts," concerned that people in poor households receiving cash might work less or might use the money to buy alcohol, tobacco, or drugs. Recent research shows no evidence of this kind of misspending or a reduction in the number of hours worked.† Advocates of cash transfers also point to the *multiplier effect*, which is the positive, macro effect of cash spent on goods and services in the local economy.‡

This shift to cash is taking place not just within governments. As we will see in the next chapter, large humanitarian organizations are moving toward cash in their relief efforts. For example, the World Food Program increased its cash programming from $10 million in 2009 to $3 billion in 2015. In the United States, the philanthropic community has taken note. GiveDirectly, a U.S.-based nonprofit that allows individuals to send cash directly to the poor in Kenya and Uganda, appeals to donors because of its extremely low over-head, extensive monitoring, and demonstrable poverty-fighting results. In 2014, its founders launched Segovia, a company and technology platform that seek to improve the logistics associated with cash transfers and payments in developing countries.

\* This is comparable in size to the estimated $560 billion in remittances to developing countries.

† David K. Evans and Anna Popova, "Cash Transfers and Temptation Goods: A Review of Global Evidence" (policy research working paper, No. 6886, World Bank, Washington, DC, May 2014). For an extensive literature review of the evidence on cash transfers, see "Cash Transfer Literature Review," UK Department for International Development, 2011, http://r4d.dfid.gov.uk/PDF/Articles/cash-transfers-literature-review.pdf. See also "Research on Cash Transfers," GiveDirectly, https://www.givedirectly.org/research -on-cash-transfers.html; "Latest Innovations in Cash Transfers," Integrated Regional Infor-mation Networks, July 2014, http://www.irinnews.org/report/100420/latest-innovations -in-cash-transfers; and Josephine Hutton, Shawn Boesser, and Floor Grootenhuis, "A Review of Cash Transfer Programming and the Cash Learning Partnership: 2005–2015 and Beyond," Cash Learning Partnership, 2014, http://www.cashlearning.org/downloads /calp-review-web.pdf.

‡ Paul Harvey and Sarah Bailey, "Cash Transfer Program and the Humanitarian System: Background Note for the High Level Panel on Humanitarian Cash Transfers," Overseas Development Institute, March 2015, http://www.odi.org/sites/odi.org.uk/files/odi-assets /publications-opinion-files/9592.pdf.

## Where Are the Women?

There is no doubt that digital and mobile technologies have improved financial inclusion worldwide, particularly in places like Africa. Yet, when it comes to financial services and participation, a stubborn and costly gender gap remains.[40] We have long recognized this as a market failure. Accord-ingly, much of the global development agenda is built around the social and economic returns that come from empowering women. "Financing gender equality should be seen as an investment in the future," proclaims UN Women,[41] as it lies at the heart of every social and development issue.

In recent years, numerous initiatives have emerged to target the financial needs of women. Like the broader microfinance evolution, many of these are moving beyond lending. For example, WWB has developed a range of new savings and insurance products and programs to complement their credit offerings. Consider the BETA savings account, launched by the WWB with Enhancing Financial Innovation and Access (EFInA), Visa, and Diamond Savings Bank in Nigeria—where 73 percent of women are unbanked and distrustful of banks which brings the service to the customer. Trusted agents frequently visit places like open markets, allowing women who are working or shopping to conveniently open an account with no fees via a mobile app.[42]

Similarly, WWB has helped develop new health insurance schemes for women, predicated on data that show they forgo their own health needs and insurance to pay for those of others in their family. Accordingly, WWB worked with one of its partners, Jordan Microfund for Women (MFW), to create a unique type of health insurance, a caregiver policy that provides a cash benefit after hospitalization for costs associated with loss of business, transportation, and ongoing medical expenses, including those related to pregnancy. Since the launch of the product, nearly half of the claims have been for pregnancy-related health issues, resulting in significant demand from MFW clients, with more than 90,000 policies outstanding.

A gaping gender gap persists at the enterprise level as well—with significant macroeconomic costs. Goldman Sachs has estimated that closing the credit gap for women-owned businesses, estimated to be approximately $285 billion per year, could boost income per capita growth rates by as much as 1 percent per year.[43] Accordingly, many new partnerships focus on the capital needs of female entrepreneurs in ways that attempt to address some of the shortcomings of earlier microlending models. For example, the IFC's Banking on Women efforts, funded in part by the issuance of a "women's Bond" has invested $800 million in institutions that serve women who are starting and leading small businesses in seventeen developing countries.[44] More recently, the IFC has teamed up with Goldman Sachs, which cut its teeth on its own 10,000 Women initiative, to create the Women Entrepreneurs Opportunity Facility, which is raising $600 million to provide business training, advice, and access to finance for up to 100,000 women entrepreneurs in emerging markets. Similarly, in 2014, Bank of America joined forces with the Calvert Foundation to make loans to support women in developing countries in Latin America, Asia, Africa, and Eastern Europe. The microfinance partnership between Citi and the Overseas Private Investment Corporation (OPIC)—a "plan to empower more than one million women"—has made nearly $400 million in loans to forty MFIs in more than twenty countries to date.[45] In Singapore, Impact Investment Exchange Asia (IIX) is launching a Women's Livelihood Bond in early 2016. This will be the first of its sustainability bonds, intended to raise $20 million in capital for a pool of underlying issuers, consisting of women-focused social enterprises and MFIs.

The gender gap, and its drain on economic progress, is not limited to developing countries. Although efforts focused on financial inclusion and access to capital are critical, they need to be part of a much larger investment agenda. As seen in the case of microlending, these supports are necessary, but not sufficient on their own, to achieve true gender parity and broad-based prosperity. Therefore, if innovative finance is to empower women, it must to go well beyond the realm of financial services and include things like financing for health interventions, access to clean energy, and education.

## Access to Capital for Small- and Medium-Sized Enterprises

Our brief treatment of the gender gap in credit brings us to the larger set of constraints that leave small- and medium-sized businesses (SMEs) without sufficient capital to grow their operations. These businesses not only provide much-needed goods and services but also are sources of employment, particularly when it comes to job creation: SMEs generate the most new jobs.[46] Access to capital for these engines of economic growth is an important public good. Yet across the globe new and small businesses lack sufficient capital. In emerging economies in particular, only one-third of firms have bank loans versus half in more-developed countries.[47]

SMEs are different than microenterprises, which are typically defined as businesses having fewer than five employees and often can access credit via microfinance institutions. The research on the efficacy of microcredit in raising microentrepreneurs and their families out of poverty is mixed. However, additional financial products can lift families out of poverty and provide them with the resilience to stay out. Similarly, microentrepreneurs can benefit from supports in starting and operating their businesses— sometimes in the form of technical assistance and sometimes in the form

## Evolutions in Microenterprise: Microfranchise and Microconsignment

Capacity building for microenterprises is challenging but not without precedent. The recognition that microentrepreneurs need more than credit to start and grow a successful business is the driving force behind many new business approaches that build finance into the business model and reduce risk for the entrepreneur.

In recent years, a number of microfranchise models have evolved that supply entrepreneurs with complete "kits" to start them off, essentially prefinancing the inventory of the businesses. For example, the HealthStore Foundation in Kenya franchises entire pharmacies to Kenyan villages, and Solar Sister gives women a "business in a bag" so they can sell solar lamps. Grameenphone, now the leading telecom operator in Bangladesh, began by franchising cell phone posts in rural villages. The best-known franchise model is that of Living Goods, which operates "Avon-like" networks of independent agents who sell affordable health products door-to-door in Uganda and Kenya. The organization franchises its brand and business model to these entrepreneurs, who receive a below-market inventory loan and a free "business in a bag," including uniforms, signs, a locker, and basic health and business tools. They also receive ongoing support through training, mentoring, and performance monitoring. Mobile has become central to the Living Goods model, providing direct marketing to customers about the benefits of specific health products and a range of health innovations like patient registry, treatment information, and reminders.

Even more micro is the microconsignment model (MCM), developed by Ashoka Fellow Greg Van Kirk, which allows rural villagers to "test drive" a business by investing their time selling products like eyeglasses, water filtration buckets, cook stoves, or solar lamps. They do not have to own the inventory; rather, the goods are consigned, removing the risk of outstanding loans for failed franchises. In addition to the products, the entrepreneurs are provided education and training. First developed in Guatemala in 2004, the MCM has expanded to Ecuador, Nicaragua, and South Africa.[*]

[*] Brett Smith, "Social Entrepreneurship: The MicroConsignment Model," Forbes, May 10, 2011, http://www.forbes.com/sites/ciocentral/2011/05/10/social-entrepreneurship-the -microconsignment-model/#2d011a5f206a.

of new business approaches, like microfranchising and microconsignment, which reduce risk for the entrepreneurs by changing their financing model.

SMEs, or larger firms with fewer than 100 employees (or fewer than 300 employees in some cases), are a different story. They require larger amounts of credit than they can access through MFIs, but they are often ineligible for commercial finance from other banks. This is why they are known as "the missing middle," or, on account of their major role in developing economies, "the missing majority."[48]

By some estimates, SMEs account for 50 percent of employees in developing countries. As in developed countries, they also create a greater share of jobs relative to large firms. Yet SMEs are capital constrained for a number of reasons. Like poor people, they often lack collateral and require significant lender diligence, which translates into unaffordable interest rates. Their businesses might not be sufficiently profitable to warrant commercial investment in the first place. Furthermore, SMEs, like individuals, often need financial services beyond conventional loans, like leasing or equity. The IFC estimates that the SMEs' global unmet need for credit is $2.1 to $2.5 trillion.[49] (In chapter 5, we will explore this financing gap as a significant issue in more-developed countries as well. In the United States, community development finance institutions have played an instrumental role in channeling capital to SMEs.) Development experts call this lack of capital in emerging economies the "valley of death" and a significant market failure. Improving access to credit for SMEs has become a priority of the global development agenda, as their growth is recognized as a global public good.

## Attracting Foreign Capital

### Innovation at Traditional Development Finance Institutions

For decades, the world's development finance institutions have worked to bring investment capital to SMEs in developing, emerging, or "frontier" markets. OPIC does this primarily through debt instruments, guarantees, and different kinds of insurance. Although OPIC cannot make equity investments itself, it can insure private equity firms and participate in private equity investment through senior secured loans. It can also participate in local markets and currencies through American partners on the ground. For example, its partnership with Citi Inclusive Finance provides financing in local currencies to MFIs in emerging markets around the world—most recently in Senegal and Armenia. As we have seen, the U.S. Agency for International Development has adopted more of an investment versus a grant approach to aid.

Outside the United States, the development finance agencies in the UK and Germany—CDC and KfW, respectively—have more investing latitude because their finance tool kits include equity. From a multilateral perspective, the Multilateral Investment Guarantee Agency, like OPIC, offers political risk insurance and credit enhancement to investors and lenders, which lower the cost of capital for investment in SMEs. The IFC provides financing to SMEs and recently launched a targeted SMEs Ventures Project.

### Venture Capital, Private Equity, and Impact Investors

In recent years, development finance institutions have gone a long way toward removing the risk of investing in emerging markets by promoting equity or equity-like structures. However, for venture capital and private equity investors, the risks, both perceived and real, of investing in frontier markets, particularly in small or early-stage companies, remain high, with the cost of diligence higher still.

As we have seen, there is growing investor interest in the "mass market," particularly in proven industries like microlending, insurance, and other financial services—those the Omidyar Network calls "asset light"—which are driven by the growth of smart phones and other digital technologies.[50] Some of these investors, like LeapFrog, self-identify as impact oriented. Although it is hard to define *impact investing* or estimate its market size, we do know that it's growing. The most recent estimates from JPMorgan and the Global Impact Investing Network suggest that the total global impact-investing market stands at about $60 billion, up from $45 billion in 2014.[51] In their sample, the majority of the assets are owned and managed in developed countries, but roughly half are invested in emerging markets. The majority of investments are made directly in SME-like companies, not indirectly through funds. Private debt and private equity account for more than three-fourths of the instruments used.

Yet significant barriers remain. Transaction sizes remain small—for example, in 2012, the average deal size was approximately $2 million—compared to the growth capital deals of traditional private equity—which average an estimated $36 million.[52] This limits the kind of investor, often to those with patient capital who might not require traditional market rate returns. Additionally, there have been few "exits," which investors are looking for as a proof point of returns. The field is an emerging one, with individual countries, development banks, and larger G8 efforts gaining momentum in shaping the right policy frameworks for further advancement of the impact-investing sector.

## Developing Domestic Capital Markets

While the flow of foreign direct investment is critical for SME financing, local market development, or the ability of domestic investors to identify and support market opportunities with debt or equity, is equally critical to long-term growth. The development of local capital markets and economies has become a public-good priority of the G8 and G20 macroeconomic development agendas. This discussion is not intended to comprehensively assess the broad range of local policies and initiatives emerging-market governments can undertake to attract foreign direct investment or to foster their own capital markets, nor to examine which countries have the most conducive policy or regulatory environments for lending and investment. Rather, we highlight recent and innovative efforts that support the development of local capital markets. The problem, and the market failure, is not a lack of capital. There is an estimated $9 trillion in local institutional investments—among them, emerging-market savings and pension funds.[53] Recall that the World Bank and infoDev are optimistic that over the next ten years, technology can unlock as much as $96 billion in local and "crowdfunded" investment for SMEs.[54] The hope is that with the right financial infrastructure—and with a high level of credit protection and risk mitigation, in particular—countries can deploy their own assets into local SMEs, funding their own development. Stronger local capital markets will also be more appealing to foreign investors.

### Hedging Strategies and Currency Risk

One place we have seen innovative finance solutions is in the emergence of new hedging strategies and tools to guard against currency risk, which is a major barrier to investment. Currency fluctuation is widely viewed as the "original sin" of development finance, posing an enormous challenge to entrepreneurs and investors alike. Typically, enterprises need funds in their own currencies to buy materials from local suppliers, to pay employees, and to build and run the business, but the foreign capital they borrow to make these payments is in dollars or euros. There is a mismatch in available currency and a risk that the value of one currency will fluctuate. If the local currency depreciates, as is often the case, these companies become overindebted and cannot repay their loans. This is also true of countries. This prospect discourages local and foreign investment in the first place.

Innovations in finance are taking place to mitigate some of these risks for microenterprises and SMEs. For example, MFX Solutions, a Washington, D.C., company, supports lending to entrepreneurs in low-income countries with affordable hedging, derivative products, and risk-management education. MFX aims to lower the cost of lending to entrepreneurs at the bottom of the pyramid, reaching more of them by helping lenders manage currency risk. It believes that better access to foreign-exchange hedging tools and financial education can profoundly affect global poverty.

"We stand in the middle and redistribute the risk," says Brian Cox, MFX's founder. "The lender gets repaid in dollars, and the borrower repays in his own currency." Since its launch in 2009, the company has hedged nearly half a billion dollars in loans to small entrepreneurs in developing countries covering more than thirty currencies, transferring the risk to large pools of international risk capital. "It's like shipping cargo: the most efficient way to carry a small load across the ocean is to find a big ship going the same direction," Cox says.[55] MFX's education programs have trained hundreds of SME bankers across Africa on managing market risk. Although the company started in microfinance, it has begun to expand its services and products to the growing field of impact investing and to other investment areas where currency fluctuation and lack of access to hedging products are major obstacles. This could go a long way toward strengthening SME growth.

Others are looking to strengthen domestic markets through local bond issuances, which are an important method of raising capital. The ability to borrow in local currency is critical. Created in 2012, the African Loan Currency Bond (ALCB) Fund allows SMEs to hedge against local currency risk (and political risk) by issuing bonds in their own currencies. Seeded with funds from KfW, Germany's largest development bank, and managed by Lion's Head Capital, ALCB Fund offers anchor investments to facilitate local currency bond issuance by nonsovereigns. As of 2015, it had invested $16 million in six local currency bonds, unlocking an additional $200 million in investment from local banks and raising capital for microfinance in Zambia and Botswana, SMEs in Gabon, and housing finance in Kenya, Ghana, and West Africa. In the ALCB Fund structure, government takes the first loss, the development finance institutions come in at the mezzanine level, and private capital is series A. The fund plans to grow to $100 million in investments over the next two to three years.

Another new player focused on local bond issuances as a tool of autonomous emerging-market economic development is Ascending Markets

Financial Guarantee Corporation (AMF). By providing monoline guarantees for local bond issuances, the company can ensure investors timely repayment (in local currency) of principal and interest for creditworthy bond issues and bank loans, whether microfinance, SMEs, consumer debt, agriculture, housing, health care, education, energy, infrastructure, or government debt. This kind of guarantee facility is not new. Monolines provide insurance for bond issuance and finance public-sector infrastructure by lowering the cost of capital, and have been used extensively in wealthier countries. The innovation here is the developing-country application. AMF uses local currency—in the form of guaranteed development bonds—as the vehicle to inject capital into SMEs' "missing middle."

In the wake of the financial crisis, monolines became the target of criticism, as they used derivatives to insure mortgage-backed securities and CDOs, inflating the credit bubble and exposing the market to greater risk. Yet AMF's CEO David Stevens asserts that, when these kinds of financial instruments are applied to good use and leveraged responsibly, they can have significant positive social impact, particularly in low-income countries where they do not simply lower the cost of capital; their guarantee wrap may be the only way the bond gets issued in the first place. Stevens describes the "stereo" benefit of this kind of financing. First, there is the fact of financing for a project itself. Second is the project's demonstration effect. Once a local currency debt market is proven, Stevens says, "you can open the floodgates to private capital.[56]

## What About Agriculture?

Concerns about capital constraints for developing-country SMEs are most pronounced when it comes to agriculture. This is true at both the household and the enterprise levels. Globally, the more than 2 billion poor people who depend on agriculture for their livelihood are consistently underbanked and underrepresented in the financial system. This has a number of negative externalities, including large costs borne by families and society at large. Without access to capital to invest in improved seed, fertilizer, and other supports, millions of smallholder farmers around the world do not produce enough food to feed their families. Moreover, it is estimated that the agricultural sector is the primary source of income and employment for 70 percent of the world's poor. Therefore, its growth and improved productivity are an important way to reduce extreme poverty.[57] On an even larger scale, the world's 450 million smallholder farms are needed to feed the rest of the world, but these farmers lack the resources necessary to invest in their farms and reach markets to sell their goods. Although it is hard to precisely calculate what the capital gap is for smallholder farmers, some suggest the demand could be as much as $450 billion.[58] What little lending there is, an estimated $8 billion, primarily comes from local "public policy banks." Only a small portion comes from commercial or microfinance lenders.[59]

The barriers to lending in this sector are numerous and should be familiar at this point. The first is simply geographic. Farmers find it hard to access banks from remote locations, and banks do not open branches in rural, sparsely populated areas. Therefore, access to credit and a broader suite of financial products has been limited. Risk is also a significant factor, as farmers and agricultural SMEs face natural disasters and extreme weather conditions. For financial institutions, these are both systemic and concentrated risks, which make diversification challenging (e.g., all the farmers in a particular region will be hit at the same time by drought or flooding). Other risks, as seen in the case of microcredit for women, involve collateral and credit histories, both of which are challenging for poor farmers to supply. All of these factors reinforce market failure and a vicious cycle. The absence of agricultural finance infrastructure means that in many places farmers have no experience with financial products or services and do not trust banks, even when products or services are available.

Although many of the obstacles facing smallholder farmers resemble those affecting other underserved groups, the same solutions do not always apply. For example, traditional joint-liability loans, used in microfinance to surmount the collateral problem, work best in cities, where most micro-lending takes place. In the case of agricultural laborers, borrowers are not close to each other. Furthermore, the funding cycles and needs of agricultural clients are different from those of urban workers, where the norm is the high-inventory-turnover model of street or market vendors. In agriculture, cash flow cycles are longer, typically seasonal: many smallholder farmers need cash for inputs during the planting season but do not have cash to repay loans until after the harvest. Other household expenses may arise when liquidity from farming is low.

Accordingly, a number of agriculture-specific financing models are taking shape. For example, warehouse receipt financing helps farmers obtain credit by using nonperishable goods deposited in a warehouse as collateral for their loans. Leasing allows farmers to acquire machinery and other kinds of farm equipment, even livestock, through flexible payment structures.[60] In these cases, the assets themselves serve as collateral. In factoring, farmers can use accounts receivable as collateral for loans.

The proliferation of new financial products also includes things like seasonal agricultural loans, in which disbursement happens during the planting season but repayment occurs during the harvest. For example, in 2014, the IFC, AccessBank Tanzania, and the MasterCard Foundation piloted a new agricultural loan that offered an initial grace period, which enabled farmers to plant, allowed for seasonally adjusted repayments to account for harvest income, and accepted livestock as collateral. Repayment rates and uptake have been high.[61] In addition, the bundling of products—agricultural loans with savings, life insurance, and index crop or weather insurance—can serve as collateral for lenders.[62]

Bundling can also occur through technical assistance. Credit and other financial products have limited utility if farmers don't know how to use them in order to improve yields and productivity. One-Acre Fund, a non-profit organization founded in Kenya, serves smallholder farmers using a four-part model that includes credit, training, inputs, storage, and insurance. It provides farmers with improved seed and fertilizer for stable crop production, financing through in-kind loans, on-farm agriculture training, and postharvest assistance in the form of storage and market facilitation. Farmers also have the flexibility to repay loans at their convenience as long as they fully repay at harvest time. The fund currently serves 135,000 farmers in East Africa, but the demand for its financing and services is vast. It has partnered with the MasterCard Foundation to provide training and financial services to farmers in Kenya, Rwanda, and Burundi. The fund's goal is to "build a farm microfinance movement" and to strengthen the commitment of microfinance institutions to expand into rural areas.[63]

## Aggregation, Value Chain Finance, and the Hope for Scale

It should be no surprise that there are benefits to farmer aggregation when they are closely integrated with each other and with the larger "value chain" of buyers and commercial banks that provide financing. However, less than 10 percent of smallholder farmers work as aggregated or collective producers.

In recent years, much work has been done to improve value chain finance—to better link small farmers to multinational firms like Nestle, Unilever, Coca-Cola, and Starbucks that will purchase their products and finance investments in productivity. In the last decade, impact-driven agricultural lenders have pioneered models for lending to smallholders through producer organizations, including access to finance with technical assistance.

One important pioneer in this space is Root Capital, a nonprofit social investment fund that offers credit, financial training, and other technical assistance to SME agricultural producer organizations in Africa's and Latin America's "missing middle." These businesses are too big for microfinance but are generally unable to secure credit from conventional commercial banks. Root Capital clients are farmer cooperatives, associations of growers, or federations of small enterprises that build sustainable livelihoods by aggregating hundreds or thousands of rural producers. Since 1999, Root Capital has disbursed more than $740 million in credit to over 530 businesses that improve the livelihoods of more than 500,000 rural households by paying these farmers better prices for their crops, improving their productivity, and providing them with steady access to markets. Root Capital's loans range from $50,000 to $2 million and are typically either short-term credit or preharvest loans, used by borrowers to cover the costs of purchasing "raw product" (commodities) from their farmer suppliers, or longer-term fixed-asset loans with terms of up to five years, used for equipment and infrastructure. With capital and training, Root Capital's clients have increased the volume, quality, and consistency of their products and have become trusted suppliers of more than 120 buyers, including Equal Exchange, Body Shop, General Mills, Keurig Green Mountain, Starbucks, Pier 1 Imports, and Whole Foods. Many of these companies, including Starbucks and Keurig Green Mountain, are also investors in Root Capital.[64]

Root Capital has also received program-related investments from the Gates Foundation and a recent $10 million investment from OPIC. In June 2015, Root Capital partnered with German development bank KfW and AgDevCo to create the Lending for African Farming Company, a $15 million lending facility that will finance agricultural enterprises throughout sub-Saharan Africa by providing working capital loans, lines of credit, and other flexible debt products worth up to $4 million in dollars and local currencies. Root Capital plays a number of critical innovative finance roles, including brokering capital, supplying technical assistance, and proving that there is a thriving, successful market for agricultural finance at various points in the value chain. This demonstration role is as essential as the first two if we are to attract the private capital necessary to bridge the "missing middle" finance gap.

## Mobile Technologies Redux

Mobile technologies have made dramatic improvements in finance for agriculture, where transaction and information costs are high. In addition to providing mobile banking, payments, credit, and movable collateral registries, these technologies link remote farmers to commodities exchange markets, which have themselves grown more sophisticated. Commodities futures, forwards, options, derivatives, and swaps (all of which lock in the price of an agricultural crop) have a prominent history in Asia and Latin America and are now being piloted in several African countries. These financial products can be useful tools for farmers to hedge against price fluctuations.

Technology, including mobile, satellite, and data collecting weather stations, has also fostered the growth of index insurance, which in turn helps to mitigate some of systemic risk of agricultural activities. On a regular basis, events like natural hazards and extreme weather conditions can devastate farming households and communities. They also therefore discourage large-scale investment in entire vulnerable regions. The emergence of new kinds of weather insurance—particularly index insurance that allows for payments based on proxies for damage—has led to significant cost reductions and opportunities for risk transfer. This means more protection for farmers and potentially more capital in the agricultural sector.

These innovations in technology, as in finance, are a means to an end: tools that enable us to build more-inclusive economies and more-resilient societies. And as we have explored in this chapter, there are moments in history when technological innovation changes the economics of markets sufficiently to disrupt and transform industries—and create opportunity. Such has been the impact of mobile on financial services as phones have become digital wallets that allow people to pay for goods and services and that provide access to financial products like savings and loans for the first time. We have seen how mobile money has ushered in new consumer finance models like PAYG that have enormous implications for the delivery of public goods like clean energy. However, we have also seen that when it comes to financial services, technology may be just a starting point. Often the right combination of finance, technology, and trust—the personal interactions that make new products or services seem less complicated, daunting or suspect—is what makes financial inclusion possible. We saw this in the case of microfinance 2.0 innovators IFMR Trust and Women's World Banking's BETA Friends initiative.

IFMR's other innovative finance breakthrough—using structured finance to unlock commercial capital for its local, customized banking on the ground pilot—reminds us that, despite the gains we have made toward financial inclusion, we still have a long way to go in bringing financial services to the unbanked, along with investment capital to the millions of SMEs that drive economic growth worldwide. Mindful of the tensions inherent in scale—the potential pitfalls that come with wholesale commercialization—the challenge and the opportunity for innovative finance in the twenty-first century is to make markets more inclusive and autonomous as engines of local and global growth.

# 4

## Toward a New Disaster Finance
### *Redefining Risk, Response, and Resilience*

In March 2014, Médecins Sans Frontières sounded the alarm: Ebola had reared its head in West Africa. Earlier that month a Guinea newspaper had reported that eight patients suffered from nasal and anal bleeding, and within two weeks, there were seventy-two confirmed deaths. The World Health Organization (WHO) did not declare an international emergency until August, and donor country and World Bank funds did not begin to flow until November. This Ebola epidemic would claim the lives of more than 10,000 people in Sierra Leone, Guinea, and Liberia. Families and communities across the region are still reeling from the devastation. The human toll is incalculable, and the disease is estimated to have cost these countries between $3 and $7 billion in GDP losses in the short term alone. "Ebola acts both as a serial killer and a loan shark," says risk management expert Gordon Woo. "If money is not made available rapidly to deal with an outbreak, many more will suffer and die, and yet more money will be extorted from reluctant donors ... like a fire, infectious disease spreads at an exponential rate."[1] The WHO estimates that in April it might have cost $5 million to control the disease. By July, it was $100 million and, by October, $1 billion. The next pandemic could be one of any number of pathogens more contagious than Ebola. Unless our response system changes, it might also be costlier, in lives and dollars (see figure 4.1).

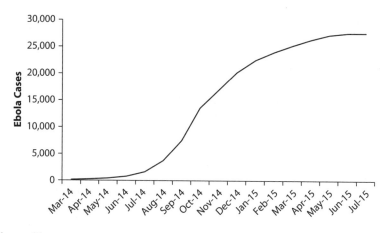

Figure 4.1
Global Ebola Cases, 2014–2015 Outbreak
*Source*: World Health Organization.

Nearly a decade before this Ebola outbreak, development experts Joanna Syroka and Richard Wilcox warned that "the timing of humanitarian assistance in the developing world has critical consequences," as delay is a "matter of mortal peril." They were not health workers but senior officials at the World Food Program (WFP)—and they were not the first to critique the inefficiencies of the international emergency response system, in which UN agencies like the WFP, WHO, UNICEF, and Office of the UN High Commissioner for Refugees (UNHCR) issue an appeal to donor countries after an emergency is under way and hope for an adequate response. Instead, Syroka and Wilcox argued for a "conceptual shift from a reactive emergency aid business model to a proactive risk management investment model"—one that would make emergency response and relief more rapid, less political, and more effective and that would form the blueprint for a new kind of disaster finance.[2]

～

This century has been no stranger to disaster. Although it is challenging to estimate these costs—in loss of life, disruptions to households and communities, and GDP—we know that humanitarian crises from natural disasters and political turmoil are both increasing and increasingly intertwined.

An estimated 93 percent of people who live in extreme poverty are in countries that are politically or environmentally fragile, or both.[3] Over the last ten years, natural disasters alone have disrupted the lives of 1.7 billion people, and economic losses are estimated to be on the order of $1.4 trillion,[4] nearly double the average of the previous decade. We also know that climate change exacerbates the conditions that trigger disasters and that investments in resilience and prevention are more cost effective than crisis responses. By some estimates, and depending on the measure, we spend nearly forty times more money responding to disasters than preventing or preparing for them.[5]

How can we better manage these disasters? Many recent efforts, within and beyond the formal UN and multilateral development system, have investigated how we can improve our investments in prevention and resilience, risk assessment, response and relief, and long-term rebuilding and development work.[6] Although funds are not a cure-all for these complex global challenges, there is room to enhance the amount and efficiency of resources available for disasters. Therefore, there is a role for innovative finance in securing this critical public good.

Let's begin with natural disasters.

In 2013 alone, there were approximately 150 major catastrophic natural events in which 26,000 people went missing or lost their lives. The estimated economic loss was $140 billion.[7] In the last decade, more than 700,000 people have died from natural disasters. According to the UN Office for Disaster Risk Reduction, 90 percent of these disasters—drought, floods, storms, and other extreme weather events—are attributed to climate change. By some estimates, drought in Africa accounts for almost one-third of all deaths from natural disasters.

This shouldn't surprise us. Nearly 70 percent of the 1.4 billion people in extreme poverty live in rural, agriculture-dependent communities that are vulnerable to risks from land degradation and the price volatility of crops. This will only worsen as global warming magnifies weather-related disasters like droughts and floods.[8] Although food shortages are the most immediate consequence, they are not the only climate-change threat for poor communities, agricultural or otherwise. The *Lancet* argues that climate change may be the greatest threat to public health of the twenty-first century.[9] All of these hardships will exacerbate the tensions and costs of large-scale migration.

Consider for a moment *food insecurity*, a term for hunger and starvation when drought strikes. Across the globe, half the world's hungry people live on small farms, relying on rain-fed crops and pastures for their live-stock. They cultivate exhausted land and have little access to markets to sell their goods. Crop yields are low and savings are lower still, especially when crops fail. Many suffer from seasonal or chronic food shortages. Layer onto this already fragile subsistence increasing weather variability, which threatens more than 40 percent of farmers in developing countries. The consequences are disastrous. Even the most conservative projections about climate change suggest that in the next few years 100 to 200 million more people will be food insecure.[10]

What does this mean for families? In the face of drought, poor house-holds cope in ways that are rational for short-term survival but that com-promise their ability to invest in long-term well-being. Families respond to the shock and stress of drought by eating less, taking children out of school, depleting savings, and selling off productive assets they own. When entire communities are affected, as they often are by drought or flood, fam-ilies cannot rely on friends, neighbors, or other supports. There is little in the way of a safety net or insurance against natural disasters and their consequences.

Although the costs of climate change are felt everywhere, the region most vulnerable to weather risks and shocks is sub-Saharan Africa. It is there that we are an estimated $14 to $17 billion in investments away from adapting to a climate that is warmer by 2 degrees Celsius. Weather-related disasters are particularly damaging for agriculture, food security, and liveli-hood across the continent and are already adversely affecting gains in eco-nomic growth. Over the last decade, more than one-third of the WFP's operations in Africa—a reasonable proxy for larger aid flows—went to combat drought. Some estimate that a widespread catastrophic drought in sub-Saharan Africa today could cost as much as $3 billion in emergency assistance, an enormous strain on African budgets and the fatigued donor governments.

So can finance help?

Because so many of Africa's disasters are weather related, they are, in some ways, predictable. Or at least, with good historical data, they can be modeled, assessed, priced, and insured against. Enter weather-*risk transfer*—that is, an insurance mechanism that can help Africans countries better manage some of these risks and therefore also their response to disasters.

There is nothing new about insurance. It is a long-standing, vital func-tion of finance that allows individuals and institutions to manage their risks by transferring the costs of potential losses to another entity—usually one with deeper pockets—in exchange for a payment or premium. The insurer provides a payment guarantee for a predetermined loss; seeks to identify and combine multiple risks, ideally uncorrelated, into a pool; and profits on the sum of the premiums. Although insurance has been around in various forms for millennia, it is relatively new to global disaster response. The subject of risk transfer has taken on increased urgency; it was most recently addressed in 2015 at both the World Conference on Disaster Risk Reduction in Sendai, Japan,[11] and the COP21 Paris Climate Conference as governments, multilateral institutions, philanthropies, banks, nongovernmental organizations (NGOs), and others considered how insurance can prefinance disaster response.

Though nominally about monetary payments, insurance is a useful instrument of innovative finance because of the larger security it affords households and governments, freeing resources that would be spent on immediate crises for longer term and future-facing investments.

## African Risk Capacity

Such was the thinking behind the African Risk Capacity (ARC), a specialized agency of the African Union (AU) created in 2012 by its member states to better prepare for and respond to natural disasters by using a new set of risk transfer tools.

The original concept for ARC was born out of frustration with the international emergency aid system, which experts like Syroka and Wilcox have long noted is ad hoc, uncoordinated, dated, and insufficiently matched to the magnitude and complexity of today's disasters. The flaws are structural. There is too much of what economists call *moral hazard*: countries often do not pay or plan for the bulk of the response efforts. Instead, funds come from the international donor community. This lack of ownership of both the process and the payments hinders effective disaster response. Moreover, the international response system is purely reactive. The formal appeals process occurs *after* disaster strikes, when governments reallocate funds in their national budgets intended for development to crisis response, while households have already begun to deplete vital resources. In their vision for ARC, Syroka and Wilcox imagined a more proactive entity that would use the tools of risk management for faster disaster response. Insurance could also make aid more equitable, as payouts are data driven, determined by demonstrated need and not the politics of the international appeals process.[12]

This shift would require new thinking about risk transfer. Effectively, Syroka and Wilcox argued, large humanitarian relief agencies like the WFP are responsible for so much of the world's disaster relief that they play the role of insurers. However, these insurers of last resort have not adopted valuable tools like pooled portfolio risk and other insurance mechanisms that were developed over centuries in the commercial capital markets.

In Africa, it turns out that most natural disasters are meteorological and can be modeled. For a number of historical reasons, including assiduous colonial rule, there is good historical data about the frequency of extreme weather events. Investments in technologies like satellite data and weather stations mean there is ample real-time data about weather—like rainfall and ocean levels—which, in combination with historical benchmarks, can be used to predict events like drought and flooding. The availability of such weather data also allows us to create indices—and therefore index insurance.

We begin to see here the important ingredients in the recipe for early warning and early intervention systems. The combination of real-time and historical data can be used to model weather and cost estimates, which allows for risk transfer and insurance payouts in the event of extreme events and for disaster response earlier in the season—before drought becomes famine. It helps significantly that many weather-related events across sub-Saharan Africa are uncorrelated to each other and to the stock market. This means that weather risks from different countries can be bundled together and transferred to an insurer in the form of a portfolio. It also means that reinsurers and larger institutional investors in the larger capital markets will take on weather risks for diversification, as these risks do not tend to correspond to larger macroeconomic fluctuations.

### The Power of the Portfolio: Risk Pooling and Transfer

Thus, ARC was formed in 2012 to be a pooled contingency fund linked to early warning systems that Syroka and Wilcox hoped would ensure "more timely and predictable aid in times of crisis, risk price information for sound development portfolio decisions, and dignity for the beneficiaries."[13] Risk pooling for disaster is not new, but for the first time, African countries can take advantage of the diversification of weather risks across the continent. The ARC pool takes on the risk profile of the group rather than that of each individual country. Because it is unlikely that droughts will

### Index Insurance

Index insurance uses data collected via satellites or weather stations as a proxy for a larger set of conditions on the ground. It allows agencies to predict the severity and consequences of potential weather events without having to assess local damage after the fact. As a result, it reduces transaction costs because assessors do not need to do farm-by-farm or household-by-household examinations to determine the cost of damage from drought or flooding. This is important because insurers historically have not offered farmers insurance coverage, affordable or otherwise, due to the expense of inspection and assessment. In contrast, weather stations can measure rainfall and compare it to an agronomic model specifying rainfall needs for a particular farm or region. If the rainfall needs are not met, all farmers insured in that region receive a payout. Index insurance also has the value of being apolitical or equitable. The claims adjustment process is established before insurance is offered to anyone—households or governments—using an ex ante assessment of risk exposure based on an independent, objective, and verifiable set of data. Evidence from pilots and studies shows that index insurance can minimize moral hazard and adverse selection, encouraging farmers to make riskier, but more profitable, investments. And its use is growing globally.[*]

However, challenges to the broad adoption of index insurance remain, including issues of cost, distribution, education, and trust.[†] Furthermore, index insurance is only as good as the quality of its data and the technology that enables data collection. Even in places where index insurance has seen significant adoption, like India, its growth remains limited by inadequate investment in infrastructure. There simply aren't enough weather stations to measure rainfall.

[*] See, for example, Dean Karlan et al., "Examining Underinvestment in Agriculture: Measuring Returns to Capital and Insurance," Poverty Action Lab, 2012, http://www.povertyactionlab.org/evaluation/examining-underinvestment-agriculture-returns-capital-and-insurance-among-farmers-ghana.
[†] "Financial Inclusion," World Bank, 2014, https://openknowledge.worldbank.org/bitstream/handle/10986/16238/9780821399859.pdf?sequence=4.

occur in the same year in all parts of the continent, not every country in the pool receives a payout in any given year. This means the pool can manage drought risk with less funds than if each country insured itself individually. Like all insurance, coverage through ARC is substantially cheaper than what any one country could obtain alone. The collective cost of capital reduces the cost for each country by an estimated 50 percent. ARC's hope is that countries will invest the savings in long-term development projects and resilience-building activities. This is an important distinction. Although insurance is a critical tool for major, but infrequent, disaster response, chronic development challenges require investment.

### Data, Technology, Early Warnings, and Early Payouts

The ARC financial model relies on Africa RiskView, advanced satellite weather surveillance, and software first developed by the WFP that projects crop losses and cost implications for food security based on rainfall data from past droughts and emergency operations. The information provided by these data creates the opportunity for early warnings, early payouts, and early interventions, which is the crux of the innovation. "Whereas in the developed world, waiting a few months for a car insurance claim settlement or the payment of a hospital bill is not a matter of mortal peril," explain Wilcox and Syroka, "the timing of humanitarian assistance in the developing world has critical consequences."[14]

Early payouts arrive in a country's national treasury within two to four weeks of harvest season. The intent is that financial assistance reach households within 120 days, the time when families begin to deplete critical assets. This timing shaves several months off the typical disaster response period. A number of independent cost-benefit evaluations of ARC have shown that these early payouts have significant economic and welfare benefits for participating governments and their vulnerable households. According to one study from the Boston Consulting Group, every dollar spent on early intervention through ARC saves four and half dollars after a crisis is under way.[15]

### Operations, Ownership, and Agency

ARC was premised on an insurance scheme, but its successful practice—and its importance for innovative finance—is all about implementation: operations, ownership, and agency. "This really isn't an insurance story," says Syroka. "It's about early intervention: there is no point in getting the money out quickly if it isn't used quickly. And it's about governance, governments owning their own response."[16]

Before countries can sign on for ARC insurance and pay a premium, they must present detailed implementation plans that show how they will use the insurance payments in a timely and effective manner. The ARC Agency Governing Board's Peer Review Mechanism evaluates the plans before signing off. Thus, there is a kind of forcing function inherent in the model, a pay-for-preparedness aspect, not unlike other insurance schemes. Auto insurers make premiums cheaper for drivers who have safe records. Health insurers offer cheaper coverage in exchange for health and wellness activities on the part of the insured. Some of these simply lower the risks and the probability of payouts. Others reduce what those payouts might need to be. In the case of drought, we know that earlier response means lower costs. These required contingency plans are also a way of building assurances about good government and governance in places where these factors have long been a development concern. This is important to the initial donors of ARC. In addition to the premiums, ARC has been funded with $200 million from the UK's Department for International Development; KfW, Germany's development bank; the International Fund for Agricultural Development; the Rockefeller Foundation; the Swiss Agency for Development and Cooperation; the Swedish International Development Cooperation Agency; and the WFP. From the perspective of the participating governments, ARC payouts are attractive because of the objective, transparent process through which they are determined. The predictability of the funds is extremely valuable for national budget directors in charge of allocating resources through the agricultural season and beyond.

These contingency plans are also critical to a government's ownership of the process. "With ARC," notes Wilcox, "the national government pays the premium through its budget, where it is embedded, which is different from how disasters have been managed in Africa." Countries pay premiums into an insurance pool and company they own—the ARC Insurance Company Limited is a mutual insurance company owned by the participating countries—which removes the moral hazard and encourages active participation, especially in preparedness planning. Wilcox maintains that sovereign and shared ownership reinforces the most basic principles of insurance—mutual coverage, reciprocity, and solidarity—and improves the countries' agency in financing natural disaster responses. In the words of Dr. Ngozi Okonjo-Iweala, coordinating minister for the economy in Nigeria and chair of the ARC Agency Governing Board, "This African-owned approach is addressing specific country-level climate change concerns, decreasing reliance on external aid, and promoting a sustainable solution to one of our continent's biggest challenges."[17]

### First Payouts and Next Steps

The inaugural pool was set up in in 2014, with Kenya, Mauritania, Niger, and Senegal becoming the first African countries to sign on. ARC worked with these countries to customize their profiles, calculate premiums, and allocate payouts. Countries could select the level at which they wished to participate. Each paid premiums of about $3 to $4 million in return for annual drought coverage of up to $30 million. In January 2015, ARC made its first payment: $25 million in drought insurance claims to Mauritania, Niger, and Senegal, which had paid a combined premium of $8 million. These countries used the payout to mobilize early interventions in response to drought, based on their preapproved contingency plans. Although ARC's model is still new, it is garnering significant enthusiasm in the development and disaster response community. The insurance payments do not cover all of the disaster response needs, but they do represent new, additional capital in addition to the preparedness and governance benefits. According to Robert Piper, the UN regional humanitarian coordinator for the Sahel, "These first payouts by ARC represent a milestone in government leadership and financial innovation for emergency response across the Sahel."[18]

ARC is now investigating other hazards, including floods and Ebola. It looks to scale its portfolio to $1 billion, offering coverage to approximately twenty countries by 2020 via the newly created Extreme Climate Facility (XCF). XCF will securitize its financial obligations to African countries by issuing a series of climate change catastrophe bonds, which will provide additional financing to participating AU countries affected by weather shocks, including extreme heat, droughts, floods, and cyclones. The bonds will be financed by capital provided through private investors, and donors will support the annual bond coupon payments. Like ARC's pooled financing facility, the XCF will be designed around historical weather data—in this case, the Extreme Climate Index, a multihazard index for each African climatic region that will use Africa's meteorological climate data from the last thirty years as a baseline. ARC plans to issue the first catastrophe bonds in 2016.

## Epidemics: The Disaster of Disease

In 2014, as Ebola ravaged much of West Africa, members of the AU recognized that their ARC architecture might lend itself to disease risk management.[19]

As with natural disasters, fighting the spread of contagions requires immediate funding to manage outbreaks—to prevent them from escalating into epidemics—but the response is often ad hoc and riddled with delays. The hope is that insurance-like tools can speed the timing of the response to these outbreaks: the difference between life and death. Again, as with drought response, risk transfer for disease is a vital public good that the market has not otherwise provided. It is hard to capture Ebola's toll—the loss of life and the economic consequences—and the fact that both are compounding in nature. We may not be able to prevent the next outbreak, but we can certainly improve our response to it.

As many have noted, there are diseases that are even more infectious and more deadly than Ebola.[20] The Spanish flu of 1918–1919 killed between 50 and 100 million people in one year. Between 1997 and 2009, six major outbreaks of highly fatal zoonoses—animal-borne diseases that are transmitted to humans, such as Ebola, SARS, avian flu, and H1N1—caused an estimated $80 billion in economic losses. The human and social costs are incalculable. According to a 2013 survey of insurance industry experts around the world, pandemics topped the list of extreme risks (along with costs and potential coverage) that they are closely monitoring.

In 2015, World Bank President Jim Yong Kim, a former WHO physician, argued that investing in the world's capacity to respond to epidemics "is really investing in the resilience of the global economic system." Accordingly, the World Bank outlined its plan to create a Pandemic Emergency Financing Facility (PEF), built on lessons learned from the Ebola scourge, that would put the WHO at the center of response efforts, requiring coordination between many UN agencies, including the WHO, the WFP, and UNICEF—and private-sector partners—including insurance, pharmaceutical, transport, and communications companies. When it comes to paying for these response efforts, the idea, similar to ARC, is to prefinance interventions, allocating funds to governments, multilateral agencies, and NGOs to contain dangerous epidemics *before* they become pandemics. Also like ARC, the PEF will have a kind of pay-for-preparedness feature, linking financing to robust country-level pandemic emergency preparedness plans.[21] (Many have suggested that adequate preparedness will require better medicines—like the Ebola vaccine or the newly developed cholera vaccine—to make early response effective.[22] This is the side of the finance equation we explored in chapter 2.) The PEF will also be financed in part through an ARC or XCF risk transfer mechanism, likely one that uses a catastrophe bond to unlock private capital for this purpose.

## Cat Bonds[23]

Catastrophe, or "cat," bonds are not entirely new, though demand has grown substantially in the last few years. They now represent a market of over $25 billion, with record issuances in 2014 (figure 4.2). Cat bonds were first explored in 1992, when Hurricane Andrew devastated much of south Florida, and with it the ability of insurance companies to cover their losses. More than ten insurance companies went bankrupt trying to cover $15 billion in damage. Over time, as the frequency and intensity of these storms increased, striking places that were well developed and therefore vulnerable to billions of dollars in damage, it became clear that traditional insurance instruments were no longer adequate. In response, reinsurance companies, which provide insurance for insurers, turned to the capital markets to transfer and mitigate their own risk.

Hanover Re ("re" being short for reinsurer) created the first successful cat bond in 1994. Since then, approximately 230 have been issued to investors. Hurricanes in the United States represent 70 percent of the total market. Insurers use cat bonds as a way to transfer risk off their balance sheets for a range of natural disasters, from earthquakes in California and Japan to windstorms in Europe and "extreme mortality" that could result from things like nuclear disasters. Recently, there has been discussion by

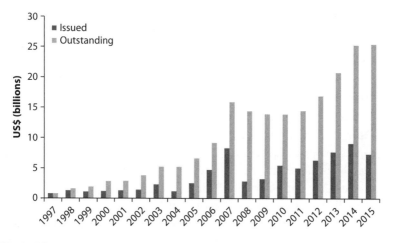

Figure 4.2
Growth in Issued and Outstanding Catastrophe Bonds, 1997–2015
*Source*: Artemis Deal Directory.

insurers and policy makers about whether cat bonds might be adapted to cover man-made perils like terrorist attacks[24] or even financial crises. Nearly any risk with a probability that can be accurately modeled to occur within set parameters can lend itself to a cat bond. This is why these could cover a multitude of weather risks in Africa and why ARC and the World Bank are exploring their efficacy for pandemics like Ebola.

The theory behind cat bonds is simple: insurers transfer their risk to capital market investors who are betting *against* catastrophe—for instance, that a hurricane won't hit a particular place at a specific time. If there is no disaster, the cat bond investors are repaid their principal plus relatively high interest. However, if disaster strikes, they are on the hook and lose their principal. In practice, the bonds have a number of complex parts. They require the creation of a special-purpose reinsurance entity, and they are structured around sophisticated modeling of the risk of catastrophe, which must occur at a specific "event level" (e.g., wind gust intensity or earthquake magnitude), geographic area, and time period to trigger a payout. Unlike green bonds, cat bonds have a higher return because the risk is higher. In innovative finance terms, there are two valuable pieces: the first is the bond, and the second is the insurance coverage.

To date, most cat bonds have been issued to protect against disasters in developed economies with mature insurance markets, where the probabilities and potential losses associated with hurricanes and earthquakes can be well modeled. In the case of ARC we see that developing countries are hoping cat bonds will bring much-needed private-sector investors to absorb some of the risk from natural disasters.[25] In these cases, cat bonds serve as an important tool for economic development and a way for developing countries to more actively participate in and shape their own development and risk management.

These rationales underpinned the World Bank's MultiCat Program, created in 2009 to enable member countries to enter the cat bond market. This program allowed Mexico to issue cat bonds in 2009 and 2012 to protect against earthquakes and hurricanes. In 2014, the bank issued its own cat bond linked to natural hazard risks. This three-year, $30 million Capital-at-Risk Notes Program[26] provides reinsurance to the Caribbean Catastrophe Risk Insurance Facility for cyclones and earthquakes.

The Capital-at-Risk Notes Program is a harbinger for other public-sector issuers at the multilateral or sovereign level. Developing countries are looking to access the cat bond market independent of the World Bank. For example, in April 2013, Turkey issued a $400 million cat bond for earthquake protection. China, which relies heavily on agriculture and whose coasts are populated with commercial and residential development, issued its first cat bond in 2015. Although the bond is relatively small—$50 million for earthquake coverage—it represents China's first public-private insurance coverage scheme and marks a notable shift from postdisaster finance toward preemptive risk management.[27] Many believe India is next, as its agricultural land is vulnerable to drought.[28]

Only a handful of the 300 or so cat bonds sold have generated a payout following a natural disaster. Hurricane Katrina in 2005 and the earthquake and tsunami in Japan in 2011 are two. Payouts are infrequent because the parameters used to measure the risk—location, time period, and specific intensity of the event—are so narrowly defined. A hurricane the scale of Katrina triggered only one of nine cat bonds in the Gulf of Mexico region. Even so, the increased frequency and intensity of storms have whet the appetite for the instruments on the reinsurance side. Though expensive, they sometimes prove to be the most cost-effective coverage in the aftermath of a catastrophe, when traditional insurance prices spike.

Consider the circumstances faced by New York's Metropolitan Transportation Authority (MTA) in the wake of Hurricane Sandy in 2012. Although it had shut down the New York City subway system in preparation for the hurricane, 14-foot storm surges at Manhattan's Battery swamped the city's rail stations and tunnels, flooded tracks, corroded antiquated electric controls, and wreaked $5 billion in damage on the largest regional transportation provider in the Western Hemisphere. When it emerged from Sandy's wreckage, the MTA found it impossible to buy any conventional insurance against future storms.

In response, the MTA issued a cat bond, the first specifically designed to protect against storm surges. Working with the First Mutual Transportation Assurance Company (FMTAC; its in-house insurer), GC Securities, and Goldman Sachs, the MTA created MetroCat Re, a reinsurer that could collateralize the reinsurance coverage it provided to FMTAC by selling $200 million in cat bonds to twenty investors. These investors were betting that the city would be safe from Sandy-level storm surges for the next three years, and they had a good chance of being right. Gordon Woo's Risk Management Solutions, the firm that assessed the risk, calculated that there was only a 1.67 percent chance of this kind of storm surge each year.

There are a number of innovative finance firsts in the MTA deal. It is the first cat bond specifically designed to protect public transportation infrastructure. Much of the cat bond market has grown up around coverage of private property. As noted above, it is also the first in which the payout trigger is linked solely to storm surge levels. This means that investors in the MetroCat Re cat bond pay only if coastal waters rise above 8.5 feet in the Battery, Sandy Hook, and the Rockaways, where much of the damage to the subway system from Hurricane Sandy occurred, or higher than 15.5 feet in East Creek and Kings Point. If there are no such storm surges before August 2016, they get their principal investment and annual returns of 4.5 percent above Treasury rates.

These yields explain why the MetroCat Re placement was oversubscribed—and why the cat bond market has grown exponentially. Over $40 billion in bonds has been issued in the last decade, and there is now approximately $25 billion outstanding, up from $4 billion in 2004.[29] Institutional investors like cat bonds for the returns—the demand for them has increased substantially in a period of low interest rates—and use them as a way to diversify as natural disasters are not typically correlated with other economic conditions or the stock market. They seem to believe the returns are commensurate with the risk. In the last year, yields compressed, meaning the returns were lower than they have been compared to conventional bonds. Development experts believe investor demand will remain strong and more than adequate to cover public finance needs, but the market is worth watching.

Cat bonds may be compelling for investors, but do they make for good public policy? Cat bonds aren't cheap and, as in the case of New York's MTA, must be weighed against the alternatives. In theory, the vast resources of the U.S. government should allow for self-insurance, absorbing the risk of catastrophe without paying a premium for coverage in the private markets. Typically, however, natural disasters strike locally, and state and city governments are on the hook for much of the immediate response and rebuilding. As in the global disaster relief context, there is often a delay in getting response and rebuilding funds to people and places in need. In New York, Governor Andrew Cuomo unveiled a plan to invest billions of dollars of federal disaster aid to improve the city's and state's infrastructure to withstand future shocks, but this was announced more than a year after Sandy struck.

Whether in New York City or sub-Saharan Africa, strengthening resilience is not just about building better or smarter; it is also about creative financing. New York's MTA, in the face of significantly increased prices in the traditional insurance market, found an inventive way to target the specific, costliest source of property damage: the storm surge. ARC created a risk transfer mechanism under different, but analogous, circumstances. "This is now an important risk financing tool for us," said Laureen Coyne, the director of risk and insurance management at the MTA.[30] Although this tool was tailored to the specific needs of the transportation assets of the MTA, and small relative to the total magnitude of Sandy's destruction, it may lend itself to use in other vulnerable municipalities. There are more than a few. By some estimates, 90 percent of the world's cities have developed along waterways (lake, rivers, or oceans) and are prone to flooding. And those along a coast, like New York, are exposed to wind-induced storm surge.

Whether this kind of innovative finance becomes a regular tool of municipal risk management in the United States remains to be seen. In March 2015, following a winter of record snowfall and havoc, the Massachusetts Bay Transportation Authority (MBTA) began to explore the possibility of insuring against another storm of that magnitude by issuing cat bonds—an option it is still considering. Once the MBTA exhausts its property insurance coverage, it must look to the Federal Emergency Management Agency for additional emergency support.[31] The Boston area experienced a record 110 inches of snowfall during the winter of 2014–2015, which shut down MBTA operations for long periods. By March, the MBTA had incurred costs of at least $35 million due to the snowfall (outages, removal, and repairs), an amount that did not include the estimated $1 to $2 billion in lost productivity.[32]

Recently, 100 Resilient Cities, an effort to strengthen cities' capacity to respond to shocks like natural disasters and other climate change events, forged a partnership with Risk Management Solutions (RMS) to allow urban leaders to better understand and manage their risks. RMS, which provides the cities with its models and technologies, will work first with San Francisco, where it is based. This partnership will educate cities about their disaster, catastrophe, and weather risks, quantifying their exposure. As they better manage their risk, some, like New York and the MTA, may transfer that risk to the capital markets. Perhaps more important than how they weather the weather are the security and autonomy that come with better risk management and disaster planning.

### Microinsurance: Can This Kind of Security Be Brought to Households?

Cat bonds offer a creative way for sovereigns and cities to manage risk at the macro level. But how well do these protections serve the poor and vulnerable in practice—and at the household level? For years, effective micro insurance for the poor has been a holy grail of development. In the previous chapter, we looked at insurance products when it comes to things like health or accidents. The question is whether there are similar retail instruments to protect against the kinds of shocks we discuss here—events like flood or drought—that threaten the food security of more than 1 billion people across the globe who live on less than $1 dollar a day and depend on agriculture for their survival.

For poor people on the rural margins, insurance can be the difference between security and ruin. As we have seen, insurance is a public good, but 98 percent of the 1 billion poorest people in Africa and Asia don't have it. What explains this market failure?

There are many obstacles to broad insurance adoption, but the primary one is cost. Although it makes economic sense to purchase agricultural insurance, a farmer may be too poor to pay regular premiums. Sometimes the problems of cost are compounded by access: there aren't always insurance products available for rural households to buy. Culture can also be a stumbling block. Without the traditions of insurance, poor households don't trust a product (or the person selling it) if they aren't familiar with it. Until they experience insurance and see the benefits, they won't buy it. Accordingly, there have been a number of experiments to stimulate farmers' demand for insurance by removing the obstacles to its purchase and demonstrating its value. The hope is also, in the process, to prove to the larger marketplace that there is a potential commercial insurance industry at the micro level of poor consumers.

## HARITA and R4

The Horn of Africa Risk Transfer for Adaptation (HARITA) is one such initiative to stimulate the demand for agricultural insurance. It was launched in 2008 to protect the poor against drought in Ethiopia, where 85 percent of the population depends on farming for their livelihood. When drought hits, these farmers, many of whom are poor, sell productive assets, pull children out of school, deplete their savings, and survive on the next year's seed money, causing them to fall into debt and deeper into poverty. Although crop insurance could mitigate the risk of this kind of disaster, only 0.4 percent of Ethiopia's 85 million people have insurance.

Through HARITA, Swiss Re, Oxfam, and other aid organization partners designed a risk management package that addressed affordability by allowing farmers to work for their premiums by participating in community-identified projects. The participating families helped to design the program, identifying the resilience activities that would benefit their communities and that would count as work toward premiums.[33] This process was essential to ownership, buy-in, and agency. Two hundred families at Adi Ha, in the Tigray Region, participated in the initial pilot. The project succeeded as a demonstration, showing farmers the benefits of insurance and showing potential investors and providers the early signs of a microinsurance market. The HARITA pilot was expanded, and by 2010, it served 13,000 households. Evaluations of the program, including the most recent, show that many families—and women, in particular—benefit from this insurance.

Three years later the R4 Rural Resilience Initiative was created on the HARITA model, allowing poor farmers and rural households to contribute their time and labor to crop irrigation or forestry projects to pay for their own insurance.[34] In 2014, it reached over 26,000 farmers, allowing them to manage risks to their livelihoods, particularly food insecurity, and it has since expanded beyond Ethiopia to include farmers in Senegal, Malawi, and Zambia. According to a recent Institute of Development Studies evaluation, R4 contributes positively in a number of ways, including women's empowerment. In addition to having improved access to land, seeds, and water for irrigation and drinking, women who participated in R4 benefited from training in numeracy, literacy, and business. They also reported reduced stress and more confidence in their abilities to pay for school fees and expenses through their insurance-related financial gains. The insurance product served its larger purpose: it helped households break the depletion cycle, providing cash, when necessary, in the short term and allowing them to invest for the long term. This study also showed that in Ethiopia, where farmers can obtain insurance through either cash or work, the percentage of those who paid in cash improved substantially.[35] This is an important outcome because one of the chief aims of these pilots is to demonstrate the commercial viability of the microinsurance markets.

## Kilimo Salama and the Challenge of Scale

And of course commercial viability matters when it comes to questions of whether these pilots can expanded—and, if so, whether they can remain faithful to the original models in the process. R4 is perhaps the best-known pilot in agricultural microinsurance, but there have been others, from Mexico to Rwanda. In India, the commercial insurer ICICI Lombard sells some 40,000 to 50,000 policies per season, but even after five years, the company considers itself in the early stages of product development and market penetration.

One way to get at scale is to grapple with the price of premiums, as was done with R4. Another is to improve access and distribution. Still another is to simply build trust. *Kilimo Salama*, or "safe agriculture" in Swahili, is a mobile index insurance product that attempts to get at all three. It was launched in 2009 by a partnership among Syngenta Foundation for Sustainable Agriculture, the African insurance company UAP, the NGO CNFA/AGMARK, the Kenya Meteorological Department, and Safariacom. Mobile phones are used to sell and track the insurance and to distribute payouts.

The original design was based on a pay-as-you-go experiment in the Laikipia district to demonstrate the value of insurance to farmers. In Kenya, as in other countries, farmers are unfamiliar with and suspicious of insurance, which was priced exorbitantly high prior to index and mobile.[36]

Kilimo Salama offers a "pay as you plant" mechanism so farmers can insure as little as 1 kilogram of maize seed or fertilizer at a time and thus test the insurance in a low-risk and low-cost way. When drought strikes, they immediately receive a payout. Drought is measured by insufficient rainfall at a weather station, and the payouts are delivered via M-Pesa on their mobile phones. The index structure, enhanced by mobile, means that the transaction costs are much smaller, and Kilimo Salama can offer low premiums for small insurance amounts. This helps build trust, as farmers can make a low-cost investment in insurance, observe its benefits, buy more, and over time use the savings to make larger investments in their farms, thereby improving productivity and economic security.

There are other innovations in the Kilimo Salama scheme. Because farmers do not often buy index crop insurance as a separate product, the Syngenta Foundation takes advantage of the existing mobile payment infrastructure and bundles sales of inputs like seeds and fertilizer that they are already buying with sales of insurance. Farmers pay only half the insurance premium. The agribusiness selling the seeds or fertilizer pays the other half. This kind of shared cost is a first in microinsurance (it is also considered a kind of insurance for the agribusiness, rather than a donor subsidy). Kilimo Salama is distributed through local agrovets, of which there are an estimated 8,400 in Kenya. The agrovets use a scanner with software that allows for low-cost, paperless registration and immediately confirms a customer's policy. They also collect premiums and transfer these in bundles through

M-Pesa to the insurance company. Agrovets are already trusted sellers of agricultural inputs, often giving advice on farm management, spraying, and other services, now enhanced by the fact that they and the farmers now have improved access to real-time weather information via connections to the local weather stations. As we have seen in the case of IFMR wealth managers and BETA Friends, the innovation comes at the intersection of finance, technology, and trusted human interaction. In its fourth year of operations in 2013, Kilimo Salama enrolled 150,000 smallholders in Kenya and Rwanda, assisted in part with support from the International Finance Corporation's Global Index Insurance Facility. This model seems to be making inroads on scale.

## Unnatural Disaster: Coping with Man-Made Crises

Although catastrophic in size and scope, the natural disasters described above are only one piece of the disaster story. In some ways, despite their staggering destruction and loss, weather risks are relatively easy to manage.

What of vast and man-made disasters, the humanitarian crises caused by conflict and persecution that are unfolding, with unprecedented sweep, across the globe? Is there any way for innovative finance to ease these human emergencies—particularly as prolonged refugee crises begin to look more like long-term development challenges?

The insurance industry includes in its definition of man-made disasters events like fires, train derailments, oil spills, and even some political conflicts: human accidents that often reoccur in some way can, even crudely, be predicted in some way and insured against.[37] We very specifically consider here the kinds of complex humanitarian catastrophes like war and conflict that do not lend themselves as readily to risk transfer. Globally, these kinds of disasters affect not only populations within countries at the center of turmoil but also those on the receiving end of refugees fleeing turbulence and violence. And while these intensely complex political crises are not always obvious candidates for financial solutions, innovative or otherwise, there is an emerging consensus in the humanitarian community that we need to rethink, reform, and improve how we pay for humanitarian assistance along the prevention, response, and rebuilding continuum.

What constitutes humanitarian assistance is multifaceted and complex and eludes any single definition. Yet it is generally agreed that humanitarian aid is intended to save lives, alleviate suffering, and preserve human dignity during and in the aftermath of emergencies.[38] Indisputably, the rate of displacement and suffering far outstrips the voluntary contributions of governments and private donors to meet these needs. The issue is clearly about negative externalities and global public goods. The question is whether some of the creative financing techniques explored here and in the previous chapters—pay-for-success, pooling and risk transfer, and mobile payments, for example—can harness new sources of funding or improve response time or deploy existing resources more efficiently.[39]

In 2014 and 2015, we saw record levels of need for humanitarian assistance. It is difficult to estimate exactly how many lives have been severely affected by crises like those in Syria, South Sudan, and Iraq because many people are unreached or go uncounted and because situations change quickly. That said, it is estimated that in 2015 an unprecedented 60 million people—half of them children—were driven from their homes by war, persecution, and violence.[40] Conflicts around the world have caused the numbers of internally displaced people and refugees to rise dramatically.

In response to these crises, in 2014, the international community volunteered $12 billion through the UN appeals process, which is more than this process had ever raised in the past—but still well short of the official request of $19.5 billion.[41] The unmet requirements—that is, the shortfall of $7.5 billion, or 40 percent of the need—were also the highest to date. The situation in 2015 was equally daunting. By March 2015, the international community's appeals for funds to address humanitarian crises worldwide had reached $18.7 billion—although this amount was needed to assist 74.7 million people in thirty-three countries, $5 billion was required by the Syrian refugee crisis alone, which was rapidly spilling beyond Syria's borders in a tragic, costly, and destabilizing way.

The United States is the world's largest humanitarian donor, and has been for some time (in 2014, it provided 32 percent of all government assistance). Roughly half of all international humanitarian assistance from government donors goes to the UN agencies that play a central role in humanitarian response and coordination, including the WFP (the largest) and the UNHCR. Private donors—primarily individuals but also trusts, corporations, foundations, and companies—provide nearly one-quarter of all humanitarian assistance, though they respond more generously to natural disasters like earthquakes and tsunamis than they do to chronic and conflict-related crises. International NGOs, which receive approximately 20 percent of humanitarian assistance funding, are the largest mobilizers of private funding.[42] Although there is a growing insistence on the importance of national and local NGOs in humanitarian activity, their direct share of total funding is less than 1 percent. Not surprisingly, it is challenging for countries affected by political crises to harness the development resources described in previous chapters: foreign direct investment and remittance flows, for example, are lower for conflict-ridden countries. Although development finance institutions like the Overseas Private Investment Corporation and Multilateral Investment Guarantee Agency offer some political risk insurance, many of the hazards associated with severe political conflict are simply not insurable. Unlike drought, civil war and religious conflict are not mathematically elegant problems because their risks are hard to transfer.

Is there any promise of improvement in the system? Is there any room for innovation in how we finance it—with new and better sources and uses of funds?

## New Sources of Funds

While European countries are, very visibly and viscerally, experiencing the pressures of large waves of refugees, most displaced people—86 percent—still flee from one poor country to another.[43] However, recent shifts in the geography of displacement, driven largely by the conflicts in Syria and Iraq, mean that the largest numbers of displaced people are no longer only in Africa, in countries like Ethiopia and Kenya, but also in the Middle East, in more middle-income countries like Turkey, Iran, and Pakistan.[44] By 2015, Turkey had become the nation hosting the largest number of refugees, with more than 2 million Syrians fleeing there from the violent conflict in their country.[45]

This situation has numerous funding implications. For starters it means that host countries, out of necessity, have assumed a greater share of the cost burden. Turkey, for example, has spent $6 billion on integrating its Syrian refugee population as of 2015. This geographical shift has also catalyzed a change in the global donor profile as Persian Gulf states like Saudi Arabia and the United Arab Emirates take on a larger role in humanitarian financing.[46] In 2014, Saudi Arabia became one of the ten largest contributors to humanitarian assistance, while the United Arab Emirates joined the top twenty. Overall, assistance from donor governments in the Middle East increased 120 percent from 2013 to $1.7 billion in 2014.

Accordingly, the international community has its eye on Middle Eastern and Islamic sources of funding. The hope is that these countries will participate even more fully in disaster response and development assistance, in the form of investment along the lines of the International Finance Facility for Immunization *sukuk* or through *zakat,* the Muslim practice of giving 2.5 percent of accumulated wealth annually for charitable purposes. Indeed all the world's major religions have a tradition of almsgiving, some of which goes to the faith-based humanitarian relief across the world. By some estimates, faith-based giving accounts for more 15 percent of all funding for humanitarian relief NGOs.[47]

While we try to increase the voluntary contributions from governments, philanthropic groups, and individuals, are there ways to improve how we deploy the humanitarian funds at hand? In recent years, as some of the protracted humanitarian crises begin to look like long-term development challenges, the shift to thinking about relief as resilience building has led to some innovations in disaster relief finance.

## New Approaches

### POOLED FUNDS

As with natural disasters, early warning and early action are critical for human emergencies. However, and perhaps by definition, most humanitarian responses will be too late. As we saw in the case of the WFP, an insurer of last resort, relief comes when local resources prove absent or insufficient to meet the severity of need. In contrast, ARC has showed us that it is possible to intervene sooner by pooling funds.

Even if they don't lend themselves to insurance-like risk transfer, pooled funds can play an important role in expediting the response to man-made disasters. The UN first used pooled humanitarian funds in 2006 in an effort to make crisis funding more timely and efficient. The idea was to create reserves outside of the formal appeals process that would reduce transaction costs and allow for flexibility and speed in response time[48] and that could fill in gaps where aid was directed.[49] Although these funds are relatively small and major donors like the United States and Japan do not participate much, they are drawing increased attention as a way to make humanitarian funding more efficient.[50] Pooling is only one of a number of avenues along these lines that the UN is exploring. In 2014, the UN Office for the Coordination of Humanitarian Affairs created a Social Impact Innovation Fund and Incubator to explore how innovative finance could improve our collective work in disaster relief.

## CASH TRANSFERS

In recent years, cash transfers—giving people money instead of goods—have come to play a more prominent role in the delivery of humanitarian assistance. Research, pilots, and programming in the last decade have shown that these transfers can be an effective form of humanitarian aid. When local markets are functioning, cash allows people to choose the goods and services they need, stimulating the local economy. This stimulus—what economists call a "positive multiplier effect"—can speed the recovery of local communities.[51]

Although in-kind aid is still the predominant form of assistance around the world, cash transfers are being used more frequently, and they have grown in importance in developing-country safety nets. For example, the responses to the 2004 Indian Ocean tsunami, the 2010 floods in Pakistan, and the 2011 drought-induced famine in Somalia included significant cash components. In the aftermath of Typhoon Haiyan, the WFP provided cash via the Philippine government's social safety-net scheme.[52]

Cash and vouchers have been used extensively for Syrian refugees. The WFP now refers to itself as a *food assistance* rather than a *food aid* agency because of the significant increase in its use of cash to allow people to purchase food. In 2014, it provided 98 percent of its food assistance to Syrian refugees through food vouchers. This is the WFP's largest program of its kind: with over $1 billion spent so far, it reaches 1 million Syrian refugees in camp and noncamp settings in the countries that comprise the Syria Regional Refugee and Resilience Plan (3RP): Egypt, Iraq, Turkey, Jordan, and Lebanon. In many cases, instead of a fixed basket of food rations, people are given paper or electronic card vouchers to spend in participating shops. The WFP has been working with MasterCard to develop a single electronic card that could be used by multiple agencies in different countries and contexts. In 2015, UNICEF launched a cash program in Jordan with these WFP electronic cards, and a similar pilot is under way in Lebanon with a consortium of six NGOs.

Vouchers are not equivalent to cash because they offer less choice and, given limited vendors and reduced competition, may mean higher prices. Cash also has its drawbacks: autonomy and choice mean less oversight. There is concern about misuse, which is related to gender equity in some cases: Who in a household controls the money and where is it spent? However, the evidence to date on cash and vouchers in the humanitarian context suggests they work well. For example, evaluations of credit vouchers in Jordan find that they have helped to boost employment, government tax receipts, and investment in local infrastructure: their value amounts to an estimated 1 percent of Jordan's GDP.[53]

Many believe that cash and vouchers, although still a relatively small percentage of overall humanitarian relief, have the potential to radically alter how we deliver humanitarian relief as we begin to understand it in terms of development over a longer horizon. According to a recent High Level Panel on Humanitarian Cash Transfers, these innovative finance mechanisms "challenge the 'business model' of humanitarian aid—the way that such aid has traditionally been funded, delivered, and organized" and "could have transformative implications for humanitarian action and the humanitarian system."[54]

## The Fusion of Relief with Development Goals

The refugee crises in general—and the case of Syria in particular—have brought together the discussions about humanitarian relief, resilience, and long-term development needs. One indication of this fusion—and a notable change in the appeals process—has to do with time horizons. Until 2013, UN-coordinated appeals had always been for one year or less. The first multiyear appeal took place in December 2012 for Somalia. By 2015, there were fourteen multiyear appeals, most for the Sahel. Many of these appeals target long-term resilience initiatives, and the needs covered by these multiyear appeals affected more than 45 million people in 2014.[55] In fact, in 2014, resilience became an official framing concept for the Syrian refugee response with the launch of the Syrian 3RP, which called for durable, long-term political and economic solutions to a refugee crisis turned development challenge.[56]

### THE CASE OF LEBANON

As a major recipient of Syrian refugees, Lebanon represents this fusion of humanitarian relief with long-term development goals. By the spring of 2015, the refugee population from Syria neared half the population of Lebanon.[57] This has led to all kinds of turbulence and dislocation, from severe unemployment, particularly for unskilled youth, to disruptive educational challenges, as schools have moved to three shifts to absorb the newcomers. The World Bank estimates that as a result of the refugee crisis, hundreds of thousands of additional Lebanese have been pushed into poverty, on top of the 1 million that had already been considered poor.[58] Lebanon is a small country—4.5 million Lebanese live on 10,000 square kilometers—and this influx has put tremendous strain on its local resources, particularly as raising support from international relief organizations has become more challenging.

In these circumstances, is there room for innovative finance? And if so, what is it?

The World Bank and the International Finance Corporation are both active in Lebanon, but their efforts have not been enough to mitigate the massive human emergency. Furthermore, official and multilateral relief and response in places like Lebanon and Jordan are highly politicized. Although they cannot offer the resources of the multilateral development finance institutions, local NGOs, often by necessity, operate outside of the politics of the international appeals process. In Lebanon, where human emergencies have morphed into development projects, local organizations with expertise in economic development and financial inclusion are stepping in to fill the void.

For example, Al Majmoua, the largest microfinance institution in Lebanon, with 50,000 clients, has begun to work with Syrian refugees. It now offers 13,000 Syrian refugees (many of them women heading households) a range of services related to business training and technical skills. It is also piloting group lending that would include both Syrian refugees and Lebanese citizens. The idea is to finance income-raising activities while enhancing social cohesion between the populations.[59]


## Finance for Economic Prosperity and Peace

This marriage of humanitarian relief with development brings us, in some ways, full circle—a return to the principles of the original Bretton Woods institutions like the World Bank and the International Monetary Fund which were created to rebuild the economies shattered by World War II and promote international economic cooperation. Although the focus at the time was on monetary policy, the intent was to use financial institutions to further economic development and prosperity and create global political stability—the ultimate public good.

## Swords Into Bank Shares

In recent years, we have seen a rekindled interest in the explicit application of these tenets: economic development for stability, or turning "swords into bank shares."[60] At a recent Economic Prosperity for Peace conference, former Treasury Secretary Larry Summers called these age-old linkages—economics and politics—"the right leg and the left leg" of global prosperity.[61]

Much of the recent activity regarding investment, SME development, and other efforts to stimulate entrepreneurship and business development as an antidote to conflict—a kind of Bretton Woods 2.0—has focused on the Middle East. These activities have included innovative initiatives like the Tunisian American Enterprise Development Fund, created by the Obama administration in the wake of the Tunisian revolution and seeded with funds from the U.S. Agency for International Development (USAID). This fund promotes economic development in Tunisia by catalyzing investment and encouraging business growth, with a particular focus on job opportunities for Tunisia's youth. Both it and a similar fund created for Egypt were modeled on the highly successful enterprise funds that USAID created in the 1990s to support Eastern European countries as they transitioned from centrally planned to market-based economies after the collapse of the Soviet Union.

Outside of these government-led initiatives, there have emerged a number of philanthropic and commercial investment efforts, including the Palestine Investment Fund and the Portland Trust, both focused on developing the Palestinian private sector and stimulating entrepreneurship and investment as a way of promoting peace and stability. The Middle East Investment Initiative, headed by former Secretary of State Madeleine Albright, takes a similar but regional approach. These innovative finance approaches return us to long-held beliefs about and hopes for economic development, prosperity, and peace—what some have called *expeditionary* economics[62]—that entrepreneurship, business, and job creation offer a way out of conflict toward stronger, resilient economies over the long term.

There is nothing easy about catastrophe—and little room for optimism, given the scale and scope of disasters unfolding across the globe. Yet in the case of natural disasters, the technology-finance nexus may be producing important breakthroughs when it comes to risk management. ARC showed us this was true at the sovereign and continent levels. HARITA, R4, Kilimo Salama, and others have demonstrated the march of index insurance into rural communities. Each reminds us that insurance is about something larger than money. It is a financing tool that gives families the security to make long-term investments in their well-being, whether it is through farm equipment, fertilizer, or a child's education. It is also a way to give countries the confidence and certainty to invest in their long-term resilience needs. For individuals and institutions, we saw how insurance can empower, bringing ownership, agency, and autonomy to the fore—whether it is Ethiopian farmers designing their own work-for-premium programs or African countries financing their own development through an AU-owned insurance company. Finally, we learned the importance of insurance in facilitating early intervention. The ability to act sooner—to prevent drought from escalating to famine or outbreak from metastasizing into pandemic—means exponentially more lives, and dollars, saved.

The complex and wrenching world of humanitarian crises is another story. Although we are a long way from devising financial solutions, it is clear that the line between prolonged human emergencies and long-term development challenges has blurred. This suggests that creative approaches to development—whether they involve pooled funds, cash transfers, insurance, microfinance, or something else—are one of the more urgent areas for further exploration in the world of innovative finance.

# 5

# Innovative Finance in Communities Across the United States

In 2015, a one-way subway or bus ride in New York City cost $2.75. That is no small fee for a daily commuter, who makes 500 of those trips a year. The good news is that the New York Metropolitan Transportation Authority (MTA) offers a thirty-day card, good for an unlimited number of trips, at a substantial discount. The bad news is that many who rely on this transportation do not have the $116 to pay up front for this monthly pass. Together, New Yorkers overpay $500,000 per day because they cannot afford the bulk fare. What's the solution? Go ask ALICE, a new start-up that allows New Yorkers to pay for the thirty-day card in affordable weekly installments, using their mobile phones.

∽

So far we have focused on the needs of the developing world and the ways that innovative finance can address them. Wealthier countries also face urgent capital challenges but often lack the public resources or political will to invest in the future. This means more-mature economies across the globe need robust, lasting partnerships, not to mention innovative finance, in order to meet the demands of the twenty-first century: strong economic growth, shared prosperity, and resilient and inclusive societies. Whether it's ride-by-ride microfinancing for subway commuters or billions of dollars in blended capital to build new rail lines, innovative finance has a critical role to play in harnessing more and better resources for communities across the United States.

## U.S. Community and Economic Development

We begin with community development in the United States, an approach to local economic growth and a sector that offers one of the first and most successful road maps for innovative finance. As with every chapter, this one could be a book unto itself. This discussion is not meant to be comprehensive; rather, it provides compelling examples of creative finance, public and private, that address market failure and stubborn issues of intergenerational poverty and that improve opportunities for America's most vulnerable.

Community development in the United States sometimes focuses on place—neighborhoods, housing, and commercial facilities—and sometimes on people—the health, education, and employment needs of those who live and work in these places. A holistic vision of community well-being, one that encompasses investment in people and place, is rooted in the nineteenth-century settlement house movements and work of the New Deal reformers. More recent and successful efforts to attract large infusions of private capital to underserved communities have centered on physical assets: on real estate and housing development, in particular. This is not surprising, as it is possible, under the right conditions, to use these assets to create monetary returns for would-be capital market investors. The question is whether we can apply the tools of innovative finance to support a comprehensive community development agenda, one that advances and fuses the needs of people and the places where they live.

What we call *community development* today has its origins in the urban renewal movement of the 1950s and 1960s, along with the emergence of the first community development corporations (CDCs), which embraced business models to tackle social and economic problems. Vibrant cities with broad-based prosperity have always been considered a public good—but one that policy makers and community activists recognized was not provided by the market alone. Accordingly, these early CDCs were first supported by philanthropic dollars and subsequently by federal block grants to states and cities, which in turn allowed the CDCs to attract more philanthropy. Community development also benefited significantly from the emergence of nonprofit intermediaries like Coastal Enterprises, Inc.; Enterprise; the Local Initiatives Support Corporation (LISC); and similar initiatives across the country. Today, for example, LISC is active in more than thirty U.S. cities, bringing together corporate, government, and philanthropic resources to provide local community development organizations with grants, loans, equity investments, and management assistance.[1]

## Housing

If the arc of this sector's development sounds familiar, it is because the community development field, like the microfinance industry, was born and proven with philanthropic and public dollars, but would grow to scale with commercial capital. It is hard to overstate the importance of the Community Reinvestment Act of 1977 (CRA) as a catalyst for innovative finance. The CRA was introduced and passed in 1977 to prohibit *redlining*, the use of discriminatory lending practices in low-income neighborhoods. That term dates to the 1930s, when the government-backed Home Owner's Loan Corporation drafted and color-coded maps of U.S. neighborhoods to indicate those they deemed creditworthy. "Inharmonious" racial groups were D-rated and circled in red, a practice adopted by a broader set of commercial lenders. As we have seen, credit—including credit for low-income people and neighborhoods—is a critical public good. The CRA was meant to overcome market and nonmarket failures by requiring commercial banks to lend in *all* communities in which they were chartered.

Although the CRA has been revised and amended over the years, it is largely recognized as a cost-effective way to substantially increase access to credit for low- and moderate-income and minority borrowers.[2] Moreover, it did *not* contribute to the subprime lending and overindebtedness—a kind of reverse redlining—that, in turn, exacerbated the collapse of the mortgage markets and the larger financial crisis.[3] All told, the CRA—and a set of innovative finance tax credits that it inspired and helped to fuel—has ushered in billions of dollars for community-based lending and affordable housing development.

Perhaps the most notable and transformative of these follow-on innovations in finance and policy is the Low-Income Housing Tax Credit (LIHTC). Like the CRA it depends on, the LIHTC is a successful case study in innovative finance. Initially a provision of the 1986 Tax Reform Act, the LIHTC was decidedly about place-based development in general, and housing in particular.

Decent housing is often described as a public good—but one the market fails to deliver without the visible hand of innovative finance. There is nothing new about this conundrum. The supply of and demand for affordable housing have long been challenging issues in communities across the United States. The fundamental economics of housing construction show that the market-rate costs of capital, operations, and investor returns translate into rents that are beyond the reach of lower-income families.

After World War II, U.S. policy makers attempted to address this market failure by funding and overseeing the construction of massive public housing projects. But over time it became clear that much of the public housing built in the 1950s and 1960s was serving neither poor people, nor the cities in which they lived, particularly well. In the 1970s, there was an emergence of *demand*-side solutions, initiatives like Section 8 housing vouchers that would allow poor people to pay closer to market-rate rents in areas in which they chose to live. The rationale—that government was a poor real estate developer and that outside market forces should have some degree of impact on the housing landscape—also informed the LIHTC. However, unlike Section 8 vouchers, the LIHTC tax credits are operated by the U.S. Treasury; it allocates the credits to the states, which then make them available to private developers to build affordable housing across the country, particularly in high-cost regions. This represents a decidedly *supply*-side approach.

Although different in shape and design from those we've seen in other chapters, the LIHTC represents a pay-for-success kind of innovative finance. The credit is structured so that the benefits flow only to units that meet the public affordability objective: rents that do not exceed 30 or 60 percent of the area median income. Importantly, no credit is available unless a minimum percentage of the units meets this income test. Under the program, private investors front the money for a developer to construct rental housing that is affordable to low-income families. In exchange, the investors receive a tax credit from the federal government, redeemable only when construction is completed and the renters move in. Investors receive the benefits of the credits only if the developer maintains the buildings as affordable for fifteen to thirty years. If the rent does not remain affordable for the specified period, the government can recapture the tax credit. In summary, the government pays only if the program is successful—if the investors, who bear the risk, build and supply affordable housing for at least fifteen years.[4]

The subsidy is not perfect. It is static and meant only to decrease the cost of capital for developers. It does not track or look to create positive outcomes related to a tenant's well-being over time. The fixed rent target does not adjust up or down to accommodate a range of tenant incomes once they are below the threshold, as the deal is struck before the specific tenants are identified. Tenants significantly below the threshold can often use additional subsidies, including Section 8 vouchers, to cover the difference between the rent and what they can afford. Tenants can also remain in the property if their income increases. This means that LIHTC units often serve residents with somewhat higher incomes than those served by traditional direct subsidy programs. Going forward, the LIHTC design could be improved along these lines to serve lower-income residents and account for a more holistic measure of their broader needs.

Today the LIHTC accounts for 90 percent of new funds for the construction of affordable housing in the United States, having leveraged an estimated $100 billion in private investment—roughly $8 billion a year for the last few years—to develop 2.6 million rental homes in urban, suburban, and rural communities (figure 5.1). It is also estimated that the construction of these properties supports approximately 95,000 jobs each year.[5] The LIHTC has achieved these gains through an almost-zero default record, no scandal, and strong bipartisan support.[6]

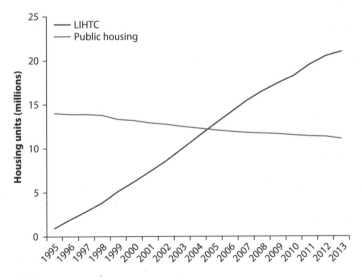

Figure 5.1

Total Housing Units from LIHTC Versus Total Public Housing Units, 1995–2013
*Source*: U.S. Department of Housing and Urban Development.

Despite these gains, affordable housing remains a major challenge in communities throughout the United States. The Joint Center for Housing Studies at Harvard University estimated that in 2013 half of all renters in the United States were paying more than 30 percent of their income for rent, the threshold generally accepted in definitions of affordability. For poorer families, it's even worse. Most families below the poverty line spend more than half of their income on rent, forcing them to cut back on food, health care, and other vital expenditures. In the meantime, the supply of affordable housing has been shrinking for decades.[7] This suggests the need to expand the LIHTC or devise similarly effective programs, thinking creatively about ways to finance them. In June 2015, for example, the New York City Housing Development Corporation issued the first Sustainable Neighborhood Bonds, raising $590 million for the construction and preservation of affordable housing in the city. These bonds, modeled in part on green bonds (and inspired by the demand for them, and for socially investment more broadly), were underwritten by a consortium of the City's banks, including Citi and Morgan Stanley.

In 2000, in part because of the success of the LIHTC in mobilizing private capital, Congress authorized the creation of the New Markets Tax Credit (NMTC) Program to motivate private investors to provide capital to real estate and business ventures in poor communities through community development entities. Between 2003 and 2013, direct NMTC investments of $35 billion were made, leveraging nearly $70 billion in total capital investment in businesses and revitalization projects in impoverished communities and generating around 750,000 jobs in the process. The NMTC expired at the end of 2014, but the New Markets Tax Credit Extension Act, introduced in 2015, looks to extend the NMTC program.

### Enterprise Capital

Although much of the NMTC flows to real estate development, the field's enterprise component has, by design, grown significantly in recent years. Our discussion in this chapter focuses more on the financing needs of individuals and families than on those of small businesses. Yet it is as true in the United States as it is in developing countries that access to capital for small- and medium-sized enterprises (SMEs) is vital for economic development— and an important public good. For decades, policy makers have sought to shape market forces accordingly. The Small Business Administration serves

The rental market is, of course, only a piece of the affordable housing puzzle. Homeownership has been an aspiration of Americans and their policy makers for centuries. It is rooted in the American dream—and in the Homestead Act of 1862, the National Housing Act of 1934, the creation of government-backed mortgage finance entities like Fannie Mae and Freddie Mac, and even the deregulations that sought to expand credit and instead birthed the subprime mortgage debacle. In the community development field, advocates of both place-based and people-based prosperity have argued that increased homeownership benefits individuals, families, and communities. Through the 1990s and early 2000s, the United States saw significant increases in homeownership, particularly for lower-income families, which, in turn, helped narrow racial wealth disparities.

As Americans know all too well, the financial crisis reversed these gains. Changes to lending practices and bank oversight led unscrupulous subprime lenders and often poorly informed borrowers into disastrous financing schemes, which have resulted in millions of defaults, foreclosures, ruined credit scores that prevent future home purchases, and enormous setbacks in terms of asset building.

The most recent data from Harvard University's Joint Center for Housing Studies show that in 2015 the homeownership rate had fallen to 64.5 percent, a twenty-year low, erasing all of the increase of the last two decades.[8] In the wake of the housing market's collapse, there is renewed debate about the value of homeownership, once a gospel of wealth building and development. Some evidence suggests millennials lack faith in the housing market and/or in their financial capacity (including the necessary credit history) to make homeownership a reality.[9] Many low- and middle-income families whose credit ratings were destroyed by the financial crisis are now locked out of the mortgage markets. This episode also reminds us that financial innovation is not innovative finance, where inventions and creativity must be used or intended to improve lives. Innovation that is opportunistically predatory is bad business for everyone.

The housing market may improve for those with some degree of financial security. In the meantime, a number of new developments are emerging in the field of housing finance that might ultimately alter the long-term homeownership landscape. For example, new kinds of *shared equity* mortgages are altering the all-or-nothing ownership structure of our housing market—in which you either rent or own the property 100 percent. Shared equity recalibrates this arrangement, offering buyers an opportunity for fractional ownership—to effectively issue equity. In these arrangements, banks or others can take some of the ownership or equity in exchange for reduced liability or debt.

At the same time, institutional investors are becoming more creative in the rental market. In November 2013, private equity firm Blackstone issued the first single-family rental bond, serviced by payments from 3,000 homes across the South and Southwest. In 2014, there were nine additional securitizations along those lines from a wide variety of real estate investors, ultimately increasing the availability of rental properties. These properties do not fall within the scope of what might be considered affordable housing and do not solve that crisis in community and economic development. However, they do begin to address some of the structural problems of the U.S. housing market.

this purpose, as do numerous state and local initiatives. Although community banking, lending, and venture capital organizations have existed for decades, the industry gained steam in 1994 with the creation of the Community Development Financial Institutions (CDFI) Fund at the U.S. Treasury, which supports CDFI activity locally, including lending and community development venture capital. As with the LIHTC, investment in local CDFIs can satisfy CRA requirements to serve low- and moderate-income neighborhoods.[10] All told, it is estimated that U.S. financial institutions make about $200 billion worth of CRA-related loans annually, including $47 billion in community development lending. Between 1992 and 2007, lenders committed approximately $4.5 trillion in CRA loans.[11]

In recent years, newer players in SME financing have emerged in the United States, including microfinance institutions like Accion that offer grants, credit, and technical assistance to small businesses. Yet microcredit in the U.S. remains relatively small. In addition, the impact-investing industry—more often considered in the context of emerging or frontier markets than in the U.S.—is a growing presence. JPMorgan estimates that 40 percent of the $60 billion impact-investing industry is invested in North America, in funds like Bridges Ventures U.S.

Some of these impact investors are seasoned CDFIs pursuing new ways to invest. The Calvert Foundation's Community Investment Note, for example, allows for broad investor participation in community development. Individuals can invest as little as $20 and select an investment term of one to ten years and an interest rate of 0 to 3 percent. As of 2014, the foundation had passed the $1 billion cumulative mark in notes, from

15,000 investors, invested over twenty years. In 2015, it had approximately $229 million invested in 250 community organizations across all 50 U.S. states and more than 100 countries. Calvert Foundation's Vested.org website has the look and feel of a crowdfunding site, allowing investors to purchase their notes with one click.

Calvert recently launched the Ours to Own campaign in Denver and the Twin Cities, enabling people to make small investments through the Community Investment Note to support projects and businesses in their own neighborhoods. One of Calvert's partners in this work is the equally innovative Community Reinvestment Fund (CRF), a CDFI that has been a leader in using structured finance and securitization to substantially increase the capital available for small businesses in disadvantaged communities. CRF is also beginning to explore the possibility of specialized online or marketplace lending for the kinds of small businesses typically served by CDFIs. As we have seen, there has been an explosion in what used to be called peer-to-peer lending, a new kind of credit marketplace that has disrupted the traditional banking industry. Even though many view this new lending paradigm as a boon to small businesses—providing access to capital when there wasn't any—CDFIs like CRF are beginning to see signs that small businesses are borrowing unwittingly and in inappropriate ways. For example, small businesses that need working capital but that borrow from OnDeck in a merchant cash advance can get into trouble. Designing the right online banking tools for small businesses, particularly in underserved communities, is an important frontier of innovative finance.[12]

## Place to People

Whether they encourage the development of new enterprises or of commercial or residential real estate, these capital flows represent, for the most part, place-based approaches to community development. This makes sense as a strategy for crowding in private capital, as it is possible with these kinds of projects to gauge risk and measure returns in ways that can satisfy investors.

For years, there has been a simultaneous focus in community development on *social infrastructure,* that is health, education, and employment for the poor. Unsurprisingly, it is more challenging to attract financial investment, subsidized or other, for these kinds of activities. That is even true for investments in things like early childhood education or maternal health, which have demonstrably strong returns, as the time horizons of the returns and the ability to measure and monetize them do not often match the requirements of private capital. Going forward, an important role for innovative finance is to encourage investors and social service providers to think differently about the ways capital can be harnessed to improve social infrastructure; the well-being of individuals and families.

## Financial Inclusion and Asset Building

Some of the most important innovations in people-centric community development have to do with asset building. First articulated in the 1990s by Michael Sherraden, asset building posits that wealth is a better measure of well-being than income alone—and a more secure route out of poverty. In *Assets and the Poor*, he shows that asset building increases household stability and provides the security families need to plan for the future, allowing them to take short-term investment risks for long-term gains. In addition, he posits that asset building enhances opportunities for community involvement and civic participation.[13]

To begin accumulating assets, people need access to basic financial services. Approximately one-third of Americans lack a basic bank account or are "underbanked"[14]—and most of them are poor.[15] But perhaps more relevant than whether they have a bank account is whether they are using appropriate and affordable financial services and whether they can plan and save, all of which would provide a better picture of financial health. Recent findings from the Center for Financial Services Innovation (CFSI) suggest that more than 50 percent of Americans are financially unhealthy. This doesn't mean they don't need finance; the explosion in a broad range of shadow banking services like pawn shops, check cashing, overdraft fees, auto loans, and payday lending (the last originates about $27 billion in loans each year) is evidence that they do.[16] In fact, in 2015, the financially underserved spent approximately $147 billion in fees and interest to access a range of these kinds of products and services.[17] This tells us that poor people rely on more expensive and informal kinds of personal finance. Access to affordable credit is even more limited since the Great Recession.[18]

This means, as we saw in chapter 3 on financial inclusion in the developing world, that there is ample room to improve products and services for poor people—including for poor Americans. But what is available for them? And what is the role for further innovation?

Sherraden and others—including Reid Cramer, whose work on asset building over the last decade has shaped and advanced the field—have shown that although there are a number of programs in place to help families build wealth via the tax code—including subsidized mortgage payments, contributions to retirement savings accounts, and 529 college plans—the poor are effectively excluded from many of these schemes because they do not earn enough to save for them in the first place.[19] Furthermore, when it comes to asset building, there are sometimes unintended consequences from well-intentioned government programs for low-income families. Section 8 housing vouchers, for example, are asset capped, so they can discourage savings or other investments, keeping families outside of the financial mainstream. Among the innovations Sherraden, Cramer, the Corporation for Enterprise Development and others have championed that would allow the poor to increase their wealth are individual development accounts and universal children's savings accounts, both of which pay in dollars to match those saved by individuals or households. Pilots of these products in various cities in the United States, the UK, and Singapore show that they improve the long-term economic security of individuals and families.[20] Saving becomes all the more important as the prospects for reform of Social Security, no doubt the most powerful antipoverty program in the social policy arsenal, are in doubt. At current replacement rates, Social Security cannot be relied on, as it has been in the past, to keep seniors, children, and the disabled out of poverty.[21]

Additional research suggests that, although saving is critical, financial products beyond traditional savings accounts may be necessary to enable poor households to manage short-term fluctuations in income and cash flow, pay down debt, and plan for the future. For example, development economist Jonathan Morduch has recently undertaken a U.S. Financial Diaries (USFD) research initiative (not unlike the financial diaries of the poor referenced in chapter 3) in conjunction with the CFSI. USFD found that the uncertainty from "spikes and dips" in cash flows challenges households who strive for economic stability as much as mobility; this volatility "complicates choices over jobs, budgeting, making appointments and personal plans, and deciding to borrow or save." The USFD results suggest that these families would benefit from tools or products that manage finances for the short term, like emergency or automated savings, or simply from better financial education about products, programs, and services, like government benefits, that people are already eligible for.[22]

## The Earned Income Tax Credit

The observation that poor people in the United States would benefit from improved access to existing public resources is worthy of book-length treatment itself, but a few sentences must suffice. The need for better access is particularly apparent with regard to one of the most effective antipoverty initiatives of recent decades, the Earned Income Tax Credit (EITC). Though rarely included in the discussion of innovative finance, taxes and tax credits, whether they are solidarity airline levies or the LIHTC for real estate developers, can have a tremendous impact in generating new, additional resources for public goods. Although income tax credits, a kind of negative tax, do not crowd in additional private resources, they can achieve tremendous benefits for low-income people and significantly contribute to welfare and economic development. The EITC is a "refund" above owed taxes (usually a low amount or even zero) for low-income workers that increases with every dollar earned up to a maximum level. First crafted in 1975 and expanded significantly as part of the same 1986 tax reform that introduced the LIHTC, the EITC has been extended and enhanced a number of times—most recently as part of the 2009 Recovery Act. In 2013, it lifted more than 6 million people out of poverty, half of them children. It also reduced the severity of poverty for another 21 million people, including 8 million children.[23] Although the EITC does not leverage additional direct investment, it does make antipoverty spending both more efficient and more effective, providing individuals and households with additional income they need to consume, save, or invest.

Critics of the EITC contend that these programs, although effective, hinge on work; they are therefore not available to those who are out of work—and who are often the most marginalized.[24] Indeed the EITC does encourage and reward work, but the critique has proven to be relevant, especially in the last few years, given the weak economy and high unemployment rates. Critics also suggest that tax credit–based programs—the EITC, NMTC, and LIHTC among them—let the government off the hook for spending more directly on a variety of pro-poor initiatives. This critique, part of the larger set of concerns about the "financialization" of society, assumes there is a viable counterfactual in which the government is spending these dollars. For the most part, those who work on fighting poverty have called for significant expansion of the EITC at the federal and state levels.[25]

Some of the more compelling innovative finance developments surrounding the EITC and other benefits have come from outside government, from leading creative nonprofit organizations and companies that help people access resources for which they are already eligible. Single Stop USA is a good example. Originally incubated at the Robin Hood Foundation, it was launched in 2007 to connect people to a range of government benefits, from financial aid and food stamps to child-care subsidies, health insurance, and the EITC. McKinsey & Company estimates that approximately $65 billion in benefits go unclaimed each year because people don't know about them or because the logistics of filing for and claiming them can be complex and expensive and are uncoordinated among city, state, and federal agencies. Through trained personnel, partners like community colleges that already reach large numbers of people, and smart software, Single Stop matches supply and demand by determining a host of benefits for which an individual might be eligible. On average, every dollar the organization spends has produced approximately $20 for clients, much of this from the EITC. To date, Single Stop has served 1 million households, across eight states, helping them collect nearly $1 billion in benefits. To reduce costs and increase scale, Single Stop has improved its software to become more self-service. It is also developing an app. However, the program's historical success has depended on innovation at the intersection of human interaction and technological advance.

*Fin Tech*

Leveraging technology to serve people in need is one of the most promising areas of exploration for innovative finance. The Social Entrepreneurs Fund (TSEF), an impact-investing fund that invests in the technology-poverty nexus, has a number of Single Stop like companies in its portfolio that match people to resources. Aunt Bertha, for example, allows people to enter their zip codes and find human services, including places like Single Stop locations. Benestream, another TSEF investment, is an outsourced Medicaid enrollment system, enabling employers to save 90 percent of the health insurance costs for their low-income workers while connecting millions of eligible working-poor families to health insurance and food stamp benefits. Other TSEF investments are in new kinds of financial technology, or fin tech—pay-as-you-go financing devices, data analytics for credit scoring, and energy efficiency. Similarly, Blue Ridge Labs at Robin Hood provides fellowships, grants, and other supports to social innovators creating tech products and services for the 75 million Americans who live in households earning less than $25,000 a year, including Propel, an app for enrolling in SNAP, or food stamps, and Rebank, a website that allows low-income New Yorkers to better shop and assess their banking options.

Another Blue Ridge Labs and Robin Hood spin-off is ALICE Financial, the company that finances thirty-day unlimited-ride MetroCards for New Yorkers who cannot afford the $116 up front but who would benefit substantially from the bulk savings. New Yorkers overpay $500,000 per day by using a daily or seven-day MetroCard instead of the thirty-day card. ALICE offers a pay-as-you-go installment payment plan, allowing riders to pay $28.50 a week for the card. Although users receive their MetroCards in the mail, most communication about the cards, including payments, is by mobile phone. ALICE may not be a complete solution to poverty in New York, but it makes a difference in the lives of many residents, especially as the geography of poverty has changed. Many of the poorest New Yorkers no longer live in the inner city but have substantial commutes to work in the city center.

Although it is still early to assess results, ALICE has shown tremendous growth because of its creative partnerships. These include, for example, Neighborhood Trust Financial Partners (NT), a New York City organization that has turned the twentieth-century credit union model into a twenty-first-century innovative finance institution. NT started a community development credit union, a cooperative financial services organization owned and operated by its members, and, over time, evolved into a financial empowerment organization built on the trusted relationship between advisors and low-income clients. NT's advisors work closely with clients to create a customized financial plan, typically focused on debt reduction, improved credit scores, and savings. In order to scale this trust model, NT has begun to work with employers, using the workplace and workplace systems (e.g., payroll) as a way to reach and empower clients.

More recently, NT has begun developing new fin tech products along the lines of ALICE, introducing the Trust Card, one of the country's first "socially responsible" credit cards. This card allows users to establish manageable repayment schedules tailored to their financial circumstances so they can pay off their high-interest debt and repair their credit histories. It also makes credit available in proportion to a client's demonstrated ability to manage and pay down debt. In addition, NT is developing a variety of mobile-enabled tools, including a credit snapshot, digital financial plans, and PayGoal, an app that will help people save.

Neighborhood Trust exemplifies the importance of technological innovation combined with personal interaction—the finance, technology, and trust nexus we have seen before. The success of its financial empowerment products and services depends on education and counseling, and its financial advisors look and sound a lot like IFMR Trust's wealth managers. In both cases, they seek to win the trust of clients and match them with the right offerings. NT is now a national model of financial empowerment.

Interestingly, countries like Kenya that have extremely high rates of mobile use have been pioneering more digital payment and mobile financial services than wealthier countries like the United States. Most recent innovations in fin tech in the United States—whether they are ATMs, debit cards, point-of-sale terminals, online banking, consumer payment and financial services from Google, PayPal, Facebook, Apple, or "wallet-to-wallet" payment platforms like Venmo, Dwolla, Lemon, Isis, and Chirpify—are not directly aimed at serving the poor or improving financial inclusion. However, they suggest there is a demand for products and services that do. Harnessing technological innovation for greater financial inclusion is one of the most exciting and promising areas of innovative finance.

## Social Impact Bonds and Pay-for-Success

As we have seen throughout this book, a critical question bedeviling the economic development field is how to think about about human capital in the same way we think about physical assets. How do we translate highly valuable investments in education, health, or workforce development into language and structures amenable to innovative finance? This is a different proposition than simply devising new financial products. It means considering return on investment rather than just up-front cost and attempting to quantify social and economic value that accrues in the future so it can be "monetized" today. Often this is as much about costs avoided as it is about positive benefits.

We have also seen that prevention pays. Providing vaccines is a far more cost-effective public health intervention than treating full-blown diseases. Early response is the difference between drought and famine, outbreak and pandemic. Preventing pollution in the first place is cheaper than remedying the catastrophic effects of climate change. The same is true for human capital development. We invest in high-quality education at all levels along the pre-K through secondary continuum because we believe a range of important benefits will accrue over time for both individuals and society at large. In the U.S., every dollar spent on high-quality early childhood education for low-income children returns $7 in improved life prospects and can save large sums that might have been spent on remediation services. It is cheaper to house the homeless than to treat them in shelters and emergency rooms. Crime prevention costs less than mass incarceration.

And yet, although we know prevention pays, governments do not always make adequate investments in preventive programs. Sometimes these kinds of interventions for the homeless, convicted criminals, or troubled teens are politically unpopular. Often the benefits from the investments are either difficult to observe or are realized only after an elected official leaves office, distorting the investment decision so that it is based on cost rather than value or long-term return on investment. Most often, it's simply the result of budgetary realities, insufficient resources for immediate needs, and fewer investments for the long term. This was particularly true after 2008, when government coffers worldwide—and especially at the state and local levels in the United States, where many human services are funded—were eviscerated by the financial crisis and the ensuing recession. This focus on the short term represents both a government and a market failure.[26]

For years, scholars and practitioners have grappled with ways to surmount this investment-in-prevention conundrum: how to get governments to pay for these interventions despite the obstacles. In the face of this, social impact bonds (SIBs) represent a new, innovative kind of public financing instrument premised on the not-so-new notions that prevention pays—and that we can put a dollar value on these preventive investments.

Given the massive costs of social problems and the significant savings from avoiding these costs, some asked whether it was possible to enlist private sources of capital, such as philanthropies or commercial investors, to underwrite the prevention in return for a portion of the dollars saved. If private investors could share in the savings, they could also shoulder risk, meaning that, if the interventions did not work, they could lose their investments. This was an important design feature of the SIB: governments would pay only for successful outcomes. The SIB theory was built on these two pillars: investments in prevention must have measurable, "monetizable" value, and taxpayers should pay only for those interventions once success is proven.

What about SIBs in practice? The record is both new and mixed. SIBs continue to evolve as an instrument of innovative finance and we are just beginning. We are beginning to understand the implications of the various SIB experiments.

The first SIB pilot was launched in 2010 in Peterborough, England, a town with a large prison and high rates of recidivism. Each year nearly 60 percent of Peterborough's released prisoners reoffended and were reincarcerated within twelve months. This cycle was costly in terms of crime in the community as well as the expense of putting someone back in jail—£30,000 to £40,000 per prisoner per year. This was far more than the cost of programs or services that could keep someone *out* of jail.

The Peterborough SIB pilot looked to test whether privately funded interventions could reduce recidivism rates. The SIB contract—which Social Finance UK, a nonprofit intermediary, arranged among the British Ministry of Justice, philanthropic investors, and four nonprofit service providers—called for intensive supports for 3,000 prisoners—given first inside prison and then in the community following their release. The philanthropies provided working capital to the service providers to work with these prisoners. At the end of six years, investors would be repaid if the interventions reached a reduction threshold in recidivism. The greater the improvement, the greater the financial return. In this case, if the nonprofits succeeded in reducing recidivism by 7.5 percent or more, the British government would pay investors up to a 13 percent return on their investment out of the long-term cost savings. Below 7.5 percent, the investors would get nothing.

## Pay-for-Success

In the sense that its return varies based on performance, the SIB is misnamed: it is not a bond but more of an equity investment. With returns shifting both up and down with performance, investors share in the upside and the risk. Governments repay only if the intervention works.

Pay-for-success is not entirely new. In the United States, state and local governments have been experimenting with different types of pay-for-success contracts—such as those covering the construction of affordable housing, as the LIHTC example shows, or of infrastructure like roads or bridges—when vendors are paid only after the project is successfully completed. Historically, the world of social services has worked differently.

Nonprofit service providers lack the cash reserves to fund interventions in advance of government repayment, so governments and philanthropies provide grants in advance of the interventions. SIBs translate the physical capital model into human capital by making payments after the work is done and the results are demonstrated. In the case of Peterborough, this meant after rates of recidivism had come down. Proving success requires rigorous measurement and evaluation. In Peterborough, this meant using a "randomized control" group of prisoners who would not receive services in order to better assess the impact of the intervention.

## A Field Is Born

Peterborough was both product of and spark for a larger revolution in how we think about financing entrenched social problems. In the five years since the first SIB pilot, a "pay-for-success" industry has emerged to test SIB models beyond the UK and recidivism (see figure 5.2). (In the United States, the term pay-for-success has become nearly synonymous with SIBs.) At this time, there are more than forty SIBs operating worldwide, and twice that many in active development, across North America, Europe, Asia, and the Middle East (table 5.1). They address a range of issues from health, workforce development, foster care, education, housing, and veteran reentry to criminal justice. The global market, currently about $150 million, is expected to grow to $300–$500 million over the next few years.

The first U.S. SIB, a contract put in place in 2012 in New York City by Mayor Michael Bloomberg, was aimed at reducing the high rates of recidivism of young men leaving Rikers Island Correctional Facility. The deal garnered much attention at its launch. It was an American first, taking on one of the country's toughest prisons. Its lead investor was not a philanthropy but one of the world's preeminent investment banks, Goldman Sachs. The investment marked an early innovation in SIB design, as it came not from Goldman's foundation but from the Urban Investment Group (a unit of the firm whose investments satisfy Goldman's CRA obligations). However, the capital structure also included a hefty loan guarantee. Goldman Sachs's $9.6 million stake was backstopped by $7.2 million from Bloomberg Philanthropies. The Goldman-Bloomberg-Rikers SIB received even more attention two years in, when it was deemed a "failure." The interventions had failed to generate the reduction in recidivism that each party had hoped to see. The city shut down the pilot, and Goldman and Bloomberg absorbed the losses.

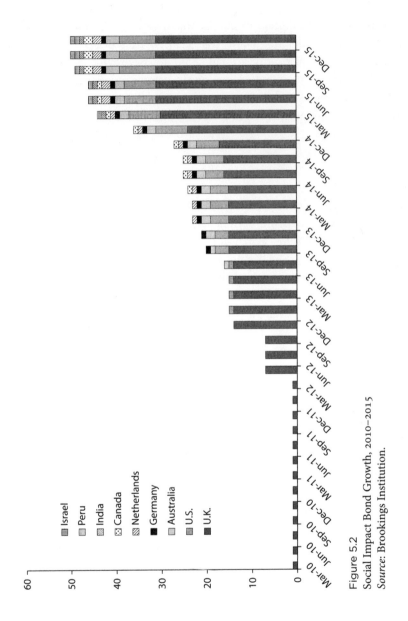

Figure 5.2
Social Impact Bond Growth, 2010–2015
*Source:* Brookings Institution.

Table 5.1 Social Impact Bonds Worldwide, 2014

| Country | Impact Bonds in Design Stage | Impact Bonds in Implementation Stage |
|---|---|---|
| United Kingdom | 8 | 25 |
| United States | 8 | 11 |
| Netherlands | 0 | 2 |
| Australia | 1 | 2 |
| Austria | 0 | 1 |
| Belgium | 0 | 1 |
| Finland | 1 | 1 |
| Germany | 0 | 1 |
| Ireland | 0 | 1 |
| Portugal | 0 | 1 |
| Switzerland | 0 | 1 |
| Peru | 0 | 1 |
| Canada | 0 | 1 |
| Israel | 4 | 1 |
| India | 0 | 1 |
| South Korea | 0 | 1 |
| Colombia | 1 | 0 |
| Costa Rica | 1 | 0 |
| Chile | 1 | 0 |
| Uganda | 1 | 0 |
| Mexico | 1 | 0 |
| New Zealand | 1 | 0 |
| South Africa | 1 | 0 |
| **TOTAL** | **29** | **52** |

*Source*: Instiglio, Interactive Impact Bond Map, as of January 2016, http://www.instiglio.org/en /sibs-worldwide/. Deal numbers are constantly changing as new deals come into the design stage and those into design move into implementation. Another terrific source for social impact bond number and type is Emily Gustafsson-Wright at the Brookings Institution, who refreshes the data from her important report, "The Potential and Limitations of Impact Bonds: Lessons Learned from the First Five Years of Experience Worldwide," Brookings Institution," July 2015. http:// www.brookings.edu/~/media/Research/Files/Reports/2015/07/social-impact-bonds-potential -limitations/Impact-Bondsweb.pdf?la=en. See also the Nonprofit Finance Fund Pay for Success Activity Map: http://www.payforsuccess.org/pay-success-deals-united-states

## What Have We Learned?

Although it is early, the New York City SIB, as well as the dozens of others that are now in place across the United States and across the globe, give us insight into how this innovative finance approach is evolving. In the case of New York City, it is fair to say that as a test of a new financing instrument, the contract worked. If SIBs, like other innovative finance instruments, are meant to identify, price, and transfer risk, that is what happened. This is important. Although it is unfortunate that young men returned to prison at rates no lower than before, the city and the New York taxpayers were not on the hook for a cognitive therapy intervention that did not work; Goldman Sachs was. Some have argued that Goldman should not have been shielded by Bloomberg Philanthropies' loan guarantee, but it has long been an important role for philanthropy: to test experiments in the social sector that government should not, and to bring additional, commercial capital investors into the mix by mitigating risk.[27]

We saw this, for example, in the case of the Global Health Investment Fund when the loan guarantee from the Gates Foundation helped attract investors who might not otherwise have participated. This is a larger theme of innovative finance; philanthropy can help alleviate risk and unlock new sources of private capital. When it comes to pay-for-success contracts, nearly all of the deals in the United States that followed the New York City SIB—in Massachusetts, Utah, Chicago, and Cuyahoga County, Ohio—have involved some kind of philanthropic participation in the form of grants or guarantees.[28]

Philanthropy is also important because foundation grants build the ecosystem necessary to support the emerging field. In 2009, before the Peterborough SIB was transacted, the Rockefeller Foundation provided operating support to Social Finance UK to assess the feasibility of this financing arrangement. In fact, since 2010, a number of foundations—such as the Pershing Square Foundation, the Bank of America Charitable Foundation, the California Health Foundation, various Pritzker charitable arms, Omidyar Network, and the Laura and John Arnold Foundation—have supported R&D, assessments, feasibility studies, policy recommendations, and information hubs to advance the SIB field. They have also supported the growing number of intermediaries, like Social Finance US and Third Sector Capital, that work with government and the private sector to ready and implement SIB deals and that continue to innovate in the SIB space.[29]

Among other things, these intermediaries manage the significant operational complexity and risk of SIB deals. The challenges and risks of implementation may be the chief lesson of the New York City experiment. The Moral Reconation Therapy that Osborne Associates brought to Rikers Island was an evidence-based approach because it had been shown to improve recidivism in young people. However, operational context matters, and the population at Rikers was older. This meant that the intervention was tweaked for Rikers, arguably one of the most challenging criminal justice environments, in the United States.[30] All of this suggests that Rikers might not have been the optimal location in which to test out a new rehabilitation strategy. It also reminds us that, no matter how elegant the theory of the financial instrument, the devil is in the implementation details.[31] In the same month New York City called for an end to its SIB, the results of three UK SIBs were announced. They were all contracted in 2012 between the Department of Work and Pensions and programs run by Career Connects, Teens and Toddlers, and Adviza. Each focused on the education, training, or employment of disconnected youth. These SIBs performed above expectations and delivered outcomes sufficient to return investor capital earlier than expected. In each of these deals, the interventions were more or less straightforward, and the operational and implementation risks were lower.

Operations matter because SIBs are not just about overcoming market failure, especially given the complexity of poverty and its social pathologies. As seen in chapter 2, simply making drugs cheaper and more accessible can go a long way toward improving health, especially for the world's poor. In places like the United States, however, interventions can be more complicated, as they often involve behavior change. "If you build it, they will come" does not always hold true because people do not always seek out the educational, vocational, or health services they need or could benefit from, even when they are available. Bringing people out of poverty often involves investments in prevention *and* behavior change, demonstrating to people that opening a bank account, purchasing agriculture insurance, or acquiring the skills they need to parent more effectively or find a job is a sound use of their resources. This relies on good implementation and service delivery.

## Evolution of SIBs

SIBs are rapidly evolving. Each new SIB brings with it an innovation in structure, approach, and sector. This change is what Clay Christensen calls a sustaining innovation, one that continuously improves on the value of a product or service.[32]

It is not surprising that the first SIB deals focused on recidivism: incarceration is costly, and the costs are well known.[33] Recidivism often occurs within a year, so the time frames for assessing the success of an intervention are short. Politically, there is little public sympathy for the issue. Therefore, there is little taxpayer support for services for convicted criminals, even if the potential cost savings from these services are vast.[34] Even the criminal justice SIBs have quickly iterated on the first models. For example, we saw that the New York City deal combined a bank investment with a philanthropic backstop. The following year a New York State SIB involving recidivism—executed by Social Finance, the Center for Employment Opportunities, the Harvard SIB Lab, and Bank of America Merrill Lynch (BAML)—combined foundation support with a private placement with BAML clients.

More notable is the evolution beyond criminal justice to include issues of homelessness and supportive housing, workforce development, and the needs of children, families, and young people in the areas of health and education (see figure 5.3). Two U.S. SIB deals, one in Salt Lake City and the other in Chicago, have focused on early childhood education. Although the benefits of these interventions accrue in later years, when children grow into productive adults, some value can actually be monetized earlier, as high-quality pre-K can reduce the need for special education supports for students as early as kindergarten.[35] The pre-K examples have helped

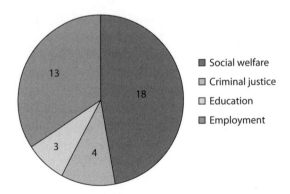

Figure 5.3
Social Impact Bonds by Sector, 2015
*Source*: Brookings Institution.

nudge SIB thinking further down the prevention continuum. In February 2016, the Nurse Family Partnership (NFP), the leading home-visiting program to promote maternal and child health in families living in poverty, with a strong evidence in breaking the cycle of intergenerational poverty, and Social Finance, announced the largest SIB to date, $30 million, in the South Carolina. Other states have been exploring similar maternal health intervention SIBs.

Over the long term, health may prove to be the most promising area for SIB exploration and application. In addition to looking at maternal and child health, several states are considering how to adapt SIBs to better manage "super users" of their health-care systems. Others are examining how SIBs can achieve savings through the prevention of chronic conditions like diabetes or asthma, the latter being the most prevalent chronic condition among children in the United States.

Approximately 7 million children under the age of eighteen have asthma, and poor minority children suffer disproportionately. Asthma is the third leading cause of hospitalization among children under the age of fifteen and is associated with increased emergency room visits. It is also one of the leading causes of absenteeism from school, accounting for 14.4 million lost school days and 14.2 million days of missed work for caretakers.[36] It is estimated that pediatric asthma costs the U.S. health-care system $56 billion a year in direct health-care expenditures and indirect costs from lost productivity. Nonmedical treatments of the disease—including removal of household and other environmental triggers, home visits, and child and parental education—can play a critical role in reducing asthma attacks and related emergency room visits and hospitalizations and have been shown to have a significant return on investment ($5.30 to $14 for each dollar invested in preventive treatments).[37]

In Sacramento, 20 percent of children have asthma, and twenty children end up in the emergency room each day to treat their asthma, which costs the city $35 million a year. Sacramento is exploring a health impact bond to address prevention. The pilot is projected to reduce emergency room visits by 30 percent and hospitalizations by 50 percent and to save between $1,000 and $5,000 per child. Similar efforts are under way in Baltimore and Alameda County, California. Local governments are not the only ones watching the asthma pilots. Others, including state and federal health insurers like Medicaid and private insurance companies, stand to gain from the cost reductions. Therefore, they could also serve as the ultimate repayers in a SIB-like innovative finance structure.

## Variations on the SIB Theme

The alternative payer model has application beyond Sacramento. In recent years, development economists have been investigating whether the SIB structure is relevant for poorer countries. Initially, the thinking was no: SIBs rely on repayment from governments that experience savings when they don't have to spend as much of their large safety-net budgets, and governments in poorer countries often don't have the funds needed for such repayment. In 2013, the Development Impact Working Group produced initial recommendations for how best to proceed with development impact bonds (DIBs) in ways that would allow donors or development finance institutions to play the role of payer.[38]

The first DIB to launch was one focused on girls' education in Rajasthan, India, where 40 percent of girls drop out of school before fifth grade. In this small arrangement (less than $250,000), the UBS Optimus Foundation will fund the efforts of the Indian nongovernmental organization Educate Girls to improve enrollment and learning. The Children's Investment Fund Foundation is the outcome funder, and Instiglio is the project manager. Social Finance UK has been exploring the feasibility of a DIB to address sleeping sickness in Africa, and the private equity firm D. Capital has been trying to structure an impact bond for malaria in Mozambique.

A more recent innovation along these alternative-payer-for-development lines comes from Grameen Social Business, a social business accelerator and offshoot of the Grameen Bank. Working with the Rockefeller Foundation, Grameen Social Business is testing the feasibility of a Social Success Note—a pay-for-success financing mechanism designed to attract mainstream capital to social enterprises in poor countries. With this note, a private investor agrees to invest equity in or make a low-interest loan to a social business. The business has to repay the investment, but if it hits a set of predetermined and SIB-like social impact targets, a philanthropic donor pays the investor a kind of impact "bonus," or payment for the outcome that wouldn't have been achievable without the initial investment.

Another recent SIB-inspired pay-for-success instrument is the Forest Resilience Impact Bond, premised on the idea that it costs forty times more to put out a wildfire than to prevent it. The bond raises capital from private investors to fund forest restoration and increase water availability for local utilities. It was designed by Blue Forest Conservation, the 2015 winner of the Morgan Stanley Sustainable Investing Challenge, which has gone on to raise additional philanthropic and impact investor support.

This flourishing of innovation is encouraging—and the most important legacy of the original SIBs. But many of these efforts are in their infancy, and each has required a long planning period and is labor intensive. This is the primary critique of the larger SIB movement: that each of these deals remains relatively complex and time consuming to structure. Each trans-action has multiple actors, including, but not limited to, a government agency, a set of investors, a third-party evaluator, and an intermediary, all structuring the deal and overseeing its implementation. Deals in the United States have ranged from $3 to $30 million, whereas the typical amount of capital raised in the UK, Europe, and Canada is between $1 and $5 million. Remember that these are all still pilots. Of the forty or so deals still under way, most serve populations of fewer than 1,000 people.[39]

The hope is that, with time and some standardization, both the transac-tion costs of the contracts and the time taken to structure them will decrease. Although the field is steadily maturing and participants are learning the best practices from each arrangement, those decreases have not yet happened. The economics are such that, for a particular deal, large scale remains elu-sive. (To date, the high costs beg the question of whether it would simply be cheaper for government to pay for the service directly.) In the meantime, the perceived risk also remains a barrier for mainstream, commercial inves-tors seeking market-rate returns. At present, investors remain in the philan-thropic and socially motivated impact investor category.

Concerns about SIB risk are not limited to returns. SIBs require precise measurement and evaluation in identifying the right outcomes, which is not always easy and not always available. Many nonprofit providers, even if their services are effective, lack the evidence base that would qualify them for SIBs. For reasons of time horizon, complexity in isolating specific desired outcomes, and other important measurement challenges, some social prob-lems do not readily lend themselves to SIBs in the first place. Some worry that enthusiasm for instruments like SIBs and innovative finance more gen-erally can skew government priorities not just to "what works" but also to "what can be measured," which isn't always the same thing. This represents a kind of metric drift, an unintended consequence of the adage and practice that what gets measured gets done. This bias is an important one. Though some issues related to poverty and injustice are hard to quantify, they still need to be addressed. Furthermore, sometimes a laser-like insistence on proof and evidence can discourage innovation and risk taking.[40]

## SIBs and Good Governance

The larger lessons we can glean to date about SIBs are less about financing structure than about the changes in governance they encourage. Like the African Risk Capacity and other innovative finance instruments, SIBs are about early intervention. They also demonstrate the power of measurement and evaluation to foster evidence-based policy making. In New York City, the outcomes-based contract meant the city could pull the plug on the recidivism project, at zero taxpayer expense, when the data showed it wasn't working. Additionally, the contract was not a Bloomberg administration one-off; it extended beyond the Mayor's term. The same is true of the Massachusetts SIBs put in place by Governor Deval Patrick. In both cases, and in other municipalities, SIBs have established a methodology related to evidence-based policy making that may be shifting how government works, or can work, when it comes to program design, evaluation, and funding—regardless of who pays the bill.[41]

In that sense, SIBs and pay-for-success more broadly are part of a larger push toward evidence-based policy making that is taking place both inside and outside of government. At the federal level, identifying and scaling "what works" was an early hallmark of the Obama administration, in part because the president and his budget team assumed office in the midst of a financial crisis—a time when all social spending was under scrutiny—and faced pressure to fund only programs with "rigorous evidence."[42] This principle would inform the design and allocation of innovation funds in the Department of Education, the Department of Labor, and the new White House Office of Social Innovation and Civic Participation (OSICP). OSICP, in particular, has championed pay-for-success in numerous ways. Its innovation funds have been awarded to intermediaries like the Harvard SIB Lab, the Green and Healthy Homes Initiative, and the Nonprofit Finance Fund, among others, that build SIB capacity at the state and local levels.

Evidence-based policy making and pay-for-success enjoy bipartisan support. The president's 2014 budget included close to $500 million for pay-for-success initiatives, including a $300 million Pay for Success Incentive Fund at the Treasury Department to encourage state and local governments to pilot SIBs. That fund remains at the heart of the Social Impact Bond Act—legislation introduced in Congress in 2014 by Todd Young (R–IN9) and John Delaney (D–MD6) that was echoed by the Pay for Performance

Act, championed by Michael Bennet (D–CO) and Orin Hatch (R–UT), and reintroduced as the Social Impact Partnership Bill in 2015.[43] On February 16, 2016, Governors Nikki Haley of South Carolina and Dan Malloy of Connecticut, a Republican and Democrat respectively, both announced pay-for-success initiatives in their states. This common ground is important as we think about the future of policy-led innovative finance.

The evidenced-based policy movement also thrives outside of government. The Coalition for Evidence-Based Policy has long been working in this area and has been joined more recently by Results for America, where Michele Jolin manages the Moneyball for Government initiative, calling for better use of data, evidence, and evaluation to inform policy.[44] Sonal Shah, the first director of the White House OSICP, and the director of Georgetown's Beeck Center for Social Innovation and Impact, regularly advocates for the use of evidence-based policy making to "drive impact."[45]

## The Larger Blended Finance Landscape

SIBs are both prod and product of a larger trend in public finance, demonstrating how blended capital structures can unlock private-sector investment for important community and economic development initiatives, whether they are place based, people based, or some holistic combination of the two. In that sense, SIBs represent a new way of thinking about public-private partnerships. The visible hand of innovative finance necessarily involves investors from across sectors.

In the field of community and economic development in the United States, a number of creative models are emerging that follow and further the blended finance approach. In the case of affordable housing, policy makers are increasingly looking to investments from foundations, often in the form of low-interest program-related investments, that will crowd in or subsidize investment from more commercial investors, expanding the overall pool of capital. This was the design of the New York City Acquisition Fund, where the city's Housing Commissioner, Shaun Donovan, used public and philanthropic dollars, along with loan guarantees, to attract commercial capital (from investors like HSBC and JPMorgan Chase) to finance affordable housing. A similar, but more recent, innovation is the Housing Partnership for Equity Trust, the country's only real estate investment trust that is owned and operated by nonprofit organizations. It has used low-interest program-related investments from the Ford and MacArthur

Foundations, pioneers of that philanthropic investment tool, to attract further investment from Citigroup and Prudential Financial.

## Housing, Health, and Transit-Oriented Development

Similar initiatives link place-based investments in affordable housing and enterprise development with investment in people-centric community needs like education and health—a reaffirmation of the value of a more integrative approach to community development.[46]

By insuring millions of Americans, the Affordable Care Act has created a demand for more health centers.[47] Accordingly, funds like the Healthy Futures Fund finance new affordable housing that incorporates health programs and new health centers for low-income residents. The Healthy Futures Fund is a $100 million partnership, in which LISC's procured tax credits (LIHTC for housing and NMTC for community centers) and the Kresge Foundation's loan guarantees paved the way for Morgan Stanley to enter with $87 million in investment. Similarly, in the fall of 2015, the Kresge Foundation, the Robert Wood Johnson Foundation, KeyBank, and Goldman Sachs created the $70 million Strong Families Fund to finance affordable housing with on-site social services for low-income families. The fund takes advantage of the LIHTC for capital development with a pay-for-success model based on demonstrated outcomes for residents in health and wellness, housing stability, and education. Goldman Sachs is providing $30 equity investments in the form of the LIHTC. The deal has $20 million in debt from the Community Development Trust, and the philanthropies are providing grants and program-related investments.

In addition to the housing and health synergies, developers and advocates of community and economic development are exploring the housing-transportation nexus, with the recognition that poverty and need have expanded beyond urban centers and that opportunity may require moving people to different places. The growth of poverty in the suburbs means, among other things, that mobility is more important and that transportation lies at the heart of the new community development—and an ever more urgent public good.

As such, transit-oriented development that combines affordable housing, a mix of services and amenities, and transportation linking up local and regional destinations requires new innovative finance. The Bay Area Transit-Oriented Affordable Housing (TOAH) Fund is a recent example.

This $50 million fund provides financing for the development of affordable housing and other community services, including child-care centers, health clinics, and fresh food outlets, along transit lines throughout the Bay Area. The TOAH Fund was made possible through an initial $10 million investment from the Metropolitan Transportation Commission and is managed by the Low Income Investment Fund. Other financing partners included the Corporation for Supportive Housing, the Enterprise Community Loan Fund, LISC, the Northern California Community Loan Fund, and the Opportunity Fund. In addition, participation by the Ford Foundation, Living Cities Catalyst Fund, San Francisco Foundation, and Silicon Valley Community Foundation made possible a $25 million investment by Citi Community Capital and Morgan Stanley.[48]

Living Cities oversaw a similar initiative in Detroit as part of its Integration Initiative, which began with support for Midtown, Inc., one of the city's community development corporations, and the Woodward Corridor revitalization efforts. In 2012, Living Cities member institutions Kresge Foundation, Prudential Financial, MetLife, and Morgan Stanley helped create the $30.5 million Woodward Corridor Investment Fund that financed mixed-use, mixed-income, "transit-friendly" real estate development along the city's central artery.

These transit-oriented development projects remind us of the growing importance of regional and global economies—and especially of the need to link them. As Ben Hecht, CEO of Living Cities, notes, "the geography of opportunity today stretches far beyond neighborhood and city boundaries . . . the primacy of place has lost out to mobility."[49] This means we must connect people to opportunity and to the capital markets necessary to finance those opportunities.[50] Each of these transit-oriented development projects was made possible through blended capital: investors with lower return requirements crowd in new and additional private-sector capital. These lessons are valuable when we consider that our larger infrastructure needs will require no small amount of innovative finance.

# Conclusion

## *Financing the Future: The Lessons of Innovative Finance and the TIES That Bind*

A globalized world means that the challenges we face are not confined to any one geography or sector; nor must be the solutions. Local carbon emissions produce global warming. Epidemics spread with rapid and cruel caprice. Conflict drives people over fences and oceans in search of sanctuary. Poverty exacerbates all of these problems, and investing in its alleviation is the paramount public good. Accordingly, innovative finance allows and encourages integrative, borderless thinking that makes critical linkages and investments across issues and regions: poverty and environmental degradation, public health and global warming, humanitarian disasters and long-term resilience, and community development that is both place- and people-centric. That is why, when it comes to finance, innovation is not so much about a new product or service as it is about creative application in different circumstances: an expert in securitization who translates future development aid pledges into vaccines today; an entrepreneur who turns a mobile phone into pay-as-you-go solar electricity; the conversion of pay-for-success contracts from bridges and roads to affordable housing, early childhood education, and maternal health. This adaptive approach—the ability to think beyond bounds, to overcome market failure in one context with market solutions from another—is a hallmark of innovative finance.

By definition, innovative finance is about solving unmet needs and harnessing creativity and market forces in the service of the greater good. When our aspirations exceed our resources, we need innovative finance to unlock more and better capital: new sources of funds, and more efficient use of the funds we have. Throughout this book, we have discovered that innovative finance is only in part about money. When successful, innovative finance also gives us the right tools and incentives to make better decisions about when and how to invest, ensuring that social and economic development is inclusive, is sustainable, and supports our long-term, shared prosperity. The following sections revisit questions of time, incentives, execution, and success: the TIES that bind and guide us in the world of innovative finance.

## Time

### The Finance Front Load: Tomorrow's Resources for Today's Needs

We began this book with a review of some of the basic and most ancient functions of finance, among them what economists call *intertemporal transfer*, or *front loading*, in which people or organizations borrow from their future selves—bringing forward from the future resources we need today. The ability to pay back these debts in small and manageable increments over time, matching liabilities with assets, makes possible all kinds investments and opportunities that otherwise would not have been available.

This is important in a world of scarce resources, when our needs and aspirations, as individuals and as a society, exceed our ability to pay for them. Finance 101 gives us the mortgage as a textbook front-load example. Innovative Finance 101 explodes the possibilities of this mechanism. The International Financing Facility for Immunization (IFFIm) bonds bundle and front-load future government aid pledges into cash that can be used for vaccines today. While countries wait for government aid to arrive, Net-Guarantee and Pledge Guarantee for Health help them meet their short-term capital needs. Social impact bonds (SIBs) monetize the value of future cost savings of social interventions, effectively lending against these savings to give service providers the working capital they need to perform services today. Pay-as-you-go financing means off-the-grid households in Kenya can purchase electricity today, via their mobile phones. ALICE

Metro does the same for New York City subway riders, allowing passengers to pay for the discounted thirty-day MetroCard in smaller weekly installments. More broadly, the front-loading concept motivates solidarity levies like UNITLIFE, which attempts to convert future wealth derived from natural resources like oil or gold into current resources for social investment. It is important to note that these are all financing decisions: the mechanics of shifting resources forward, generating dollars for today, when they are most needed. When and how those resources are used (spent, saved, invested) is a separate set of decisions—and where innovative finance gets interesting.

### An Ounce of Prevention Is Worth a Pound of Cure

Throughout this book, we have seen that early intervention is often the most cost-effective approach to remedying or preventing a problem. Developing and distributing vaccines is cheaper than treating full-blown diseases. Supportive housing costs less than homelessness, and job training costs less than incarceration. Abating pollution is a whole lot more manageable than addressing the catastrophic effects of climate change. In poor countries, purchasing bed nets *before* the rainy season and responding to drought *before* it becomes famine can be the difference between life and death. Like interest, many problems compound. Recall how Ebola is both a loan shark and a serial killer: "If money is not made available rapidly to deal with an outbreak, many more will suffer and die, and yet more money will be extorted from reluctant donors."[1]

Innovative finance can free up or front-load dollars we need today, when they are most needed and often most valuable. By unlocking the value of future cost savings, SIBs give service providers the working capital they need to offer early childhood education or to work with prisoners released from jail—preventive services with a high return on investment. Loan guarantees like those provided by NetGuarantee and Pledge Guarantee for Health enable countries to make urgent commodity purchases—such as antimalaria bed nets, medicine, or contraceptives—in advance of donor aid. These expedited investments save lives and dollars. IFFIm translates aid pledges into cash for today, and the Global Alliance for Vaccines and Immunization (GAVI) converts those dollars into vaccines—a process that is cheaper than spending the same aid dollars on disease twenty years from now.

African Risk Capacity (ARC) insurance payouts allow countries to intervene early when drought occurs—months before the typical aid response. The use of catastrophe bonds, a separate financing instrument, will bring even more capital to the ARC insurance pool. Similarly, efforts to reduce carbon consumption and emissions and to channel investment into alternative energy and sustainable development are premised on the basic notion that preventing climate change costs orders of magnitude less than adapting to it later on. When the risks associated with truly catastrophic levels of climate change are weighted into investment decisions, the economics of early action become even more compelling.

### Security Pays

Paradoxically, investments in prevention today are cost effective when individuals, communities, governments, and investors take the long view. Innovative finance can further improve the time horizons of decision making when it affords security in the short term—the ability to absorb and respond to shocks—that promotes saving or investment for the future.

This is the insight of microfinance 2.0: the value of products beyond credit, particularly savings (whether pension products offered by IFMR or Individual Development Accounts in the developed countries) that allow families to weather income volatility and shocks—job loss, health emergencies—and begin to accumulate wealth and achieve better financial health in the process. The same holds for insurance, which plays a number of public-good functions, among them risk transfer and better risk management. Both allow households, businesses, and governments to plan and invest for the long term. For example, health and crop insurance strengthens the ability of poor families to withstand shocks and break the cycle of depleting critical assets in crises. The security of insurance allows people to take risks—like investing in fertilizer or farming equipment, a child's education, a mother's health, a down payment on a home—that improve the family's well-being.

As seen in the case of ARC, insurance allows countries to adopt similar long-term horizons. If natural disasters like flood or drought are predictably covered, governments can create contingency plans that account for insurance payouts. This allows governments to *prefinance* disaster, reserving and directing resources they would have spent responding to emergencies toward long-term investment and development needs.

## Incentives

### Ownership, Governance, and Voice

One hallmark of innovative finance is the way it achieves a host of important outcomes that have little to do with funding but everything to do with sound decision making. By aligning and improving incentives, innovative finance can encourage and empower individuals and organizations to act in ways that benefit themselves and the larger society over the long term. This means improved governance, accountability, and autonomy, all top of the list on the economic development agendas of wealthy and developing countries alike.

We have seen numerous ways in which ownership—literal and figurative—enhances agency. In the same way that company owners require managers to hold equity stakes, when it comes to public goods, property rights and asset ownership can encourage individuals and government leaders to make decisions that are within their own self-interest and benefit the larger society. Better decision making not only results in a more efficient use of resources; it also assuages concerns of donors and investors that supply the capital in the first place. For example, cap-and-trade creates property rights out of pollution and therefore a price for carbon and an incentive to reduce emissions. In turn, this mechanism catalyzes a broader marketplace for pollution reduction, including investments in alternative energy sources and technologies.

In the case of ARC, we saw how ownership in and of the African Union insurance pool aligns incentives to improve financing and governance when it comes to disaster response. ARC removed the moral hazard problem of traditional humanitarian relief. The property right means that ARC countries have an economic incentive to prepare cost-effective response plans. With resources freed from emergency response, they then determine how to invest in resilience for the future.

In this light, ARC succeeds because it is built on the first principle of insurance: mutual cover. There is a sense of solidarity and empowerment among the countries of the African Union that participate in the pooled insurance scheme and own the independent insurance agency. In the words of Dr. Ngozi Okonjo-Iweala, coordinating minister for the economy in Nigeria and chair of ARC's governing board: "This African-owned approach is addressing specific country-level climate change concern, decreasing reliance on external aid, and promoting a sustainable solution to one of our continent's biggest challenges."[2] This is true for many of the innovative finance approaches examined in these chapters. GAVI's model relies in part on the stake recipient countries have in the transactions as copayers for the vaccines. Similarly, the architects of the UNITLIFE levy believe it will succeed, based on the UNITAID example, because it allows African countries to tax themselves in order to finance their own development needs. The same is true when IndiGo collects payments from Indian travelers on domestic flights for their country's sustainable development projects. The IFFIm *sukuk*, the Islamic finance equivalent of a bond, raised $500 million for immunization and health systems from Islamic countries because they wanted to fund vaccinations in the Muslim world.[3] As we have seen, the Persian Gulf states are taking on a larger role in humanitarian financing for crises in the region. Although countries like Saudi Arabia are not currently providing sanctuary for refugees, the hope is that over time they will match their financial commitments with political ones.

Ownership is also about process. For years, countries in both the Global North and the Global South (rich and poor alike) have recognized the importance of autonomy in development; for emerging economies and local communities to own their own development destinies, to identify, design, and finance their own needs. Many of the innovative finance successes we see, from climate change to global health and financial inclusion, are intended to give countries and local communities a greater voice in the development process.

For example, much of the success of Reducing Emissions from Deforestation and Forest Degradation (REDD) in Brazil is attributed to the fact that Brazil remained in control of its development strategy, while funding came from Norway. By allowing Brazil to design and *own* its low-carbon development, the Norway-funded Amazon Bank strengthened Brazil's sovereignty in the development process. To that end, BNDES (Banco Nacional de Desenvolvimento Econômico e Social), the autonomous Brazilian bank, played the role of honest broker, lending trust and credibility to the arrangement on all sides. Similarly, the Global Fund succeeds in many of its projects because it relies on countries to identify their own health needs and work with partners to design and implement health interventions accordingly.

Ownership and *voice* in development are even more important at the grassroots level. They have long been a concern and important focus of REDD: that the needs, perspectives, rights and livelihoods of the indigenous people who live in the forests that the Brazilians and Norwegians are trying to protect are to be reflected in the country's development strategies. Relatedly, the HARITA and R4 microinsurance initiatives succeed because poor farmers pay for their premiums, whether through cash or work trades—an example of material ownership. These pilots have also worked well because the farmers and their families engage in the design process, creating the resilience projects they will participate in as part of the work-for-insurance arrangement.

There are important marketplace benefits related to voice. Neoclassical economic theory explains this in efficiency terms: the more decentralized the decision making, the closer it is to good, accurate information. Some call this *design thinking* or *consumer insight*; people know and understand what their needs are and what goods and services will meet them. MicroEnsure has grown exponentially because its product offerings are determined by local input and demand. In India, IFMR's wealth managers succeed because they work with each client to understand what mix of products and services would be most valuable to the long-term wealth creation of that individual or family.

Those who work in humanitarian assistance stress the importance of local participation in the relief process, especially when dignity and voice are particularly fragile. This helps explain the enthusiasm for cash transfers, which are an efficient way to allow people to pay for their own needs, stimulating local markets in the process.

Indeed the expansion of domestic markets is the holy grail of autonomous development. The growth of small- and medium-sized enterprises (SMEs) provides goods, services, and employment to a population that, in turn, experiences sufficient gains in wealth to fuel even greater demand. The innovative finance evolutions seen in chapter 3 are intended to strengthen local capital markets in different ways—from currency risk-hedging strategies like MFX Solutions to funds like the African Loan Currency Bond Fund to monoline insurance (such as that provided by the Ascending Markets Financial Guarantee Corporation) that make local bond issuances a reality for SMEs in developing countries.

## Pay-for-Success: The Role of Evidence and Outcomes

Getting the incentives right for improved governance and agency relies on proof and verification. Data and evidence can make decision making transparent and fact based, shifting risk in ways that improve outcomes—and unlocking more resources for public goods in the process. This is the power of pay-for-success.

As we discussed in chapter 2 in the context of health, pay-for-success, in the form of advanced market commitments (AMCs), prizes, and challenges, primes market activity in the face of market failure. In the case of GAVI's AMC, the purchase commitment was sufficient to eliminate the demand risk for potential manufacturers, motivating them to invest in vaccines for the world's poorest. The visible hand of the AMC design prefers the *pull* of markets to the *push* of grants. We also saw how prizes and challenges encourage a large number of innovators to try their hands at developing solutions. Because prizes are awarded to proven outcomes— classic pay-for-success—they shift risk onto the innovators, and they avoid the political challenges of "picking winners." In the process, prizes also leverage significantly more resources than the original dollar value of the prize. However, like AMCs, they are expensive to design and execute. And while we have seen the gradual emergence of prizes and challenges in the spheres of social services, they lend themselves better to technological or scientific breakthroughs that are readily observed, measured, tested, and "solved."

Pay-for-success comes in various guises, depending on the sector and the application. In the case of REDD, pay-for-success improves the effectiveness of traditional development assistance by creating an incentive to reduce deforestation and associated carbon emissions. When it works, as in Brazil, it is a powerful motivation and reinforcement for sustainable development. When it doesn't work, as in Indonesia, it reveals an important shortcoming of the laissez-faire architecture: there is no enforcement for noncompliance. REDD is not the first adventure in pay-for-success development assistance. Conditional aid has been a growing and sometimes controversial approach in the aid community, whether through grants, loan forgiveness, or debt buy-downs like Debt2Health. REDD-like aid approaches have inspired others, including a pay-for-success methane pilot facility.

Pay-for-success has a sometimes different look and feel in more-developed markets. However, the ability of this innovative finance mechanism to align incentives to overcome market failure, gain additional resources, shift risk, and encourage important nonfinancial outcomes is equally powerful in countries like the United States.

We have seen, for example, ways in which pay-for-success contracts are evolving from bricks and mortar to human services. Recall the strong record of the Low Income Housing Tax Credit, a highly successful pay-for-success contract that has crowded in billions of dollars of private investment for affordable housing. It does so in a way that shifts risk onto developers who have a financial incentive for successful outcomes. SIBs fashion this procurement model with private-sector working capital for social services. The idea is that state and local governments, and taxpayers, only pay only for interventions that work. If they don't work, the investors pick up the tab. The incentives are complicated, as the Goldman SIBs in New York and Utah show, because it is the service providers, not the funders, who are responsible for outcomes but the funders bear the risk.

Perhaps the larger lesson about SIBs relates to the role that innovative finance plays in fostering better outcomes and governance. The SIB pay-for-success contract hinges on rigorous measurement and evaluation to determine whether an intervention worked—whether it reduced recidivism, homelessness, asthma emergency room visits, the need for special education teachers in kindergarten—and whether taxpayers should pay for it. SIBs therefore focus policy makers on early interventions, doing so through multiyear contracts. This means SIBs lock in an evidence-based policy-making approach across multiple administrations, insulating long-term investment decisions from short-term political considerations.

Innovative finance plays an important role in agency and governance, even when proof and evidence are not possible. In some cases, recipient countries and donors benefit from the creation of a trusted third-party broker or auditor that can give necessary implementation assurances. This kind of arrangement may be a work around—and may not solve the longer term and underlying governance problems of corruption or incompetence—but it can align incentives in the short term to meet critical needs. This was one of the motivating principles behind the creation of the Global Fund, and we have seen numerous other incarnations. For example, UNITAID's levy on airline travel in various countries raises revenue for drugs and health care, but these countries neither collect nor distribute those funds. Instead, UNITAID, which is housed within the World Health Organization, manages the resources with a range of health partners. The same is true of the new UNITLIFE program, housed at UNICEF. UNITLIFE will use taxes on extracted resources like oil from several African countries to fund child nutrition investments there. Not unlike Debt2Health, that brokers debt conversions into health investments via the Global Fund, these initiatives are designed to channel resources in ways that avoid potential misuse by governments. The embrace of cash transfers also relates, in part, to governance concerns. Cash transfers, particularly those made via mobile, are intended to go directly to beneficiaries. Funds are not lost "leakage"—a euphemism for government mismanagement or theft.

## Execution

At the heart of governance and autonomy issues are questions of trust. The importance of trust reminds us that innovative finance is not about elegant theory. Success in earning trust depends on sound execution—operations and implementation really matter.

### The Right FITT: Finance, Technology, and Trust

We tend to correlate innovation with clever engineering—whether technological or financial. However, when it comes to solving some of the world's toughest problems, new instruments are not enough. Innovative finance often occurs at the intersection of technological breakthrough, creative finance, and human interaction. Successful innovative finance depends on trust. For example, REDD may benefit significantly from advances in satellite imagery, but it is the combination of this technology with pay-for-success financing and trusted third-party intermediaries like BNDES that makes the model effective. The same is true of ARC, which succeeds because it relies on African RiskView technologies and the solidarity and trust that come with an African Union–owned insurance company.

This confluence of finance, technology, and trust (FITT) is even more important at the community and individual levels. Consider some of the successes of microfinance 2.0 where technological innovation, particularly mobile platforms, has transformed the economics of financial services for the poor. In some cases, technological innovation is enough to create entirely new products and markets—for example, payment systems, savings, credit, pay-as-you-go consumer finance, and index insurance. Often, however, the technology is not enough for widespread adoption. In the case of IFMR, there are many reasons for success—among them a range of product offerings, including numerous loan types, savings, pensions, and various insurance products. More importantly, it uses trusted local wealth managers to enroll clients and basic technology to collect detailed household information, which in turn allows for customized offerings. Technology simplifies

the recommendation process (an algorithm suggests the appropriate products) and lets potential customers see a snapshot of their financial health—
but it is the personal relationship that helps people understand why these
products will serve them well. In IFMR's view, the wealth managers are like
doctors: their job is to improve the economic well-being of their customers.

A similar set of relationships underpins the adoption of agricultural
microinsurance in Kenya, where there has long been distrust of these kinds
of products. Recall that *Kilimo Salama*, crop insurance whose name means
"safe agriculture" in Swahili, provides payouts to insured farmers when rainfall deviates too far from the rainfall index created using information from
local weather stations. Its cost is low enough that it can be provided in small
amounts, allowing farmers to "pay as they plant" and see for themselves
whether or not it works. Yet it is the agrovets—already well known to the
farmers, who offer advice and who sell the insurance, seeds, fertilizer, and
other agricultural supplies—that are critical to the equation. Their mobile
software allows for easy and affordable registration, but it is the trusted
human dimension that makes the sale and follow-up services possible. Similarly, the success of the Women's World Banking BETA savings account in
Nigeria depends on technology for quick and convenient banking; women
can open an account in less than five minutes via a mobile app. However, the
convenience is made possible by BETA Friends, trusted agents who come to
the markets where women work and guide them through the registration
process. In New York City, the clients' personal and close connections to a
financial advisor are what accounts for the success of Neighborhood Trust
Financial Partners in advancing financial inclusion. Economic theory says
that trust makes transactions more cost effective by reducing the *counter-
party risk (*the risk that one side will not complete the transaction). This may
be true, but there is also an unquantifiable emotional component to these
connections that makes for transformative operating models.

### Complexity Made Simple

For organizations like IFMR, the operating model requires sound execution
that is both local and global; gaining trust—a good FITT—on the ground,
while accessing the capital markets for investment necessary to scale this
customized approach. This is easier said than done. In places like India, the
many financial services offered by IFMR is each regulated by a different
government entity. Successfully navigating any one of them, much less a

large suite, requires resourcefulness, fortitude, and skill. To then translate all this complexity into a set of seamless, intuitive offerings for the rural poor is an operational feat—one that has been seen throughout this book.

For example, MicroEnsure serves 15 million people across seventeen countries, with more than 200 microinsurance products. Its growth has depended on the ability to customize offerings to meet local market needs. This means working with local partners, relieving them of the recondite and costly tasks of things like customer sales and acquisition and claims management and payment. In short, MicroEnsure removes the complexity for the providers it partners with and ultimately for their clients. This is the Single Stop formula: create a one-stop shop that simplifies the web of federal, state, and local benefits for those eligible. "Moving complexity to the middle," as it is sometimes said, is the job of innovative finance intermediaries. From the perspective of consumers and investors, the process and the product look relatively simple.

The criticism of SIBs, of course, is that the complexity remains—in both structuring and implementing deals. The failure in the New York City SIB was an operational one: the attempt to apply a proven intervention in a particularly challenging criminal justice environment. If pay-for-success instruments are to work in the United States in the social services context, intermediaries need to manage this high degree of operational risk.

## Success

### Redefining Success: Quantity and Quality

In the social sector, the search for scale is elusive. Such is also the case with innovative finance: researchers want to know the so-called *success factors* that make a financing instrument or approach scalable. Often this means that an instrument has become sufficiently standardized that it is relatively simple and cost effective enough to be replicated—to reach a larger market of people or dollars. Because innovative finance is about solving entrenched social and economic problems, perhaps the better, though more difficult, metrics involve quality: Have these innovative finance tools led to significant improvements in people's lives? Have they been transformative? Are these questions of quantity or quality, or both?

We wrestled with this issue in the discussion of microfinance, and in the case of microcredit in particular. One the one hand, for microlending to begin making inroads with the billions of unbanked, it requires an infusion of commercial capital. Today the more than $80 billion in microloans that are made to 100 million borrowers annually obtain are largely fueled by private investment. Yet the industry's growth has led to legitimate concerns about the ways in which microcredit has changed. In some cases, as Nobel Laureate and microfinance pioneer Muhammad Yunus suggests, commercial capital has compromised the integrity of lending, as the urgent profit motive, particularly in the case of publicly traded microfinance companies, can lead to unscrupulous lending practices. Even if it is possible to guard against the more nefarious activities, we know the economics of scale change the nature of the loans. Commercialized microcredit does not serve marginalized borrowers in the same way that nonprofit or Grameen-style (borrower-owned) banks do at a smaller scale.

As we enter the era of microfinance 2.0 and look to expand the range of financial services from credit to savings, insurance, and other offerings, it is important to recognize the quantity-for-quality trade. In the quest for scale, we must remember that we cannot jettison or obviate the need for less-commercial alternatives. For example, as mainstream insurers and reinsurers like Munich Re, Swiss Re, and Lloyd's begin to consider the microinsurance market, their eyes are on *emerging consumers*, those in developing countries that are on their way to middle-class purchasing power. Even Leap Frog, a self-described leader in "profit with purpose investing," specializes in emerging market financial services, targeting companies that provide insurance, savings, pensions and payment services to customers earning less than $10 a day. The good news is that this is a growing market and may no longer need visible-hand interventions. We must remember however that there are billions who live on less than $1.25 a day who are in need of financial services and their inclusion remains an important public good.

The issues related to quantity and quality are not limited to financial services. Let us consider two high-profile examples from different ends of the scale spectrum: SIBs, which are not really bonds, and green bonds, which are not particularly green. As we saw in chapter 1, there is a significant appetite for green bonds, those issued by governments or companies to fund climate change mitigation or adaptation, or any other kind of "environmentally friendly" project. The market has grown substantially in recent years: 2015 marked a record $36 billion in new issuances. However, there are no formal standards or ratings for the green nature of these initiatives. There are voluntary principles and reporting guidelines for issuers, but in financial terms, there is no discount for investors and no additional risk or yield that makes them different than conventional bonds. While some advocates of green bonds call for tighter definitions of *green* or for environmental scoring akin to credit ratings, others suggest that these rules would restrict supply and reduce liquidity. In other words, it is a quantity-versus-quality trade. This doesn't mean that green bonds aren't playing an important role in satisfying investor demand for green products and in raising awareness of the need and opportunity to invest in alternative energy projects. What is evident is that the green bond market is not yet overcoming a market failure. It has achieved scale because it is directing capital to projects that are perceived to be as risky as other, nongreen infrastructure investments. We would like to see the cost of capital come down for investments in climate mitigation technologies. To date, this has not been achieved by green bonds. Hence, there is a need for more innovative finance—more work for the visible hand.

Although SIBs match green bonds when it comes to hype, the SIB market in the United States is less than $150 million. (It is estimated that the overall SIB market may grow to $300–$500 million over the several years.) Although SIBs represent a new way of doing business, each deal is small in dollar size, tailored to a specific project, and time consuming to structure. Neither the complexity nor the transaction costs have come to the point where SIBs are readily replicable in an off-the-shelf way.

Yet the SIB experiments encourage us to think differently about scale. The pay-for-success field is still nascent and evolving, and it may become easier and more affordable to reproduce a SIB deal in a new location or to increase the size of any given SIB contract. It is also possible that the legacy of the first SIBs will be their contribution to the larger fields of evidence-based policy making and good governance, as discussed above. They also provide a kind of road map when it comes to *blended finance,* illustrating how to use philanthropy and government funds and subsidy to mitigate risk for commercial investors and crowd in much larger amounts of capital for things like infrastructure. Although these are metrics related to influence rather than deal size or flow, they nevertheless can and should be understood as impact at scale.

## Partnership Finance

This brings us to the last point about innovative finance as partnership finance. Innovative finance is not simply about fusion; thinking across categories and sectors. It is also, as we have seen, an evolved approach to public-private partnerships that uses the resources of every sector to solve problems in new and better ways. Although daunting, this is also an encouraging reminder that there is a role for all of us in financing our shared future.

For philanthropy, this means a broad set of activities and influence beyond its dollar contribution. This begins with grant funding, often the lifeblood of R&D in the social sector, that can take risks where government and commercial capital will not. From these experiments come proof points, which in turn reduce risk for other public and private investors. So, too, do philanthropy's innovative financing tools—loan guarantees and first-loss investment—that can attract commercial dollars to an array of projects.

Philanthropy also plays a vital role in field building by funding research, measurement and evaluation, and intermediaries. From airline levies to SIBs, and just about every innovative finance mechanism in between, we observed how critical these intermediaries are in managing risk when we are designing, implementing, and auditing projects of all sizes and in all sectors. These intermediaries serve as the brokers or translators between the social and commercial sectors. On the investment side, we have seen the growing momentum behind impact and more mainstream capital looks to align value and values on various environmental, social, and governance dimensions. Sometimes the impetus behind cost, benefit, and risk recalibration is driven by companies themselves, who recognize there is value in long-term and sustainable operations that benefit all stakeholders: customers, employees, suppliers, and communities in which they operate. Their innovative finance activities take many forms: internal carbon pricing, supply chain finance, investments in the financial education or health and wellness of their employees.

Of course corporate leaders are central to this work, as are advocates in every sector. We have seen some very high-profile champions—Bill and Melinda Gates in health, Sir Ronald Cohen in impact investing, Norway in deforestation and climate change—but what happens for the issues that have no such loud voice? Political leadership is critical at every level, and for each area of innovative finance, there is a set of policy and political levers that can advance the field. To move these, elected officials need a different kind of capital: a groundswell of enthusiasm and support for measures that advance shared prosperity. As citizens, consumers, employees, employers, and investors, we have our work cut out for us.

# Epilogue
## *The Road Ahead*

This book is neither the last nor the definitive word on innovative finance. Instead, it is meant to introduce the subject as a way to consider our individual and collective roles in financing the public good and in developing market solutions to market failures. The omissions are many, but they are fertile ground for the next generation of innovative finance solutions. This is particularly true as we think about the two major areas of investment required for our future prosperity: education and infrastructure.

### Education: Learning from Innovative Finance

It is said that there is no greater investment nor more universal public good than education.[1] Perhaps, paradoxically, this is why it has received relatively little attention in innovative finance—because of the extent to which governments have assumed responsibility for providing and paying for education. (Of the $2.5 trillion spent annually on education around the world, the vast majority, approximately $2 trillion, comes from public or government funding.) Until recently, the education field has not explored extensively public-private partnerships for delivery or finance. Discussions of education—specifically how to improve educational opportunities—are challenging at a global level because the circumstances in poor and emerging economies are so different from those in wealthier countries. However, there is a substantial need for more and better investment in education in both spheres, as well as a role for innovative finance.

## The Developing World

Although access to education has increased dramatically over the last decade, 57 million children across the world still lack this access, and many more receive poor-quality schooling. More than half of these children are girls. Low-income countries have increased their education spending, but many cannot afford to meet their citizens' needs. This shortfall, combined with stagnating official development assistance and inflation, means that there is an estimated $26 billion funding gap.[2] The questions are whether and how innovative finance can close it. As we have seen, unlike hard assets like roads, bridges, or housing—and even technologies like vaccines—innovative finance for social services is more challenging.

In recent years, we have observed the growth in the number of impact investors looking to play a larger role in the education sector. Often, they invest directly in schools. Because, in so many places in the developing world, government schools are nonexistent or failing, for-profit and fee-based schools provide a promising alternative for millions of families. For example, Bridge International Academies, the world's largest chain of primary schools, offers high-quality education at prices affordable to families living on less than $2 a day. There are others that are similar, including The Citizens Foundation in Pakistan, or those that supplement government-funded school services through things like early childhood, after-school, and vocational training programs.

In some places, lending initiatives are emerging in the education sector. For example, microlender Kiva works with Strathmore University in Nairobi to offer low-interest tuition and laptop loans. However, there is more market interest in educational services for middle- and upper-middle-income consumers who have the ability to pay for various for-profit offerings. Increasingly, models focus on technology and ways to improve teacher training and management.

Recently, we have seen efforts to adopt some of the innovative finance approaches used in other sectors for education. These include, for example, the launch of the first development impact bond, which focuses on educational outcomes for girls in Rajasthan, India. However, a far larger transaction came last year when Citi launched the first EYE (Education, Youth, and Employment) Bond, a $500 million bond raising funds to support those areas. On behalf of the Inter-American Development Bank, this bond funds early childhood care and education, formal primary and secondary education, and labor market placement and vocational training in Latin America. Some have called for the creation of a global education investment bank.[3] In the meantime, the Every Woman Every Child International Finance Facility, formally launched in the summer of 2015 at Addis Abba and focused primarily on health, can direct funds to education. Part of the challenge, as well as the opportunity, for innovative finance involves recognizing the links among education, health, poverty, and conflict. Many of the 57 million children who are not in school live in war-torn countries or are refugees fleeing them; there is a clear need for leadership on these issues. As Julia Gillard, the former prime minister of Australia and, since 2014, chair of the board of directors of the Global Partnership for Education, has said: "We haven't as yet found the Bill Gates for education."[4]

## The United States and the Developed World

Interestingly, to the extent Bill and Melinda Gates have focused on issues in more-developed countries, they have centered on education. However, the context and the circumstances are dramatically different in wealthier countries, where we have, for the most part, achieved universal primary and secondary education. The questions pertain more to the quality and equality of this education, along with access to higher education. By and large, primary and secondary education in the United States is supplied by state and local governments. To the extent there has been a role for innovative finance, it has been in underwriting various pieces of the reform agenda. On the pure investment side, this means things like financing facilities for charter schools, which remain in the public domain but require private funds for real estate and buildings (an estimated $1.5 billion in investment each year). Technology—for curriculum, distance and customized learning—and professional development are also increasingly attractive options for investors (particularly pioneering impact investors like ReThink Education, Bridges Ventures U.S., and City Light Capital) though these investments are not without risks and the landscape is still evolving. In higher education, the debates often surround access. The growth of for-profit colleges and universities is controversial and the problem of student debt is massive. Some innovators have proposed "human-capital contracts" (a concept first advanced by Milton Friedman in 1955), in which students commit to pay investors a fixed percentage of their income for a ten-year period. This approach allows students to use equity rather than debt to finance their education, but it is also controversial.[5] A handful of crowdfunding models allow people to refinance their student loans. Nevertheless, we need a massive overhaul of the education investment system. It is a public policy question—and an area ripe for innovative finance.

## Infrastructure: Matching Supply and Demand

There is no shortage of data—and no lack of firsthand experience—to remind us of the urgent need for infrastructure investment. In the United States and across the globe infrastructure investment is vital not only for growth—the future of American business depends on improvements to roads, bridges, rail and air travel, public transportation, broadband, the electric grid—but also for a more shared prosperity. As we have seen changes to the geography of need in the United States make mobility essential to opportunity.[6] According to the World Economic Forum, the world is investing approximately $1 trillion a year *less* than it needs to on infrastructure. McKinsey estimates that we will have to spend more than $57 trillion on new infrastructure over the next decade and a half.[7]

In recent years, the debate in the United States and around the globe has centered less on whether there are sufficient public funds to meet our growing infrastructure demands (there are not) and more on how we unlock private capital. In the United States, where the call for a national infrastructure bank has been stalled since the 1990s, infrastructure is mostly financed at the state and local levels. The global infrastructure debate was rekindled last year when China announced the creation of the Asian Infrastructure Investment Bank.

What sets infrastructure and the debates about its provision apart from other public goods discussed in this book is the vast sums of commercial capital available for infrastructure investment. By some estimates, $5 trillion a year is ready to be deployed. This is because, in the last five years, many institutional investors, including pension and sovereign wealth funds, have allocated assets for infrastructure. It has become its own asset class.[8] However, the existence of these pools of capital and their infrastructure allocation do not mean that the money is flowing—or flowing to where it is needed most. One important next step in innovative finance for infrastructure is to match supply and demand.

The movement to create infrastructure exchanges is taking us in the right direction. For example, in July 2015, the World Bank launched the Global Infrastructure Facility (GIF), which helps prepare, structure, and finance infrastructure investment by bringing together emerging-market governments, development banks, and private financiers. "What we found was there was enough liquidity in the marketplace," says the World Bank's Jordan Schwartz. "We needed to match supply and demand" and improve "the quality and viability of projects."[9] The GIF, which is initially a three-year pilot program, will supply technical assistance to governments and partial financing (first losses, backstops, and other credit enhancements) to attract more commercial investment. At the international level, the GIF is part of a larger wave of exchanges, including Infradev's proposal to create a public marketplace to match supply and demand for capital infrastructure projects in developing countries[10] and the Global Finance Exchange for Social Advancement, launched in January 2016.

Although many of these efforts focus on emerging markets, there have been calls for similar exchanges in developed countries. In the United States, the West Coast Infrastructure Exchange was created in 2012 by the governors and treasurers of California, Oregon, and Washington, and the premier of British Columbia to serve as a kind of translator between the public and private sectors to develop standards, share best practices, provide technical assistance to public-sector officials, and prepare projects to enter the investment pipeline. Investors and policy makers across the United States have been interested in establishing similar local, state, or regional exchanges focused particularly on preparing deals so as to make them investable. In matching supply and demand, innovative finance for infrastructure is very much a visible hand: capital for the common good in the twenty-first century.

# NOTES

## Introduction: Innovative Finance and the Visible Hand

1. The term "visible hand" was popularized by Alfred D. Chandler in 1977 with the publication of his Pulitzer-work, *The Visible Hand: The Managerial Revolution in American Business* (Cambridge, MA: Harvard University Press, 1977). We use it here not in that corporate management sense, but instead simply in juxtaposition to Adam Smith's free market "invisible hand." When the free market, alone, fails to produce optimal social outcomes, we use the phrase "visible hand" to refer to partnerships between the public, private and nonprofit sectors to meet needs and solve problems.

2. "The Millennium Development Goals Report: 2015," United Nations, July 2015, http://www.un.org/millenniumgoals/2015_MDG_Report/pdf/MDG%202015%20 rev%20(July%201).pdf.

3. Moreover, it is important not to conflate GDP growth with comprehensive social development or progress. GDP alone is necessary, but not sufficient, to reach our broader development objectives. See, for example, Georgia Levenson Keohane, "GDP Is a Bad Measure of Our Economy; Here's a Better One," *Time*, April 19, 2015, http://time .com/3826731/is-gdp-dead/. See also "Social Progress in 2030: Developing Beyond Economic Growth," Deloitte, September 2015, http://www2.deloitte.com/global/en/pages/ about-deloitte/articles/social-progress-in-2030.html.

4. "Global Humanitarian Assistance Report 2015," Global Humanitarian Assistance, 2015, http://www.globalhumanitarianassistance.org/report/gha-report-2015.

5. "Transforming Our World: The 2030 Agenda for Sustainable Development," United Nations, adopted September 25, 2015, https://sustainabledevelopment.un.org/content/documents/7891TRANSFORMING%20OUR%20WORLD.pdf.

6. See "Outcome Document of the Third International Conference on Financing for Development: Addis Ababa Action Agenda," United Nations, July 15, 2015, http://www.un.org/africarenewal/sites/www.un.org.africarenewal/files/N1521991.pdf.

7. For more on the evolution of the innovative finance field, see "Innovative Financing for Development: Scalable Business Models That Produce Economic, Social and Environmental Outcomes," Global Development Incubator, September 2014, http://www.globaldevincubator.org/wp-content/uploads/2014/09/Innovative-Financing-for-Development.pdf; DevFin Advisors and SIDA, "Innovative Finance: Gap Analysis," DevFin Advisors and SIDA (2014); Philippe Douste-Blazy, "Innovative Financing Can Put the World's Wealth to Work for All People," International Institute for Sustainable Development, October 14, 2014, http://sd.iisd.org/guest-articles/innovative-financing-can-put-the-worlds-wealth-to-work-for-all-people/; Eytan Bensoussan, Radha Ruparell, and Lynn Taliento, "Innovative Development Financing," McKinsey and Company, August 2013, http://www.mckinsey.com/insights/social_sector/innovative_development_financing; "Innovative Financing for Development: A New Model for Development Finance," United Nations Development Program, January 2012, http://www.undp.org/content/dam/undp/library/Poverty%20Reduction/Development%20Cooperation%20and%20Finance/InnovativeFinancing_Web%20over.pdf; and The I-8 Group Leading Innovative Finance for Equity, "Innovative Financing for Development," United Nations, December 2009, http://www.un.org/esa/ffd/documents/InnovativeFinForDev.pdf.

8. Among them are the European Bank for Reconstruction and Development, Inter-American Development Bank, CAF Development Bank of Latin America, Islamic Development Bank, Asian Development Bank, and African Development Bank.

9. Gross national product (GNP) and gross domestic product (GDP) both reflect the national output and income of an economy. The primary difference is that GNP takes into account net income receipts from abroad, meaning the value of goods and services produced by nationals—including dividends, interest, and profit—whether or not they are in the country. It is worth noting that even if donor countries each hit the 0.7 percent ODA targets it would still not be enough to close the funding gap.

10. For example, in 1999, USAID launched the Development Credit Authority, which provides loan guarantees to banks in poor countries.

11. The problems of externalities and public goods are the mainstay of most economics textbooks. Perhaps the best textbook on environmental and natural resource economics is Nathaniel O. Keohane and Sheila M. Olmstead, *Markets and the Environment* (Washington, DC: Island Press, 2007). For more recent work on climate change as a global negative externality, see Gernot Wagner and Martin L. Weitzman, *Climate Shock: The Economic Consequences of a Hotter Planet* (Princeton, NJ: Princeton University, 2015). For a powerful and accessible discussion of natural capital and the value inherent in a number of natural resources, including public goods like biodiversity, see Mark R. Tercek and Jonathan S. Adams, *Nature's Fortune* (New York: Basic Books, 2013).

12. Consider, for example, the B Corp movement. See Georgia Levenson Keohane, *Social Entrepreneurship for the 21st Century* (New York: McGraw-Hill, 2013).

13. See, for example, "Sustainable Signals: The Individual Investor Perspective," Morgan Stanley Institute for Sustainable Investing, February 2015; and "2014 U.S. Trust Insights on Wealth and Worth Survey," U.S. Trust, 2014.

14. See, for example, Paul Krugman, "Destructive Creativity," *New York Times*, January 18, 2010. In 2009, Ben Bernanke, then chair of the Federal Reserve, remarked on finance's standing: "Indeed, innovation, once held up as the solution, is now more often than not perceived as the problem." Ben S. Bernanke, "Financial Innovation and Consumer Protection" (speech delivered at the Federal Reserve System's Sixth Biennial Community Affairs Research Conference, Washington, DC, April 17, 2009), http://www.federalreserve.gov/newsevents/speech/bernanke20090417a.htm.

15. See, for example, Nell Abernathy and Mike Konczal, "Defining Financialization," The Roosevelt Institute July 27th, 2015. http://rooseveltinstitute.org/sites/all/files/Defining_Financialization_Web.pdf

16. "Impact Investment: The Invisible Heart of Markets" Report of the Social Impact Investment Task Force 15 September 2014 http://www.socialimpactinvestment.org/reports/Impact%20Investment%20Report%20FINAL[3].pdf

17. See, for example, Georgia Levenson Keohane, "Will Crowdfunding Kickstart an Investment Revolution? Policy and Political Implications of Peer-to-Peer Financing," Roosevelt Institute, September 2013, http://rooseveltinstitute.org/sites/all/files/Keohane_Crowdfunding_09_04_13.pdf.

18. Danae Ringelmann, "The Innovator's New Crystal Ball: Crowdfunding," Fast Company, March 26, 2015, http://www.fastcoexist.com/3043848/techsocial/the-innovators-new-crystal-ball-crowdfunding.

19. Felix Salmon, "The Idiocy of Crowds," Reuters, September 23, 2013.

20. Massolution, "2015 CF: The Crowdfunding Industry Report," crowdsourcing.org, April 2015.

21. Charles Maldow, "A Trillion Dollar Market, by the People, for the People: How Marketplace Lending Will Remake Banking As We Know It," Foundation Capital, May 2014. For reference, even at $16 billion, crowdfunding, including lending, is still only a fraction of the total $840 billion consumer-lending business.

22. Ryan M. Nash and Eric Beardsley, "The Future of Finance:Part 1—The Rise of the New Shadow Bank," Goldman Sachs Equity Research March 3, 2015 ; "The Future of Finance: Part 2—Redefining 'The Way We Pay' in the Next Decade," Goldman Sachs Equity Research, March 10, 2015; "The Future of Finance: Part 3—The Socialization of Finance," Goldman Sachs Equity Research, March 13, 2015.

23. Michael Corkery and Nathaniel Popper, "Goldman Sachs Plans to Offer Consumer Loans Online, Adopting Start-Ups' Tactics," *New York Times*, June 15, 2015.

24. Some have suggested that crowdfunding may offer a promising channel of new and additional funding for health. At present, funds remain relatively small and philanthropic. Not surprisingly, when it comes to health, Kickstarter and other platforms have needed to tighten restrictions on the types of health products that can be funded, particularly those that are heavily regulated or claim to cure or prevent illnesses, for

obvious liability and consumer protection reasons. In recent years, a number of health-specific online platforms have emerged, mostly in the developed world, including those like MedStartr and Kangu, charitable or donation platforms for small health projects—such as free surgeries, health facilities, and prenatal and childbirth assistance—around the world. In contrast, sites like Healthfundr connect health start-ups with for-profit, accredited investors. Relative to finance need, particularly for developing-country health, these channels remain small.

25. See, for example, Georgia Levenson Keohane, "Will Crowdfunding Kickstart an Investment Revolution?"

26. These are not uncontroversial. They are potentially a very valuable workaround for untenable levels of student debt. However, critics have argued that they could potentially become a kind of indentured servitude. See, for example, Douglas Belkin, "More College Students Selling Stock in Themselves," *Wall Street Journal*, August 5, 2015, http://www.wsj.com/articles/more-college-students-selling-stockin-themselves-1438791977.

27. Amazon and Ebay offer financing options for consumers (Paypal) and short-term working-capital loans for vendors (Paypal Working Capital, OnDeck, and Kabbage). Facebook, Google, and Apple are pioneering wallet-to-wallet or digital payment systems to rival the popular Venmo, Squarecash, and others.

28. Matt Levine, "Citigroup Joins the Lending Club," Bloomberg View, April 14, 2015.

29. infoDev, "Crowdfunding's Potential for the Developing World," World Bank, 2013, http://www.infodev.org/infodev-files/wb_crowdfundingreport-v12.pdf.

30. It is estimated there are "up to 344 million households in the developing world that are able to make small crowdfund investments in community businesses," says the report. "These households have an income of at least $10,000 a year, and at least three months' savings or three months' savings in equity holdings. Together they have the ability to deploy up to $96 billion by 2025 in crowdfunding investments."

## 1. REDD Forests, Green Bonds, and the Price of Carbon

1. "Laudato Si' of the Holy Father Francis on Care for Our Common Home" (encyclical letter), The Vatican, June 18, 2015, http://i2.cdn.turner.com/cnn/2015/images/06/18/papa-francesco_20150524_enciclica-laudato-si_en.pdf.

2. Intergovernmental Panel on Climate Change, "Climate Change 2007: Synthesis Report: A Summary for Policymakers," http://www.ipcc.ch/pdf/assessment-report/ar4/syr/ar4_syr_spm.pdf; "Climate Change 2007: Working Group I: The Physical Science Basis," http://www.ipcc.ch/publications_and_data/ar4/wg1/en/spmsspm-understanding-and.html; and "Climate Change 2014: Synthesis Report," http://www.ipcc.ch/report/ar5/syr/.

3. The International Energy Agency has estimated we need to invest as much as $900 billion to $1 trillion a year above current levels. International Energy Agency, "Energy Technology Perspectives 2014: Harnessing Electricity's Potential," OECD/IEA, http://www.iea.org/publications/freepublications/publication/EnergyTechnology

Perspectives_ES.pdf. The Copenhagen Accords pledged $100 billion per year for climate finance.

4. See, for example, Nicholas Stern, *The Economics of Climate Change: The Stern Review* (Cambridge: Cambridge University Press, 2007); and "12 State Reports: Cost of Inaction," Environmental Defense Fund, 2008, http://blogs.edf.org/climate411/2008 /07/24/12_states_cost_of_inaction/?_ga=1.258795082.1980583505.1433452417. See also http:// cier.umd.edu/climateadaptation/index.html

5. Tail events—those that come at the far end of the probability distribution curve— are extremely unlikely, but when they occur, powerfully consequential. Economists Martin Weitzman and Gernot Wagner argue that climate change–related tail events would be "profound earth-as-we-know-it altering changes" with massive declines in global GDP (perhaps 30 percent) for starters. They therefore argue for policies that cut off the tail by reducing or eliminating the possibility of these highly catastrophic events (e.g., limiting temperature increase to 2 percent versus, say, 5 or 6 percent). Gernot Wagner and Martin L. Weitzman, *Climate Shock: The Economic Consequences of a Hotter Planet* (Princeton, NJ: Princeton University Press, 2015). See also Martin L. Weitzman, "On Modeling and Interpreting the Economics of Catastrophic Climate Change," *Review of Economics and Statistics* 91, no. 1 (2009), 1-19; for a critique, see William D. Nordhaus, "The Economics of Tail Events with an Application to Climate Change," *Review of Environmental Economics and Policy* 5, no. 2 (2011), 240-257.

6. Finance and risk management professor Nassim Taleb popularized the term *black swan* to describe the kind of unlikely, unexpected, and highly damaging tail events that led up to the 2008 financial crisis. Nassim Nicholas Taleb, *The Black Swan* (New York: Random House, 2010).

7. The most robust assessment of the risks of climate change and the threats to the economy in the United.States—increased flooding and storm damage, altered crop yields, lost labor productivity, higher crime, reshaped public-health patterns, strained energy systems—appears in Trevor Houser, Solomon Hsiang, Robert Kopp, and Kate Larsen, *Economic Risks of Climate Change: An American Prospectus* (New York: Columbia University Press, 2015).

8. Garrett Hardin, "The Tragedy of the Commons," *Science* 162, no. 3859 (1968): 1244.

9. Arthur Cecil Pigou, *Economics of Welfare* (London: Macmillan, 1932).

10. Formally known as the Sveriges Riksbank Prize in Economic Sciences.

11. See, for example, Ronald Coase, "The Problem of Social Cost," *Journal of Law and Economics* 3 (1960): 1–44.

12. See, for example, Franklin Allen and Glenn Yago, *Financing the Future: Market Based Innovations for Growth* (New Jersey: Prentice Hall 2010), 137.

13. Nathaniel O. Keohane and Sheila M. Olmstead, *Markets and the Environment* (Washington, DC: Island, 2007),185–89.

14. Ibid., 185.

15. Robin Finn, "The Great Air Race," *New York Times*, February 22, 2013.

16. Keohane and Olmstead, *Markets and the Environment*, 202.

17. Ibid.

18. See Regulatory In-Lieu Fee and Bank Information Tracking System, https://ribits.usace.army.mil/ribits_apex/f?p=107:2.

19. "The State of World Fisheries and Aquaculture," Food and Agriculture Organization of the United Nations, 2008, ftp://ftp.fao.org/docrep/fao/011/i0250e/i0250e.pdf.

20. See, for example, Franklin and Yago, *Financing the Future*, 139.

21. By some estimates, New Zealand's IFQ markets have halved the collapse rate for fisheries. Christopher Costello, Steven Gains, and John Lynham, "Can Catch Shares Prevent Fisheries Collapse?" *Science* 321, no. 5896 (2008): 1678–81; Environmental Defense Fund, *Sustaining America's Fisheries and Fishing Communities: An Evaluation of Incentive-Based Management* (New York: Environmental Defense Fund, 2007), 4, 18.

22. See, for example, the case of FISHE, http://www.edf.org/towards-investment-sustainable-fisheries, and also the work of EKO Asset Management Partners (now Encourage Capital), the Rockefeller Foundation, and Bloomberg Philanthropies, among others. See also, for example, David Bank, "Financing Sustainable Fisheries with Impact Investments," *National Geographic* (March 19, 2014); http://voices.nationalgeographic.com/2014/03/19/financing-sustainable-fisheries-with-impact-investments/ and Cristina Rumbaitis Del Rio, "Impact Investors Dive Into Oceans," Rockefeller Foundation, July 24, 2014, https://www.rockefellerfoundation.org/blog/impact-investors-dive-into-oceans/. We see here initiatives to forge fishery loans, investment funds, improvement projects, and efforts to increase allowable catch (and revenues) through long-term purchase agreements.

23. See, for example, Elinor Ostrom, *Governing the Commons: The Evolution of Institutions for Collective Action* (Cambridge: Cambridge University Press, 1990).

24. Eric Pooley, *The Climate War* (New York: Hachette Book Group, 2010); Ryan Lizza, "As the World Burns," *New Yorker*, October 2011 http://www.newyorker.com/magazine/2010/10/11/as-the-world-burns; Theda Skocpol, "Naming the Problem: What It Will Take to Counter Extremism and Engage Americans in the Fight Against Global Warming" (paper delivered at the Symposium of the Politics of America's Fight Against Global Warming, Harvard University, Cambridge, MA, February 2013), http://www.scholarsstrategynetwork.org/sites/default/files/skocpol_captrade_report_january_2013_0.pdf.

25. "Putting a Price on Risk: Carbon Pricing in the Corporate World," Carbon Disclosure Project, September 2015, https://www.cdp.net/CDPResults/carbon-pricing-in-the-corporate-world.pdf. See also "Why Companies Need Emission Reductions Targets," Carbon Disclosure Project, 2014, https://www.cdp.net/CDPResults/Carbon-action-report-2014.pdf.

26. David Gelles, "Microsoft Leads Movement to Offset Emissions with Internal Carbon Tax," *New York Times*, September 26, 2015.

27. "State and Trends of Carbon Pricing," World Bank, 2014, http://www-wds.worldbank.org/external/default/WDSContentServer/WDSP/IB/2014/05/27/000456286_20140527095323/Rendered/PDF/882840AR0Carbo040Box385232B00OUO090.pdf.

28. "Carbon Pricing Watch 2015: An Advance Brief from the State and Trends of Carbon Pricing 2015 Report, to Be Released Late 2015," World Bank, 2015, http://

documents.worldbank.org/curated/en/2015/05/24528977/carbon-pricing-watch
-2015-advance-brief-state-trends-carbon-pricing-2015-report-released-late-2015.

29. See, for example, Denny Ellerman and Paul L. Joskow, *The European Union's Emission Trading System in Perspective* (Arlington, VA: Pew Center for Global Climate Change, May 2008); Arthur Nelson, "European Carbon Market Reform Set for 2019," *Guardian*, February 25, 2015, http://www.theguardian.com/environment/2015/feb/24 /european-carbon-emissions-trading-market-reform-set-for-2019.

30. In the climate change community, much of what we explore in these pages has come to be known as REDD+, reflecting a broader set of activities going beyond strictly deforestation and forest degradation to include the role of conservation and sustainable management of forests and carbon stocks. Whereas REDD originally referred to "reducing emissions from deforestation in developing countries" (UNFCCC Document FCCC/CP/2005/5), REDD+ has been expanded to include a broader range of activities: "reducing emissions from deforestation and forest degradation in developing countries, and the role of conservation, sustainable management of forests, and enhancement of forest carbon stocks in developing countries" (http://unfccc.int/resource/docs/2012 /awglca15/eng/05.pdf). For simplicity and narrative purposes, we refer to all of this as REDD. It is worth noting that REDD is not the first innovative finance effort to try to stem deforestation, not the first to use pay-for-success. The debt-for-conservation swaps of the 1980s attempted to use loan forgiveness as a way to incent countries to reduce deforestation. These kinds of debt instruments are explored further in the chapter on health.

31. Mark R. Tercek and Jonathan S. Adams, *Nature's Fortune* (New York: Basic, 2013), 24.

32. The UN-REDD Program—created in 2007 by the UN Development Program, the UN Environment Program, the UN Food and Agriculture Program, and a multidonor trust fund—now includes forty-nine countries, many of which are receiving funds to prepare "readiness" activities.

33. Using a formula that converts deforested land to $CO_2$ emissions, the Union of Concerned Scientists and others estimate that this change in deforestation translates to approximately 1 billion tons of global warming $CO_2$ pollution. "Brazil's Success in Reducing Deforestation," Union of Concerned Scientists, 2011, http://www.ucsusa.org /global_warming/solutions/stop-deforestation/brazils-reduction-deforestation.html# .VlWyVVZPxAI.

34. Nancy Birdsall, William Savedoff, and Frances Seymour, "The Brazil-Norway Agreement with Performance-Based Payments for Forest Conservation: Successes, Challenges, and Lessons," Center for Global Development, August 4, 2014, http://www .cgdev.org/publication/ft/brazil-norway-agreement-performance-based-payments-for-est-conservation-successes.

35. The Green Climate Fund, created to address some of these North-South tensions, made its first investment announcements during the lead-up to the 2015 UN Climate Change Conference in Paris. Established in 2010 at the UN Climate Change Conference in Mexico and charged with channeling $100 billion for climate mitigation and adaptation in developing countries, the Korea-based fund has struggled.

Even though it is the largest public climate fund, and one that developing countries had hoped would give them more autonomy in sustainable development investment decisions, it has raised only $10 billion to date and has faced concerns about its own decision-making processes and transparency.

36. Tercek and Adams, *Nature's Fortune*, 141. See also Samuel Fankhauser, "What Is Climate Finance and Where Will It Come From?" *Guardian*, April 4, 2013, http://www.theguardian.com/environment/2013/apr/04/climate-change-renewableenergy.

37. Birdsall, Savedoff, and Seymour, "The Brazil-Norway Agreement with Performance-Based Payments for Forest Conservation."

38. Indonesia committed to reducing deforestation by at least 26 percent by 2020.

39. See, for example, Tim McDonnell, "This Could Be the Worst Climate Crisis in the World Right Now: Indonesia's Deforestation Nightmare Is Choking Thousands and Making Climate Change Worse," Mother Jones, October 27, 2015, http://www.motherjones.com/environment/2015/10/indonesia-climate-change-fires-palm-oil-el-nino.

40. Jonah Busch, "Is Indonesia's Flagship Forest Policy Lowering Emissions by Enough to Meet National Climate Targets?" Center for Global Development, January 16, 2015, http://www.cgdev.org/blog/indonesias-flagship-forest-policy-lowering-emissions-enough-meet-national-climate-targets. In April 2015, the World Resources Institute's Global Forest Watch released data (satellite imagery and an analysis from the University of Maryland) showing that rates of deforestation in Indonesia had slowed in 2013.

41. See, for example, "Tree Cover Loss Spikes in Russia and Canada, Remains High Globally," World Resources Institute, April 2, 2015, http://www.wri.org/blog/2015/04/tree-cover-loss-spikes-russia-and-canada-remains-high-globally.

42. Chris Lang, "Are Norway's REDD Deals Reducing Deforestation?" 11 March 2014 http://www.redd-monitor.org/2014/03/11/are-norways-redd-deals-reducing-deforestation/

43. Current sources of potential demand include the California Emissions Trading Scheme, the FCPC Carbon Fund, the BioCarbon Fund, the KfW REDD+ Early Movers Program, and the voluntary market. On stimulating "demand," meaning capital deployment, for REDD+, see "Stimulating Interim Demand for REDD+ Emission Reductions: The Need for a Strategic Intervention from 2015 to 2020," Interim Forest Finance Project, 2014, http://www.unepfi.org/fileadmin/documents/IFF_Report_-_Stimulating_Interim_Demand_for_REDD_Emissions_Reductions.pdf.

44. See, for example, Fankhauser, "What Is Climate Finance and Where Will It Come From?"

45. California's law is called the Global Warming Solutions Act (Assembly Bill 32). The EU ETS allows international offsets from different sectors but not deforestation. California's program is the first to do so. Michele de Nevers, "Can California's Carbon Polluters Save Brazil's Rainforests?" Center for Global Development, August 27, 2014, http://www.cgdev.org/blog/can-california's-carbon-polluters-save-brazil's-rainforests.

46. For the differences between REDD and REDD+ see note 30 in this chapter.

47. Stephan Schwartzman, "Acre: Low-Emissions, High-Growth and Sustainable Development in the Amazon," Environmental Defense Fund, April 17, 2015, https://www.edf.org/sites/default/files/acre_sustainable_development_amazon_2015.pdf.

48. "World Bank Group President: This Is the Year of Climate Action," World Bank, January 23, 2014, http://www.worldbank.org/en/news/feature/2014/01/23/davos -world-bank-president-carbon-pricing.

49. As quoted in Marc Gunther, "Can Green Bonds Bankroll a Clean Energy Revolution?" Yale Environment 360, November 24, 2014, http://e360.yale.edu/feature /can_green_bonds_bankroll_a_clean_energy_revolution/2829/.

50. See "World Bank Raises USD 91 Million with Its Pioneering Green Growth Bond" (press release), World Bank, January 8, 2015, http://treasury.worldbank.org/cmd /htm/PioneeringGreenGrowthBond.html.

51. Mara Gay, "Stringer Calls for Green Bonds in New York," Wall Street Journal, September 23, 2015. See also "A Green Bond Program for New York City," Office of the Comptroller, September 2014, http://comptroller.nyc.gov/wp-content/uploads/documents /Green_Bond_Program_-September.pdf.

52. Stefania Palma, "Masala Bond to Fuel India's Green Energy Ambitions," Financial Times, October 27, 2015, http://www.ft.com/intl/cms/s/3/4dff77c6-7c98-11e5-98fb -5a6d4728f74e.html#axzz3sXNnR400.

53. "MassGreenBonds: Investing in a Greener, Cleaner Commonwealth, 2013 Series D First Quarterly Investor Impact Report, Quarter Ended August 2013," http:// www.massbondholder.com/sites/default/files/files/QE percent20August percent202014 percent20Green percent20Report(1).pdf.

54. See, for example, "Morgan Stanley Green Bond Program," June 9, 2015, http:// www.morganstanley.com/articles/green-bond-program/.

55. See, for example, "Green Bond," EDF, http://shareholders-and-investors.edf. com/bonds/green-bond/projects-selected-for-green-bond-financing-285530.html.

56. Jim Henry, "Toyota Financial Services Claims the Industry's First 'Green' Bond," Forbes, March 31, 2014, http://www.forbes.com/sites/jimhenry/2014/03/31/toyota-financial -services-claims-the-industrys-first-green-bond/.

57. From an issuer perspective, the additional green compliance or reporting requirements add a few basis points in cost. For the most part, however, issuers absorb these costs; they do not pass them along in issuance fees.

58. See, for example, Todd Cort and Cary Krosinsky, " 'Green' Finance Environmental Impact Is Hard to Measure," Financial Times, November 4, 2015, http://www .ft.com/intl/cms/s/0/abeb036c-78a8-11e5-a95a-27d368e1ddf7.html#axzz3r0WQmQ7X.

59. "Green Bond Principles," 2014, http://www.ceres.org/resources/reports/green -bond-principles-2014-voluntary-process-guidelines-for-issuing-green-bonds/view; "Green Bond Principles," 2015, http://www.icmagroup.org/Regulatory-Policy-and-Market -Practice/green-bonds/green-bond-principles/. In addition, to further assist investors as they evaluate green bonds, MSCI/Barclays and others have recently launched green bond indices that score issuers and report on their project selection criteria and management of proceeds to support promised uses. See "Barclays and MSCI Announce Launch of Green Bond Index Family" (press release), November 13, 2014, https://www .msci.com/resources/pressreleases/Barclays_and_MSCI_announce_launch_of_Green _Bond_Index_family_Nov2014.pdf.

60. "Bank of America Issues $600 Million 'Green Bond.'" Bank of America, 2015, http://about.bankofamerica.com/en-us/green-bond-overview.html#fbid=qMFYWrTttjZ. See also Pricewaterhouse Coopers, "Bank of America Corporation Green Bond Issuance: Use of Proceeds Attestation Report of Independent Accountants as of December 31 2014," Bank of America, http://about.bankofamerica.com/assets/pdf/2014-management -assertion.pdf.

61. Gunther, "Can Green Bonds Bankroll a Clean Energy Revolution?"

62. See, for example, Sean Kidney, "MIT Issues Green Property Bonds to Refinance Green Buildings, $370M, 24 Yr, 3.959% Coupon, Aaae. We Like!" *Climate Bonds Blog*, September 27, 2014, http://www.climatebonds.net/2014/09/mit-issues-green-property -bonds-refinance-green-buildings-370m-24-yr-3959-coupon-aaae-we.

63. Mike Cherney, "'Green Bonds' for a Parking Garage?" *Wall Street Journal*, March 12, 2015.

## 2. Health: Medicine for Market Failure

1. See, for example, "The Millennium Development Goals Report: 2015," United Nations, July 2015, http://www.un.org/millenniumgoals/2015_MDG_Report/pdf/MDG %202015%20rev%20(July%201).pdf.

2. "Economic Costs of Malaria," Roll back Malaria Partnership Factsheet, 2010. http://www.rollbackmalaria.org/files/files/toolbox/RBM%20Economic%20Costs%20 of%20Malaria.pdf

3. Dr. Fatoumata Nafo-Traore, "Stretching the Dollar for Global Health: Maximizing the Impact of Investments in Malaria," *Global Health and Diplomacy*, Winter 2014, 13.

4. Ramanan Laxminarayan et al., "Economic Benefit of Tuberculosis Control" (research paper, No. 4295, World Bank, Washington, DC, 2007).

5. "World Spends More than $200 Million to Make Countries Healthier," Institute for Health Metrics and Evaluation, http://www.healthdata.org/news-release/world -spends-more-200-billion-make-countries-healthier.

6. UNAIDS Factsheet, 2014. http://www.unaids.org/en/resources/campaigns/2014 /2014gapreport/factsheet

7. For a much fuller discussion of health investment ROI, see, for example, Sergio Spinaci et al., *Tough Choices: Investing in Health for Development* (Geneva: World Health Organization, 2006).

8. Margaret Chan, head of the WHO, has stated that the estimated cost of reducing the noncommunicable disease (NCD) burden in developing countries from 2011 to 2025 is $11 billion ($1–$3 per capita), compared to $7 trillion in lost economic output associated with the four major NCDs in those countries under a "business as usual" scenario. Margaret Chan, "A Fair World for Health," *Global Health and Diplomacy*, Winter 2014, 64.

9. This is a conservative estimate, as these returns do not capture the net present value associated with things like long-term educational achievement, a healthy child's future economic prospects, or the benefits of stemming a highly contagious disease, all associated with the vaccines.

10. Bill Gates, discussing global health investments at JP Morgan Chase in September 2013. Video published September 27, 2013: https://www.youtube.com/watch?v=MohyAEijeAg.

11. Ruth Levine, Michael Kremer, and Alice Albright, *Making Markets for Vaccines: Ideas to Action* (Washington, DC: Center for Global Development, 2005). See also Georgia Levenson Keohane, *Social Entrepreneurship for the 21st Century* (New York: McGraw Hill, 2013), 58–59.

12. "Financing Global Health 2014: Shifts in Funding As the MDG Era Closes," Institute for Health Metrics and Evaluation, http://www.healthdata.org/policy-report/financing-global-health-2014-shifts-funding-mdg-era-closes.

13. Joseph Dielman and Christopher Murray, "Sources and Focus of Health Development Assistance, 1990–2014," *Journal of the American Medical Association*, June 2015, http://www.healthdata.org/research-article/sources-and-focus-health-development-assistance-1990–2014, http://jama.jamanetwork.com/article.aspx?articleid=2320320&result Click=3.

14. The United States provided $143 billion between 1990 and 2014, including $12.4 billion in 2014, for global health, with particular leadership on HIV/AIDS and malaria. Ibid.

15. N. Ravishankar et al., "Financing of Global Health: Tracking Development Assistance for Health from 1990 to 2007," *Lancet* 373, no. 9681 (June 20, 2009): 2113–2124, doi:10.1016/S0140-6736(09)60881-3.

16. This is particularly true in the push for systemwide universal health coverage in many developing countries. One of the Sustainable Development Goals (SDGs), the postmillennium goals for 2030, concerns universal health coverage, calling for universal access to health without financial burden. This linkage among equity, access, health, and development—what Dr. Margaret Chan, the head of the WHO, calls "the single most powerful concept that public health has to offer" and "one of the most powerful social equalizers among all policy options"—became a rallying cry and organizing principle for a large coalition of health advocates in the lead-up to the articulation of SDGs. See, for example, Dr. Margaret Chan, "Opening Remarks at a WHO/World Bank Ministerial-Level Meeting on Universal Health Coverage," World Health Organization, February 18, 2013, http://www.who.int/dg/speeches/2013/universal_health_coverage/en/, and "Finding New Financing Is Vital for Sustaining Health in the Post-MDGs World," *Third International Conference on Financing for Development Blog*, June 11, 2015, http://www.un.org/esa/ffd/ffd3/blog/new-financing-vital-for-sustaining-health.html. See also, for example, "Financing Global Health Post-2015," Center for Global Health and Diplomacy, Winter 2014, http://www.cghd.org/index.php/publication/view-issues-of-ghd/32-publication/149-winter-2014-financing-the-future-of-global-health.

17. http://www.theglobalfund.org/en/overview/.

18. See, for example, http://www.theglobalfund.org/en/partners/innovativefinancing/. PRODUCT (RED) partners include, among others, American Express, Apple, Bugaboo International, the Carlos Slim Foundation, Converse, Dell + Microsoft, GAP, Giorgio Armani, Hallmark, Motorola, and Starbucks Coffee. See also http://www.red.org/en/learn/manifesto.

19. "About UNITAID," http://www.unitaid.org/en/who/about-unitaid.

20. "French Contributions to The Global Fund to Fight Aids, Tuberculosis, and Malaria," Evaluation Report Number 126, French Ministère Des Affaires Étrangères 2013, http://www.diplomatie.gouv.fr/en/IMG/pdf/Web-126_UK_cle099bf6.pdf.

21. "Innovative Financing," UNITAID, http://www.unitaid.org/en/how/innovative -financing.

22. See, for example, Brookings Global Health Financing Initiative, "Airline Solidarity Contribution," Brookings Institution, http://www.brookings.edu/~/media/Projects /global-health/airline.PDF.

23. For further discussion, see, for example, Robert Hecht, Amrita Palriwala, and Aarthi Rao, "Innovative Financing for Global Health: A Moment for Expanded U.S. Engagement?" Center for Strategic and International Studies, March 2010, http://csis .org/files/publication/100316_Hecht_InnovativeFinancing_Web.pdf.

24. Richie Ahuja, "Passengers on India's Largest Airline Can Now Invest in Low-Carbon Rural Development," Environmental Defense Fund, February 10, 2014, https://www.edf.org/blog/2014/02/10/passengers-indias-largest-airline-can-now-invest -low-carbon-rural-development.

25. Sharon Nakhimovsky et al., "Domestic Innovative Financing for Health: Learning from Country Experience," USAID, October 2014, 25, http://pdf.usaid.gov /pdf_docs/PA00KF1K.pdf.

26. Miles, "UN Entrepreneur Taps African Oil for Child Health."

27. Ibid.

28. Taskforce on Innovative International Finance for Health Systems, "More Money for Health, and More Health for the Money," International Health Partnership, 2009, http://www.internationalhealthpartnership.net/fileadmin/uploads/ihp/Documents /Results___Evidence/HAE__results___lessons/Taskforce_report_EN.2009.pdf.

29. See, for example, Nakhimovsky et al., "Domestic Innovative Financing for Health," 14–15.

30. International Monetary Fund Fiscal Affairs Department, "Revenue Mobilization in Developing Countries" (policy paper, International Monetary Fund, Washington, DC, March 8, 2011, http://www.imf.org/external/np/pp/eng/2011/030811.pdf).

31. The Ghana example is also considered successful in part because of its relatively simple design, although it does demonstrate that countries with relatively higher income levels, economic reforms in place, and some degree of political transparency will have more success with a VAT than others. Nakhimovsky et al., "Domestic Innovative Financing for Health," 21.

32. "World Bank Data Migration and Remittances Data," http://econ.worldbank. org/WBSITE/EXTERNAL/EXTDEC/EXTDECPROSPECTS/0,,contentMDK:22759429 ~pagePK:64165401~piPK:64165026~theSitePK:476883,00.html.

33. Ibid.

34. Nakhimovsky et al., "Domestic Innovative Financing for Health," 15–16.

35. Jean-Baptiste Vey, "France, Austria Push to Break Deadlock on Transactions Tax," Reuters, January 22, 2015, http://www.reuters.com/article/2015/01/22/eu-tax-idUSL6N0 V117X20150122.

36. The International Monetary Fund has suggested that the lack of a VAT on financial services has led to a larger financial sector than would otherwise be the case, and others, including Nobel laureate James Mirrlees, suggested that there "was no reason financial services should be treated any differently from the provision of other services on which VAT is payable, like having a car repaired or a boiler fixed." Larry Elliot, "Taxing Times: Banks Are the Golden Goose That Won't Hiss Too Much," *Guardian*, April 5, 2015, http://www.theguardian.com/business/economics-blog/2015/apr/05/financial -sector-tobin-tax-vat-bonuses-bankshttp://www.ifs.org.uk/publications/5353. For updates on the European FTT, see http://www.kpmg.com/uk/en/services/tax/corporatetax/pages /european-financial-transaction-tax.aspx.

37. Robert Gillingham, "Fiscal Policy for Health Policy Makers," World Bank, March 2014, http://www-wds.worldbank.org/external/default/WDSContentServer/WDSP /IB/2014/05/12/000456286_20140512104354/Rendered/PDF/879810WP0Fisca00Box 385214B00PUBLIC0.pdf. See also World Health Organization, *Preventing Chronic Diseases: A Vital Investment* (Geneva: World Health Organization, 2005).

38. "From Burden to 'Best-Buys': Reducing the Economic Impact of NCDs in Low- and Middle-Income Countries," World Health Organization, 2011, http://www.who.int /nmh/publications/best_buys_summary/en/.

39. Lancet Commission on Investing in Health, "Global Health 2035: A World Converging Within a Generation," Lancet, December 3, 2013, http://www.thelancet.com /commissions/global-health-2035.

40. See, for example, "WHO Report on the Global Tobacco Epidemic, 2015: Rwanda," http://www.who.int/tobacco/surveillance/policy/country_profile/rwa.pdf. See also Karin Sternberg et al., "Responding to the Challenge of Resource Mobilization: Mechanisms for Raising Additional Domestic Resources for Health," World Health Organization, 2010, http://www.who.int/healthsystems/topics/financing/healthreport/13Innovativedo mfinancing.pdf.

41. http://tobacconomics.org.

42. Nakhimovsky et al., "Domestic Innovative Financing for Health," 27.

43. See, for example, "Report on the Global Tobacco Epidemic," World Health Organization, 2013, http://apps.who.int/iris/bitstream/10665/85380/1/9789241505871_eng .pdf?ua=1.

44. Danessa O. Rivera, "PHL Exceeds Revenue Goal for Sin Tax in First Year with P34-B Collection," GMA News, January 3, 2014, http://www.gmanetwork.com /news/story/342322/economy/finance/phl-exceeds-revenue-goal-for-sin-tax-in-first- year-with-p34-b-collection.

45. See, for example, Georgia Levenson Keohane, "The Pull of Prizes," in *Social Entrepreneurship for the 21st Century* (New York: McGraw-Hill, 2013), 55–61. See also Jonathan Bays, *"And the Winner Is …": Capturing the Promise of Philanthropic Prizes* (New York:McKinsey & Company, 2009); Liam Brunt, Josh Lerner, and Tom Nicholas, "Inducement Prizes and Innovation" (discussion paper, No. 6917, Centre for Economic Policy Research, London, 2008); and Thomas Khalil, "Prizes for Technological Innovation," Brookings Institution, December 2006, http://www.brookings.edu/~/media /research/files/papers/2006/12/healthcare-kalil/200612kalil.pdf.

46. See, for example, Challenges.gov. For further exploration, see "The Obama Administration in Theory: Social Innovation Goes to Washington" and "The Obama Administration in Practice: Unleashing the Innovation Mojo," in Keohane, *Social Entrepreneurship for the 21st Century*, 151–172.

47. USAID's Grand Challenges for Development have included, among others, Fighting Ebola, Securing Water for Food (with Sweden), Saving Lives at Birth (with Norway, the UK's Department for International Development, Grand Challenges Canada, the Gates Foundation, and the World Bank), All Children Reading (with Australia), Powering Agriculture, and Making All Voices Count. http://www.usaid.gov /grandchallenges.

48. See http://grandchallenges.org.

49. See, for example, "Innovative Financing for Global Health R&D," Milken Institute, 2012, 13–14, http://assets1c.milkeninstitute.org/assets/Publication/InnovationLab /PDF/FIL-Global-Health-Report.pdf. See also Defin Advisors, "Innovative Finance: Gap Analysis: Report to SIDA," DevFin Advisors and SIDA, "Innovative Finance: Gap Analysis," DevFin Advisors and SIDA (June 2014).

50. In the poorest countries, pneumonia and diarrhea account for 29 percent—nearly one-third—of child deaths. World Health Organization, "Ending Preventable Deaths from Pneumonia and Diarrhea by 2025," 2013. http://www.who.int/maternal_child_adolescent /news_events/news/2013/gappd_launch/en/

51. Cynthia Dailard, "HPV in the United States and Developing Nations: A Problem of Public Health or Politics?" *Guttmacher Report on Public Policy* 6, no. 3 (August 2003), http://www.guttmacher.org/pubs/tgr/06/3/gr060304.html.

52. M. L. Stack et al., "Estimated Economic Benefits During the 'Decade of Vaccines' Include Treatment Savings, Gains in Labor Productivity," *Health Affairs* 30, no. 6 (June 2011): 1021–28.

53. Levine, Kremer, and Albright, *Making Markets for Vaccines*. See also Keohane, *Social Entrepreneurship for the 21st Century* (New York: McGraw Hill, 2013), 58–59.

54. http://www.gavi.org/about/mission/facts-and-figures/.

55. This includes work with the Decade of Vaccines Collaboration. http://www .gavi.org/about/ghd/dov/. See also M. L. Stack, S. Ozawa, D. M. Bishai, A. Mirelman, Y. Tam, L. Niessen, D. G. Walker, O. S. Levine, "Estimated Economic Benefits During the 'Decade of Vaccines.'" *Health Affairs* June 2011 30:61021–1028.

56. Dalberg Global Development Advisors, "The Advance Market Commitment for Pneumococcal Vaccines: Process and Design Evaluation," GAVI, February 2013, http:// www.gavi.org/Results/Evaluations/Pneumococcal-AMC-process---design-evaluation/.

57. It is estimated that an AMC to encourage two to three manufacturers to work on this would have to be approximately $4.5–$5.0 billion. "Global Health Financing Initiative, Snapshot," Brookings Institution, http://www.brookings.edu/~/media/Projects /global-health/vaccines.PDF.

58. See Center for Accelerating Innovation and Impact, "Healthy Markets for Global Health: A Market Shaping Primer," USAID, Fall 2014, 36, http://www.usaid.gov /sites/default/files/documents/1864/healthymarkets_primer.pdf. See also "GAVI Alliance Secures Lower Price for Rotavirus Vaccine" (press release), GAVI, April 10, 2012, http://

www.gavi.org/library/news/press-releases/2012/gavi-secures-lower-price-rotavirus
-vaccine/#sthash.Y8aVZgbj.dpuf.

59. "Innovative Financing for Development: Scalable Business Models That Produce Economic, Social and Environmental Outcomes," Global Development Incubator, September 2014, 12, http://www.globaldevincubator.org/wp-content/uploads/2014/09 /Innovative-Financing-for-Development.pdf.

60. Peter Blair Henry, *Turnaround: Third World Lessons for First World Growth* (New York: Basic Books, 2013).

61. http://pdf.usaid.gov/pdf_docs/PA00KF1K.pdf; see also International Monetary Fund, "Debt Relief Under the Heavily Indebted Poor Countries (HIPC) Initiative," 2014. IMF Fact Sheet: imf.org/external/np/exr/facts/pdf/hipc.pdf. See also Sharon Nakhimovsky, John Langenbrunner, James White, Abigail Vogus, Hailu Zelelew, Carlos Avila, "Domestic Innovative Financing for Health: Learning from Country Experience," US AID, October 2014, http://pdf.usaid.gov/pdf_docs/PA00KF1K.pdf.

62. See Nakhimovsky et al., "Domestic Innovative Financing for Health," 40; Hecht, Palriwala, and Rao, "Innovative Financing for Global Health," 16.

63. Amanda Glassman and Chris Lane, "Smooth and Predictable Aid for Health: a Role for Innovative Financing?" Brookings Global Economy and Development, 2008, p. 4, http://www.brookings.edu/~/media/research/files/papers/2008/8/global-health-glassman/08 _global_health_glassman.pdf. See also Homi Kharas, "Measuring the Cost of Aid Volatility." Working paper for the Wolfensohn Center for Development at Brookings Institution, 2008.

64. Ibid., 45.

65. "U.S. Fund for UNICEF Bridge Fund," UNICEF, http://www.unicefusa.org /unicef-bridge-fund.

66. The International Finance Facility for Immunisation, Gavi and the World Bank, 3.

67. Lo's drug development mega fund would support drugs in different stages of development and might target a particular disease (say, cancer) or orphan diseases (those that reflect random mutations of genes and are therefore not well correlated). Its research-backed debt obligations could generate attractive returns for institutional investors and would not be highly correlated with the stock market. Jose-Maria Fernandez, Roger M. Stein, and Andrew W. Lo, "Commercializing Biomedical Research Through Securitization Techniques," *Nature Biotechnology* 20 (2012): 964–975, http://www.nature .com/nbt/journal/v30/n10/full/nbt.2374.html; Andrew Lo, "Wall Street's Next Bet: Cures for Rare Diseases," *Fortune*, January 21, 2014, http://fortune.com/2014/01/21/wall-streets -next-bet-cures-for-rare-diseases/?section=magazines_fortune.

68. UK: $2.98 billion over 23 years; France: $1.72 billion over 20 years; Italy: $635 million over 20 years; Norway: $264 million over 15 years; Australia: $256 million over 20 years; Spain: $240 million over 20 years; Netherlands: $114 million over 8 years; Sweden: $38 million over 15 years; South Africa: $20 million over 20 years; Brazil: $20 million over 20 years (pending). See http://www.iffim.org/donors/.

69. The IFFIm *sukuk* was coordinated by Standard Chartered Bank, working with Barwa Bank, CIMB, the National Bank of Abu Dhabi, and NCB Capital Company. http://www.iffim.org/Library/News/Press-releases/2014/International-Finance-Facility -for-Immunisation-issues-first-Sukuk,-raising-US$-500-million/

70. See, for example, Mark Pearson et al., "Evaluation of the International Finance Facility for Immunisation," GAVI, June 2011, http://www.gavi.org/results/evaluations /iffim-evaluation/.

71. IFFIm also funded tactical purchases that helped to prevent 1.4 million deaths from yellow fever, polio, and measles. In addition, dedicated IFFIm funding played a significant role in combating 600,000 cases of meningitis and maternal and neonatal tetanus.

72. In March 2013, Moody's downgraded the IFFIm from Aaa to Aa1, following its downgrade of the UK (IFFIm's largest grantor) from Aaa to Aa1. In December 2014, Fitch also downgraded from AA+ to AA with a stable outlook.

73. "Global Financing Facility Launched with Billions Already Mobilized to End Maternal and Child Mortality by 2030" (press release), World Bank, July 13, 2015, http://www.worldbank.org/en/news/press-release/2015/07/13/global-financing-facility -launched-with-billions-already-mobilized-to-end-maternal-and-child-mortality -by-2030.

74. Daniel Schafer, "Aureos Health Fund Highlights Africa Focus," *Financial Times*, December 11, 2011; see also "Africa Health Fund," Gates Foundation, http://www .gatesfoundation.org/How-We-Work/Quick-Links/Program-Related-Investments /Africa-Health-Fund. Abraaj Capital has stated that it will look to fund greenfield investments and provide growth capital to health-care companies focused on health-care services, retail pharmacies, and the distribution of medical technologies and medicine.

75. Beth Bafford and Sarah Gelfand, "Impact Investing in Global Health: Let's Get Flexible," Stanford Social Innovation Review, April 16, 2015, http://ssir.org/articles /entry/impact_investing_in_global_health_lets_get_flexible. See also Sarah Gelfand and Beth Bafford, "Strengthening Health Systems in Developing Countries Through Private Investment: Lessons from the Global Health Investment Landscaping Project (GHILP)," Calvert Foundation, January 2015, http://www.calvertfoundation.org /storage/documents/GHILP-Final-Deck-Publish-web.pdf. These issues are not unique to health impact investing, but part and parcel of larger industry maturation. See, for example, Matt Bannick and Paula Goldman, "Priming the Pump: The Case for a Sector Based Approach to Impact Investing," Omidyar Network, September 2012, https://www .omidyar.com/insights/priming-pump-case-sector-based-approach-impact-investing; and "From the Margins to the Mainstream: Assessment of the Impact Investment Sector and Opportunities to Engage Mainstream Investors," World Impact Forum, September 2013, http://www3.weforum.org/docs/WEF_II_FromMarginsMainstream_Report _2013.pdf.

## 3. Financial Inclusion and Access to Capital

1. Bindu Ananth, in discussion with the author, April 10, 2015. Unless otherwise indicated in the notes, quotes from Ananth are from this interview.

2. Asli Demirguc-Kunt et al., "The Global Findex Database 2014: Measuring Financial Inclusion Around the World" (policy research work paper, No. 7255, World Bank, Washington, DC, April 2015), http://www-wds.worldbank.org/external/default/WDSContentServer/WDSP/IB/2015/04/15/090224b082dca3aa/1_0/Rendered/PDF/TheoGlobaloFinoionoaroundotheoworld.pdf#page=3. The gender gap is global across income levels. Around the world, 58 percent of women have an account versus 65 percent of men. "Global Financial Development Report: Financial Inclusion 2014," World Bank, https://openknowledge.worldbank.org/bitstream/handle/10986/16238/9780821399859.pdf?sequence=4.

3. "Global Financial Development Report: Financial Inclusion 2014," World Bank.

4. For example, the G20 has endorsed a set of Principles for Financial Inclusion, See http://www.gpfi.org/sites/default/files/documents/G20%20Principles%20for%20Innovative%20Financial%20Inclusion%20-%20AFI%20brochure.pdf.

5. For further discussion, see Georgia Levenson Keohane, *Social Entrepreneurship for the 21st Century* (New York: McGraw-Hill, 2013), chap. 11.

6. For context, the average default rate on consumer loans in the United States since 1987 is 3.7 percent. "Delinquency Rate on Consumer Loans, All Commercial Banks," Federal Reserve Bank of St. Louis, https://research.stlouisfed.org/fred2/series/DRCLACBS.

7. Georgia Levenson Keohane, "Subprime on the Subcontinent: What Can We Learn from the Microcredit Crisis?" *Next New Deal* (blog), June 6, 2011, http://www.nextnewdeal.net/subprime-subcontinent-what-can-we-learn-microcredit-crisis.

8. These include, but are not limited to, Esther Duflo and Abhijit Banerjee, who run the Abdul Latif Jamell Poverty Action Lab at MIT; Rohini Pande of Harvard's Evidence for Policy Design Initiative; Yale's Dean Karlan and Dartmouth's Jonathan Zinman, both of Innovations for Poverty Action; and Jonathan Morduch of New York University and the Financial Access Initiative.

9. These economists have published widely on microfinance and other topics in development economics. Versions of their scholarship and field research are also included in Esther Duflo and Abhijit Banerjee, *Poor Economics: A Radical Rethinking of the Way to Fight Global Poverty* (New York, PublicAffairs, 2012); Dean Karlan and Jacob Appel, *More than Good Intentions, Improving the Ways the World's Poor Borrow, Save, Farm, Learn and Stay Healthy* (New York: Plume, 2012); and Daryl Collins and Jonathan Morduch, *Portfolios of the Poor: How the World's Poor Live on $2 a Day* (Princeton: Princeton University Press, 2010). The *American Economic Journal: Applied Economics* brought much of this research together under one intellectual roof in its January 2015 issue: https://www.aeaweb.org/articles.php?doi=10.1257/app.7.1.

10. "Global Financial Development Report: Financial Inclusion 2014," World Bank.

11. See, for example, "What Is the Impact Insurance Facility?" Impact Insurance, http://www.impactinsurance.org/about/what-is-facility.

12. Karen L. Miller, Chief Knowledge and Communications Officer, Women's World Banking, in conversation with the author, May 14, 2015.

13. Lloyd's estimated that the market for commercially viable microinsurance was 1.5 to 3 billion policies and that an annual growth rate of 10 percent per year could be

expected. Lloyd's also estimated that the current market penetration rate was 5 percent, or approximately 140 million people. http://www.lloyds.com/lloyds/press-centre/archive /2009/11/microinsurance_provides_opportunities_for_all.

14. "Eyes on the Horizon: The Impact Investor Survey," JPMorgan and Global Impact Investing Network, May 4, 2015, https://thegiin.org/assets/documents/pub/2015.04%20 Eyes%20on%20the%20Horizon.pdf.

15. Investors in LeapFrog I included, among others, the Soros Economic Development Fund, Accion, Calvert, the European Investment Bank, JPMorgan, Omidyar Network, the German Federal Ministry for Economic Cooperation and Development, Flagstone Re, Finance for Development, the IFC, KfW, Proparco, TIAA CREFF, Triodos Bank, and the Waterloo Foundation. LeapFrog II includes investment from a broader range of commercial investors and insurance and reinsurance companies, including JPMorgan, AIG, Metlife, Swiss Re, XL, and Prudential.

16. Bindu Ananth, Gregory Chen, and Stephen Rasmussen, "The Pursuit of Complete Financial Inclusion: The KGFS Model in India," Consultative Group to Assist the Poor, 2012, https://www.cgap.org/sites/default/files/CGAP-Forum-The-Pursuit-of-Complete-Financial-Inclusion-The-KGFS-Model-in-India-May-2012.pdf.

17. Ibid.

18. Ibid. See also "The Impact of KGFS in Rural Tamil Nadu: Early Evidence from a Randomised Control Trial," IFMR Trust, April 8, 2014, http://www.ifmr.co.in /blog/2014/04/08/the-impact-of-kgfs-in-rural-tamil-nadu-early-evidence-from-a -randomised-control-trial; and "KGFS: Impact on Lending Patterns," Center for International Development at Harvard University, February 2014. http://www.ifmr.co .in/blog/2014/04/08/the-impact-of-kgfs-in-rural-tamil-nadu-early-evidence-from-a -randomised-control-trial/.

19. Kshama Fernandes, "A Structured Finance Approach to Microfinance," Euromoney Handbooks. http://www.ifmr.co.in/blog/wp-content/uploads/2011/08 /Structured-finance-approach-to-Microfinance.pdf. See also Bindu Ananth and Nachiket Mor, "Finance as Noise Cancelling Headphones," Wall Street Journal, June 24, 2009.

20. "IFMR Launches Country's First Collateral Bond Deal," Times of India, June 24, 2014.

21. Laurence Chandy, Kemal Dervis, and Steven Rocker, "Clicks Into Bricks, Technology Into Transformation, and the Fight Against Poverty," Brookings Institution, 2012, http://www.brookings.edu/~/media/research/files/reports/2013/02/brookings-blum -roundtable/02-brookings-blum-roundtable.pdf.

22. World Bank Development Research Group, Better than Cash Alliance, and Bill and Melinda Gates Foundation, "The Opportunities of Digitizing Payments," Gates Foundation, August 28, 2014, https://docs.gatesfoundation.org/documents/G20%20 Report_Final.pdf. See also "Fighting Poverty Profitably: Transforming the Economics of Payments to Build Sustainable, Inclusive Financial Systems," Gates Foundation, September 2013, https://docs.gatesfoundation.org/Documents/Fighting%20Poverty%20 Profitably%20Full%20Report.pdf.

23. "The Global Findex Database 2014: Measuring Financial Inclusion Around the World," World Bank, April 2015, http://www-wds.worldbank.org/external/default /WDSContentServer/WDSP/IB/2015/04/15/090224b082dca3aa/1_0/Rendered/PDF /TheoGlobaloFinoionoaroundotheoworld.pdf#page=3; "Why Does Kenya Lead the World in Mobile Money," *The Economist Explains* (blog), May 27, 2013, http://www .economist.com/blogs/economist-explains/2013/05/economist-explains-18%20; Eric Forden, "Mobile Money in Kenya," U.S. International Trade Commission, June 2015, https:// www.usitc.gov/publications/332/executive_briefings/forden_mobile_money_kenya _june2015.pdf.

24. James Manyika et al., "Lions Go Digital: The Transformative Power of Technology in Africa," McKinsey Global Institute, November 2013, http://www.mckinsey.com /insights/high_tech_telecoms_internet/lions_go_digital_the_internets_transformative _potential_in_africa.

25. Dayo Olopade, "Africa's Tech Edge," *Atlantic*, May 2014, http://www.theatlantic .com/magazine/archive/2014/05/africas-tech-edge/359808/.

26. In 2015, the Kenyan Treasury launched the M-Akiba bond, a government security Kenyans could purchase directly on their mobile phones via M-Pesa, increasing the country's capital base and Kenyans' investment options. This first mobile money–based treasury bond is a development to watch closely, as it may be a potentially groundbreaking innovation in public finance and policy.

27. "Digital Finance Plus," Consultative Group to Assist the Poor, http://www.cgap .org/topics/digital-finance-plus.

28. "IFC Mobile Money Study 2011," International Finance Corporation, 2011, http:// www.ifc.org/wps/wcm/connect/fad057004a052eb88b23ffdd29332b51/MobileMoney Report-Summary.pdf?MOD=AJPERES.

29. Olopade, "Africa's Tech Edge."

30. Chandy, Dervis, and Rocker, "Clicks Into Bricks," chap. 2.

31. Syed Zain Al-Mahmood, "Mobile Banking Provides Lifeline for Bangladeshis," *Wall Street Journal*, June 23, 2015, http://www.wsj.com/articles/mobile-banking-provides -lifeline-for-bangladeshis-1435043314.

32. Ibid.

33. Ibid.

34. See, for example, "The Future of Finance: Part 1—The Rise of the New Shadow Bank," Goldman Sachs, March 3, 2015; "The Future of Finance: Part 2—Redefining 'The Way We Pay' in the Next Decade," Goldman Sachs, March 10, 2015; and "The Future of Finance: Part 3—The Socialization of Finance," Goldman Sachs, March 13, 2015.

35. Off-grid energy consumers in sub-Saharan Africa spend $100–$220 annually to light their homes.

36. Tilman Ehrbeck, "How Financial Innovation Helps the Poor Improve their Lives," *The Blog*, Huffington Post, May 22, 2013, http://www.huffingtonpost.com/tilman-ehrbeck/how-financial-innovation_b_3321062.html.

37. For example, Off.Grid:Electric installs solar home systems in Tanzania and Rwanda. Its distributed model, called M-Power, allows customers to use PAYG mobile finance.

38. Global Off-Grid Lighting Association, "Delivering Universal Energy Access," September 2015. https://www.gogla.org/wp-content/uploads/2013/09/Delivering-Universal -Energy-Access-The-Industry-Position-on-Building-Off-Grid-Lighting-and-Household -Electrification-Markets.pdf.

39. "Access to Energy via Digital Finance: Overview of Models and Prospects for Innovation," Consultative Group to Assist the Poor, 2014, http://www.cgap.org /publications/access-energy-digital-finance-models-innovation.

40. "Expanding Women's Access to Financial Services," World Bank, February 26, 2014, http://www.worldbank.org/en/results/2013/04/01/banking-on-women-extending -womens-access-to-financial-services.

41. OECD, Vital Voices, and UN Women, "Roundtable on Financing Gender Equality and Women's Empowerment: Summary," OECD, October 14, 2014, http://www.oecd .org/dac/gender-development/Roundtable%20Gender%20Financing%20Summary.pdf.

42. "Diamond Bank Storms the Market: A BETA Way to Save," Women's World Banking, 2014, http://www.womensworldbanking.org/wp-content/uploads/2014/03 /Womens-World-Banking-A-BETA-Way-To-Save.pdf.

43. "Giving Credit Where It Is Due: How Closing the Credit Gap for Women-Owned SMEs Can Drive Global Growth," Goldman Sachs Global Markets Institute, February 2014, http://www.goldmansachs.com/our-thinking/public-policy/gmi-folder /gmi-report-pdf.pdf. See also "Closing the Credit Gap for Formal and Informal Micro, Small and Medium Enterprises," International Finance Corporation, 2013, http://www.ifc.org/wps/wcm/connect/4d6e6400416896c09494b79e78015671/Closing +the+Credit+Gap+Report-FinalLatest.pdf?MOD=AJPERES.

44. "Banking on Women: Changing the Face of the Global Economy," International Finance Corporation, November 2013, http://www.ifc.org/wps/wcm/connect/9be5a0004 1346745b077b8df0d0e71af/BOW+FACT+SHEET+NOV+1+2013.pdf?MOD=AJPERES.

45. Bob Annibale and Elizabeth Littlefield, "A Plan to Empower 100 Million Women," Huffington Post, March 8, 2015, http://www.huffingtonpost.com/elizabeth-l -littlefield/a-plan-to-empower-more-than-one-million-women_b_6818794.html.

46. "Closing the Credit Gap for Formal and Informal Micro, Small and Medium Enterprises."

47. "Global Financial Development Report: Financial Inclusion 2014."

48. "Closing the Credit Gap for Formal and Informal Micro, Small, and Medium Enterprises."

49. Ibid. See also "IFC Enterprise Finance Gap Database," http://financegap.smefi-nanceforum.org/index.html.

50. Matt Bannick, Paula Goldman, and Michael Kubzansky, "Frontier Capital: Early Stage Investing for Financial Returns and Social Impact in Emerging Markets," Omidyar Network, October 2015, https://www.omidyar.com/sites/default/files/file_archive/insights /Frontier%20Capital%20Report%202015/ON_Frontier_Capital_Report_complete_FINAL _single_pp_100515.pdf.

51. JP Morgan and the Global Impact Investing Network, "Eyes on the Horizon," May 4th, 2015.https://thegiin.org/knowledge/publication/eyes-on-the-horizon.

52. See, for example, "From the Margins to the Mainstream: Assessment of the Impact Investment Sector and Opportunities to Engage Mainstream Investors," World Economic Forum, September 2013, http://www3.weforum.org/docs/WEF_II_FromMargins Mainstream_Report_2013.pdf.

53. This isn't just wealthier BRIC countries. Rwanda, for example, has $1 billion in pension funds.

54. infoDev, "Crowdfunding's Potential for the Developing World," World Bank, 2013, http://www.infodev.org/infodev-files/wb_crowdfundingreport-v12.pdf.

55. Thomas Heath, "Capital Buzz: Using Derivatives to Help Small Entrepreneurs," *Washington Post*, April 13, 2014, http://www.washingtonpost.com/business/capitalbusiness /capital-buzz-using-derivatives-to-help-small-entrepreneurs/2014/04/11/0df5fec4-bf44 -11e3-b574-f8748871856a_story.html.

56. Stevens, presentation at the Rockefeller Foundation conference Private Finance for Development: Connecting Supply to Demand, May 18 2015.

57. "Data: Agriculture and Rural Development," World Bank, http://data.worldbank .org/topic/agriculture-and-rural-development. See also "Global Financial Development Report: Financial Inclusion 2014," 141–42.

58. See, for example, the Initiative for Smallholder Finance, http://www .globaldevincubator.org/initiative-incubator/current-initiatives/initiative-for -smallholder-finance/.

59. "Local Bank Financing for Smallholder Farmers: A $9 Billion Drop in the Ocean," Initiative for Smallholder Finance, October 24, 2013, http://www.globaldevincubator .org/smallholderfinance/Initiative_for_Smallholder_Finance_Briefing_1.pdf.

60. "Innovative Agricultural SME Financing Models," Global Partnership for Financial Inclusion and International Finance Corporation, November 2012, http:// www.gpfi.org/sites/default/files/documents/G20%20Innovative%20Agricultural%20 SME%20Finance%20Models.pdf.

61. "Banking on Small-Scale Farmers: The Future of Agriloans?" International Finance Corporation, June 1, 2015, content/regions/sub-saharan+africa/news/za_ifc _access_bank_tanzania.

62. "Lending a Hand: How Direct-to-Farmer Finance Providers Reach Smallholders," Initiative for Smallholder Finance, October 8, 2014, http://www.globaldevincubator .org/wp-content/uploads/2014/10/Lending-a-Hand-How-Direct-to-Farmer-Finance -Providers-Reach-Smallholders.pdf.

63. https://www.oneacrefund.org/blogs/information/post/the-mastercard-foundation -and-one-acre-fund-launch-10-million-partnership/717.

64. See, for example, "Catalyzing Smallholder Agricultural Finance," Dalberg Global Development Advisors, 2012, http://dalberg.com/documents/Catalyzing_Smallholder _Ag_Finance.pdf.

## 4. Toward a New Disaster Finance

1. Gordon Woo, "Fighting Emerging Pandemics with Catastrophe Bonds," *RMS Blog*, January 28, 2015, http://www.rms.com/blog/2015/01/28/fighting-emerging-pandemics-with -catastrophe-bonds/.

2. Joanna Syroka and Richard Wilcox, "Rethinking Disaster Aid Finance," *Journal of International Affairs* 59, no. 2 (Spring/Summer 2006): 197.

3. "Global Humanitarian Assistance Report 2015," Global Humanitarian Assistance, http://www.globalhumanitarianassistance.org/report/gha-report-2015.

4. "The Economic and Human Impact of Disasters in the Last Ten Years," UN Office for Disaster Risk Reduction, 2015, http://www.unisdr.org/files/42862 _economichumanimpact20052014unisdr.pdf.

5. The Future Humanitarian Financing Initiative estimates $532 million for prevention versus $19.4 billion for disaster response. "Humanitarian Assistance in Numbers," Global Humanitarian Assistance, 2013: http://www.globalhumanitarianassistance.org/wp-content /uploads/2013/07/Humanitarian-assistance-in-numbers.pdf. See also, "Looking Beyond the Crisis," Future Humanitarian Financing, 2015, https://futurehumanitarianfinancing .files.wordpress.com/2015/05/fhf_main_report-2.pdf. And "Outcomes of the Interactive Dialogue on Humanitarian Financing," ECOSOC Humanitarian Affairs Segment 22 June 2015. https://futurehumanitarianfinancing.wordpress.com/blog/

6. For example, how we finance disaster response and relief has been on the agenda of the Third UN World Conference on Disaster Risk Reduction in Sendai, Japan; the Third International Conference in Financing for Development in Addis Ababa, Ethiopia; and the Summit for the Adoption of the Post-2015 Development Agenda in New York—and, of course, it will be front and center at the May 2016 World Humanitarian Summit in Istanbul, which falls outside of the formal UN framework.

7. Swiss Re, "Sigma," November 2014. http://www.swissre.com/media/news _releases/nr_20140326_sigma_insured_losses_in_2013.html#inline, Full report available at http://media.swissre.com/documents/sigma1_2014_en.pdf.

8. "R4 Rural Resilience Initiative: January–December 2014," Oxfam America, 2015, http://www.oxfamamerica.org/static/media/files/R4_AR_2014_WEB_2.pdf.

9. "Health and Climate Change: Policy Responses to Protect Public Health," Lancet Commission on Health and Climate Change, 2015, http://www.thelancet.com /commissions/climate-change-2015.

10. Martin Parry et al., "Climate Change and Hunger: Responding to the Challenge," World Food Program, 2009, http://home.wfp.org/stellent/groups/public/documents /newsroom/wfp212536.pdf.

11. This framework builds on the 2005–2015 United Nations Office of Disaster Risk Reduction Hyogo Framework for Action, "Building the Resilience of Nations and Communities to Disaster." See, for example, https://www.unisdr.org/we/inform/publications /1037 and https://www.unisdr.org/we/coordinate/hfa.

12. Syroka and Wilcox, "Rethinking Disaster Aid Finance."

13. Syroka and Wilcox, "Rethinking Disaster Aid Finance," 198.

14. Ibid. Also, Richard Wilcox, presentation at the "Bringing Innovation Back to Innovative Finance," convened by the Rockefeller Foundation, Bellagio Conference Center, Bellagio, Italy, April 2015; and interview with Joanna Syroka June 25, 2015.

15. See, for example, D. Clark and R. Vargas Hill, "Cost-Benefit Analysis of the African Risk Capacity Facility" (discussion paper, No. 01292, International Food Policy Research Institute, Washington, DC, September 2013).

16. Interview with Syroka, June 25 2015.

17. "Drought Triggers ARC Insurance Payout in Sahel Ahead of Humanitarian Aid," PR Newswire, January 22, 2015, http://www.prnewswire.com/news-releases /drought-triggers-insurance-payout-in-sahel-ahead-of-humanitarian-aid-300024479.html.

18. Ibid.

19. Charlie Hamilton, "An African Insurance Outbreak," Africa Report, June 2, 2015, http://www.theafricareport.com/East-Horn-Africa/an-african-insurance-outbreak .html. See also "ARC to Develop Outbreak & Epidemic Insurance for African Sovereigns" (press release), African Risk Capacity, February 3, 2015, http://www.africanriskcapacity .org/documents/350251/844579/PI_Press+Release+Outbreak+Insurance_EN _20142701_v06_FK.pdf.

20. Gillian Tett, "A Little Market Medicine to Prevent the Next Pandemic," Financial Times, January 22, 2015.

21. See, for example "Pandemic Emergency Facility: Frequently Asked Questions," http://www.worldbank.org/en/topic/pandemics/brief/pandemic-emergency-facility -frequently-asked-questions

22. See, for example, Donald G. McNeil, Jr., "Promise Is Seen in an Inexpensive Cholera Vaccine," New York Times, July 8, 2015, http://www.nytimes.com/2015/07/09 /health/promise-is-seen-in-an-inexpensive-cholera-vaccine.html?_r=0.

23. Adapted from Georgia Levenson Keohane, "Preparing for Disaster by Betting Against It," New York Times, February 12, 2015.

24. See, for example, Erwann Michel-Kerjan, "How Terror-Proof Is Your Economy?" Nature 514, no. 7522 (October 16, 2014): 275; and Howard Kunreuther et al., "TRIA After 2014: Risk Sharing Under Current and Alternative Designs," Wharton School, University of Pennsylvania, July 30, 2014, http://opim.wharton.upenn.edu/risk /library/TRIA-after-2014_full-report_WhartonRiskCenter.pdf.

25. See, for example, J. D. Cummins and O. Mahul, "Catastrophe Risk Financing in Developing Countries: Principles for Public Intervention," World Bank, 2009, http://siteresources.worldbank.org/FINANCIALSECTOR/Resources/CATRISKbook.pdf.

26. "World Bank Issues Its First Ever Catastrophe Bond Linked to Natural Hazard Risks in Sixteen Caribbean Countries" (press release), World Bank, June 2014, http:// treasury.worldbank.org/cmd/htm/FirstCatBondLinkedToNaturalHazards.html.

27. "First China Cat Bond, Panda Re 2015-1, Raises $50m for China Re," Artemis (blog), July 1, 2015, http://www.artemis.bm/blog/2015/07/01/first-china-cat-bond-panda -re-2015-1-raises-50m-for-china-re/.

28. "India Explores Catastrophe Bonds for Nuclear Liability Issue," Artemis (blog), January 23, 2015, http://www.artemis.bm/blog/2015/01/23/india-explores-catastrophe-bonds -for-nuclear-liability-issue/.

29. See "Catastrophe Bonds & ILS Issued and Outstanding by Year," Artemis, http://www.artemis.bm/deal_directory/cat_bonds_ils_issued_outstanding.html; and "Perilous Paper: Bonds That Pay Out When Disaster Strikes Are Rising in Popularity," *Economist*, October 5, 2013, http://www.economist.com/news/finance-and-economics/21587229-bonds-pay-out-when-catastrophe-strikes-are-rising-popularity-perilous-paper.

30. Keohane, "Preparing for Disaster by Betting Against It." The quote is from an interview conducted in preparing the article.

31. Felipe Ossa, "Snow Bank: Boston Takes Another Look at Catastrophe Bonds," *Structured Finance News*, March 25, 2015.

32. Patrick Gillespie, "Blizzard Mania Costs U.S. Over $1 Billion," CNN, February 16, 2015, http://money.cnn.com/2015/02/16/news/economy/boston-blizzard-2015-cost-economy/.

33. In development, it is a widely held belief that donors should not directly subsidize or pay the premiums for insurance recipients. In developed countries—in particular, the United States—premium subsidy happens on a wide scale. However, most insurance experts argue that in poor countries, where insurance markets are underdeveloped, premium sharing, rather than subsidy, is preferable. Although some invoke the moral hazard argument—the idea, in this case, that when someone else pays the premium, it can lead to risky behavior on the part of the beneficiary—most of the argument has to do with pool size and risk portfolio: that is, subsidizing or paying the premium keeps the pool small. Therein lies the importance of HARITA's labor-for-premium scheme, which is not considered a subsidy but rather provides a way to pay for premiums with productive work activities. Similar trades have been tested elsewhere, including by the World Food Program, which employs a food-for-assets design for its resilience-building initiatives.

34. The four pillars of R4 include risk transfer, risk reduction, prudent risk taking, and risk reserves.

35. "R4 Rural Resilience Initiative: January–March 2015," Oxfam America, 2015, http://www.oxfamamerica.org/static/media/files/R4_Rep_Jan_Mar15_WEB_8june_1.pdf.

36. In 2007, the Kenya FinAccess survey found that 69 percent of Kenyans believed insurance was generally unaffordable (FinAccess, 2007). Whereas the cost of general insurance is perceived as high, the actual cost of agricultural insurance is indeed high: insurance is expensive when extreme weather events happen every ten years.

37. Although insurance and reinsurance firms like Swiss Re cover what they describe as "man-made" hazards—things like fires, train derailments, oil spills, terrorist attacks, and the nebulous category of "political unrest"—we refer here more to the human emergencies caused by conflict and persecution.

38. This definition of humanitarian aid is set out in "Principles and Good Practice of Humanitarian Donorship," International Federation of the Red Cross and Red Crescent Societies, June 17, 2003, http://www.ifrc.org/Docs/idrl/I267EN.pdf.

39. See, for example, "Looking Beyond the Crisis."

40. "World at War: Global Trends: Forced Displacement in 2014," Office of the United Nations High Commissioner for Refugees, June 2015, http://unhcr.org/556725e69 .html.

41. "Global Humanitarian Assistance Report 2015."

42. Chloe Stirk, "Humanitarian Assistance from Non-state Donors: What Is It Worth?" Global Humanitarian Assistance, 2014, http://www.globalhumanitarianassistance.org /report/humanitarian-assistance-non-state-donors.

43. Somini Sengupta, "60 Million People Fleeing Chaotic Lands, U.N. Says," New York Times, June 18, 2015.

44. "Global Humanitarian Assistance Report 2015."

45. Don Murray, "World Faces Major Crisis As Number of Displaced Hits Record High," Office of the United Nations High Commissioner for Refugees, June 18, 2015, http://www.unhcr.org/5582c2f46.html.

46. "Global Humanitarian Assistance Report 2015."

47. Chloe Stirk, "An Act of Faith: Humanitarian Financing and Zakat," Global Humanitarian Assistance, March 2015, http://www.globalhumanitarianassistance.org /wp-content/uploads/2015/03/ONLINE-Zakat_report_V9a.pdf.

48. There are two types of pooled funds: the Central Emergency Response Fund, which is 45 percent of all pooled funds, and Country-Based Pooled Funds, made up of Emergency Response Funds and Common Humanitarian Funds.

49. "The CBHA Early Response Fund (ERF)," Global Humanitarian Assistance, October 30, 2012, http://www.globalhumanitarianassistance.org/the-cbha-early-response -fund-erf-3892.html.

50. "Looking Beyond the Crisis."

51. Sarah Bailey and Paul Harvey, "Cash Transfer Program and the Humanitarian System: Background Note for the High Level Panel on Humanitarian Cash Transfers," Overseas Development Institute, March 2015, http://www.odi.org/sites/odi.org.uk/files /odi-assets/publications-opinion-files/9592.pdf.

52. Sarah Bailey and Paul Harvey, "State of Evidence on Humanitarian Cash Transfers," Overseas Development Institute, March 2015, http://www.odi.org/sites/odi.org.uk /files/odi-assets/publications-opinion-files/9591.pdf.

53. Arif Husain, Jean-Martin Bauer, and Susanna Sandström, "Economic Impact Study: Direct and Indirect Impact of the WFP Food Voucher Programme in Jordan," World Food Program, April 2014, http://documents.wfp.org/stellent/groups/public /documents/ena/wfp264168.pdf.

54. Sarah Bailey, "Background Summary: High Level Panel on Humanitarian Cash Transfers" (unpublished working paper, March 2015). See also Bailey and Harvey, "State of Evidence on Humanitarian Cash Transfers." March 2015.

55. "Global Humanitarian Assistance Report 2015."

56. Ibid.

57. The Office of the United Nations High Commissioner for Refugees estimates there are 1.5 million Syrian refugees in Lebanon; the Lebanese put that estimate closer to 2 million.

58. "Lebanon: Overview," World Bank, 2015, http://www.worldbank.org/en/country /lebanon/overview.

59. Alia Farhat, "Rebuilding in Crisis Environments" (webinar), Women's World Banking, May 21, 2015, http://www.slideshare.net/womensworldbanking/rebuilding -in-crisis-environments-experiences-from-financial-institutions-webinar (summary available at http://www.womensworldbanking.org/news/blog/6-ways-financial-institutions -can-help-clients-cope-with-crisis/).

60. See, for example, Saumitra Jha, "Can Financial Innovations Mitigate Civil and Ethnic Conflict?" *World Financial Review*, March 14, 2013.

61. http://www.economicprosperityforpeace.org/#!media/c1pcx.

62. Carl J. Schramm, "Expeditionary Economics: Spurring Growth After Conflict and Disaster," *Foreign Affairs*, May/June 2010.

## 5. Innovative Finance in Communities Across the United States

1. For a longer discussion of the evolution of the community development field, see Georgia Levenson Keohane, *Social Entrepreneurship for the 21st Century* (New York: McGraw-Hill, 2013), chap. 12.

2. See, for example, Michael Barr, "Credit Where It Counts: The Community Reinvestment Act and Its Critics," *New York University Law Review* 80 (2005): 513.

3. Importantly, CRA-regulated banks made many fewer bad and subprime loans to low-income borrowers than did their unregulated counterparts. See, for example, Kevin Park, "Subprime Lending and the Community Reinvestment Act," Joint Center for Housing Studies, Harvard University, November 2008, http://www.jchs.harvard.edu /sites/jchs.harvard.edu/files/n08-2_park.pdf. See also "The CRA and Subprime Lending: Discerning the Difference," Federal Reserve Bank of Dallas, 2009, https://www .dallasfed.org/assets/documents/cd/bcp/2009/bcp0901.pdf; Testimony of Chairman Ben S. Bernanke at the Federal Reserve System's Sixth Biennial Community Affairs Research Conference, Washington, D.C. April 17, 2009, Financial Innovation and Consumer Protection," http://www.federalreserve.gov/newsevents/speech/bernanke20090417a.htm; and Paul Krugman, "Armey of Ignorance," *New York Times*, November 10, 2009.

4. Terri Ludwig, "Pay for Success: Building on 25 Years of Experience with the Low Income Housing Tax Credit," *Community Development Investment Review* 9, no. 1 (April 2013), http://www.frbsf.org/community-development/files/review-volume-9 -issue-1.pdf.

5. See, for example, Arthur I. Segel and Nicolas P. Retsinas, *Affordable Housing and Low-Income Tax Credits in the United States* (Harvard Business School Case No. 9-214-107) (Cambridge, MA: Harvard Business Publishing, April 30, 2015). See also "The Low Income Housing Tax Credit Program at Year 25: A Current Look at Its Performance," Reznick Group, 2011, http://www.cohnreznick.com/sites/default/files/reznickgroup_lihtc _survey_2011.pdf.

6. See, for example, Barry Zigas, "Learning from the Low Income Housing Tax Credit: Building a New Social Investment Model," *Community Development Investment*

*Review* 9, no. 1 (April 2013), http://www.frbsf.org/community-development/files/review-volume-9-issue-1.pdf.

7. "The State of the Nation's Housing," Joint Center for Housing Studies, Harvard University, 2015, http://www.jchs.harvard.edu/research/state_nations_housing.

8. Ibid.

9. See, for example, Monica Potts, "The Post-Ownership Society," *Washington Monthly*, June/July/August 2015, http://www.washingtonmonthly.com/magazine/junejulyaugust_2015/features/the_postownership_society055896.php?page=all#.

10. "The Community Reinvestment Act and Its Effect on Housing Tax Credit Policy," CohnReznick, 2013, http://www.cohnreznick.com/sites/default/files/CohnReznick_CRAStudy.pdf.

11. "CRA Commitments," National Community Reinvestment Coalition, September 2007, http://community-wealth.org/sites/clone.community-wealth.org/files/downloads/report-silver-brown.pdf.

12. See, for example, Harold Pettigrew and David Newville, "Are Nonbank Lenders Good for Small Businesses?" Corporation for Enterprise Development, October 20, 2015, http://cfed.org/blog/inclusiveeconomy/are_nonbank_lenders_good_for_small_businesses/.

13. Michael Sherraden, *Assets and the Poor: New American Welfare Policy* (New York: Routledge, 1992).

14. "2013 National Survey of Unbanked and Underbanked Households," Federal Deposit Insurance Corporation, 2014, https://www.fdic.gov/householdsurvey/2013execsumm.pdf.

15. Federal Deposit Insurance Corporation, *National Survey of Unbanked and Underbanked Households* (Washington, DC: FDIC, December 2009). See also "A Phoneful of Dollars," *Economist*, November 15, 2014, http://www.economist.com/news/briefing/21632441-worlds-poor-need-stability-and-security-banks-have-traditionally-offered.

16. "Payday Lending Basics," Center for Responsible Lending, http://www.responsiblelending.org/payday-lending/tools-resources/payday-lending-basics.html.

17. "Financial Health Opportunity in Dollars and Cents," Center for Financial Services Innovation, December 2015, http://www.cfsinnovation.com/CMSPages/GetFile.aspx?guid=47ad4f2b-70d3-4147-8e1c-2a50e84e081f.

18. Center for Financial Services Innovation, *CFSI Underbanked Consumer Study* (Chicago: CFSI, June 2008). An estimated 42 percent of financially underserved households face challenges accessing traditional forms of credit because of insufficient credit history.

19. Reid Cramer and Trina R. Williams Shankes, eds., *The Assets Building Perspective: The Rise of Asset Building and Its Impact on Social Policy* (New York: Palgrave Macmillan, 2014). See also Suzanne Mettler, *The Submerged State* (Chicago: University of Chicago, 2011); and Jacob Hacker and Paul Pierson, *Winner Take All Politics* (New York: Simon and Schuster, 2011).

20. Jennifer Tescher, "Household and Community Financial Stability: Essential and Interconnected," in Federal Reserve Bank of San Francisco and Low Income Investment Fund, *Investing in What Works for America's Communities: Essays on People, Place and*

*Purpose* (San Francisco: Low Income Investment Fund, 2012). See also "Children's Savings Accounts Expand Opportunity," Corporation for Enterprise Development, January 2014, http://cfed.org/assets/pdfs/Policy_Brief_-_CSAs.pdf; and "Rebuilding American Success: Savings and Financial Security for All," Corporation for Enterprise Development, April 2013, http://cfed.org/assets/pdfs/PolicyMemo_April2013_3.pdf.

21. Indeed, Social Security is arguably the most effective antipoverty tool in U.S. history. It is a savings and retirement program that keeps millions of seniors, as well as children and persons with disabilities, out of poverty each year. In the United States and across the developed world, there are fewer young people to support the growing number of retirees, making it impossible to sustain the replacement rate of 35 percent of a typical family's income and leaving a tremendous gap that cannot be filled by the savings of the average American household. This means Americans will have to work longer, save more, and/or invest their retirement savings in riskier investments. This is an area ripe for innovative finance.

22. Anthony Hannagan and Jonathan Morduch, "Income Gains and Month-to-Month Income Volatility: Household Evidence from the US Financial Diaries," U.S. Financial Diaries, March 16, 2015, http://www.usfinancialdiaries.org/paper-1/.

23. See, for example, "Policy Basics: The Earned Income Tax Credit," Center on Budget and Policy Priorities, January 20, 2015, http://www.cbpp.org/research/policy-basics-the-earned-income-tax-credit.

24. The program is also limited to people with children, although a pilot program in New York City is testing the EITC for those without children.

25. For example, the Kellogg Foundation recently made grants to organizations in Maine, Michigan, New Mexico, Virginia, and Arizona to expand an EITC rapid response, create a pooled fund, and build larger public support from state EITCs.

26. For more on the political failures related to pay-for-success and social impact bonds, see Georgia Levenson Keohane, *Can Social Impact Bonds Unlock Private Money for Public Goods? Innovation in Pay-for-Success and Social Finance* (New York: Roosevelt Institute, August 5, 2013). See also Keohane, *Social Entrepreneurship for the 21st Century*, chap. 17.

27. "MDRC Statement on the Vera Institute's Study of the Adolescent Behavioral Learning Experience (ABLE) Program at Rikers Island," MDRC, July 2, 2015, http://www.mdrc.org/news/announcement/mdrc-statement-vera-institute-s-study-adolescent-behavioral-learning-experience. See also Eduardo Porter, "Wall Street Money Meets Social Policy at Rikers Island," *New York Times*, July 28, 2015, http://www.nytimes.com/2015/07/29/business/economy/wall-st-money-meets-social-policy-at-rikers-island.html?ref=topics&_r=0; John Rowman, "Putting Evidence First: Learning from the Rikers Island Social Impact Bond," Huffington Post, July 13, 2015, http://www.huffingtonpost.com/john-roman-phd/putting-evidence-first-le_b_7738994.html; and Steven Godeke and William Burckhart, "Can Capitalism Keep People Out of Prison," Quartz, July 10, 2015, http://qz.com/435182/social-impact-bonds-catalytic-or-just-conversation/.

28. In Goldman's second SIB deal in Utah, philanthropist J. B. Pritzker provided a subordinated loan of up to $2.4 million to reduce the risk for Goldman, which came in with $4.6 million. In the 2014 New York State deal, the Rockefeller Foundation offered

a $1.3 million guarantee for nonphilanthropic investors' principal. See, for example, Emily Gustafsson-Wright, Sophie Gardiner, and Vidya Putcha, "The Potential and Limitations of Impact Bonds: Lessons from the First Five Years of Experience Worldwide," Brookings Institution, July 2015, http://www.brookings.edu/~/media/Research /Files/Reports/2015/07/social-impact-bonds-potential-limitations/Impact-Bondsweb .pdf?la=en.

29. These intermediaries—some new and some long-standing in the fields of community and economic development, nonprofit capacity building, research, knowledge building, policy formation, and cross-sector partnerships—include, but are not limited to, Social Finance; Third Sector Capital Partners; New Profits, Inc.; the Nonprofit Finance Fund; the Case Foundation; the Center for American Progress; the Harvard Kennedy School's Social Impact Bond Technical Assistance Lab (SIB Lab); Twin Cities Rise; MDRC; the Vera Institute of Justice; the Urban Institute; Living Cities; the Corporation for Supportive Housing; the National Council on Crime and Delinquency; the Green and Healthy Homes Initiative; the Institute for Child Success; the University of Utah; and Instiglio. For more on the role of philanthropy in the SIB ecosystem, see, for example, "Foundations for Social Impact Bonds: How and Why Philanthropy Is Catalyzing the Development of a New Market," Social Finance, 2014.

30. "Ending the Rikers Nightmare," New York Times, June 24, 2015, http://www .nytimes.com/2015/06/24/opinion/ending-the-rikers-nightmare.html?ref=topics. See also Neil Barksy, "Shut Down Rikers Island," New York Times, July 17, 2015.

31. Eileen Neely, a seasoned community development finance investor and the director of capital innovation at Living Cities, explains the change in mindset and investment thesis when moving from traditional community development finance to pay-for-success. Typically, she says, community development finance requires assessing 4Cs: character, collateral, capacity, and capital. Because, in a SIB, collateral and capital are either absent or entirely different, the new paradigm evaluates and relies on 4Ps: partnerships, program, policy, and process. See Eileen Neely and Andy Rachlin, "From the 4Cs of Credit to the 4Ps of Pay for Success," Living Cities, March 18, 2015, https:// www.livingcities.org/blog/798-from-the-4-cs-of-credit-to-the-4-ps-of-pay-for-success.

32. Clayton Christensen and Michael E. Raynor, The Innovator's Solution (Cambridge, MA: Harvard Business School, 2003).

33. The costs are high and known on both an aggregate and a per capita basis. In connection with its work on SIBs, McKinsey estimated that high prisoner recidivism drives corrections spending to approximately $70 billion per year in the United States, which also spends $6-$7 billion a year on remedial services for the homeless. "From Potential to Action: Bringing Social Impact Bonds to the U.S.," McKinsey & Company, May 2012, http://mckinseyonsociety.com/downloads/reports/Social-Innovation/McKinsey _Social_Impact_Bonds_Report.pdf.

34. Ibid.

35. At the time of this writing, preliminary results from the Goldman Sachs early childhood SIB in Utah have come in. Some concerns concerns have been raised about the quality of the data, some suggesting that the evaluations are "too good to be true." See, for example, Nathaniel Popper, "Success Metrics Questioned in School Program Funded

by Goldman," *New York Times*, November 3, 2015, http://www.nytimes.com/2015/11/04/business/dealbook/did-goldman-make-the-grade.html?_r=0.

36. Childhood Asthma Leadership Coalition and Green & Healthy Homes Initiative, "Issue Brief: Using Social Impact Financing to Improve Asthma Outcomes," Green and Healthy Homes, October 2014, http://www.greenandhealthyhomes.org/sites/default/files/Social-Impact-Financing-Asthma_CALC_10.14.14.pdf.

37. These findings from the U.S. Department of Health and Human Services are reported in D. D. Crocker et al., "Effectiveness of Home-Based, Multi-trigger, Multicomponent Interventions with an Environmental Focus for Reducing Asthma Morbidity: A Community Guide Systematic Review," *American Journal of Preventive Medicine* 41, no. 2, supp. 1 (2011): S5–S32.

38. "Investing in Social Outcomes: Development Impact Bonds," Development Impact Working Group, 2013, http://international.cgdev.org/sites/default/files/investing-in-social-outcomes-development-impact-bonds.pdf.

39. Emily Gustafsson-Wright, Sophie Gardiner, and Vidya Putcha, "The Potential and Limitations of Impact Bonds: Lessons from the First Five Years of Experience Worldwide," Brookings Institution, July 2015, http://www.brookings.edu/~/media/Research/Files/Reports/2015/07/social-impact-bonds-potential-limitations/Impact-Bondsweb.pdf?la=en.

40. See, for example, Amartya Sen, "Why Health Equity?" *Health Economics* 11, no. 8 (2002): 659–66. See also Jodi Halpern and Douglas Jutte, "The Ethics of Pay for Success," *Community Development Investment Review* 9, no. 1 (April 2013), http://www.frbsf.org/community-development/files/review-volume-9-issue-1.pdf.

41. See, for example, Christian Henrichson, Joshua Rinaldi and Ruth Delaney, "The Price of Jails: Measuring the Taxpayer Cost of Local Incarceration," Vera Institute of Justice, May 21, 2015, http://www.vera.org/sites/default/files/resources/downloads/price-of-jails.pdf; and John K. Roman et al., "Pay for Success and Social Impact Bonds: Funding the Infrastructure for Evidence Based Change," Urban Institute Justice Policy Center, June 2014, http://www.urban.org/sites/default/files/alfresco/publication-pdfs/413150-Pay-for-Success-and-Social-Impact-Bonds-Funding-the-Infrastructure-for-Evidence-Based.PDF.

42. See, for example, Peter Orszag, "Memorandum for the Heads of Executive Departments and Agencies: Increased Emphasis on Program Evaluations," Executive Office of the President, Office of Management and Budget, October 7, 2009, https://www.whitehouse.gov/sites/default/files/omb/assets/memoranda_2010/m10-01.pdf. See also Office of Management and Budget, "Paying for Success," 2012, https://www.whitehouse.gov/omb/factsheet/paying-for-success.

43. "Bennet, Hatch Introduce Social Impact Partnership Bill," April 28, 2015, http://www.bennet.senate.gov/?p=release&id=3323.

44. Michele Jolin, editor, *Moneyball for Government* (Disruption Books, November 2014). See also Moneyballforgov.com.

45. "Funding for Results: How Governments Can Pay for Outcomes," Beeck Center, November 2014, http://static1.squarespace.com/static/54418805e4b015161ccb0b27/t/55ad047de4b0eff766fb1420/1437402274532/May+2015+Funding+for+Results.pdf.

46. Part of the conceptual innovation that fuses place- and people-centered development involves the recognition that decent and affordable housing, although a vital human need and public good, is not sufficient by itself for a family's or neighborhood's well-being. Accordingly, in recent years, we have seen a renewed commitment to integrated and holistic community development approaches, which, in effect, combine housing with things like health or education needs. For example, Harlem's Children Zone, which concentrates on a section of Harlem that extends from 116th to 124th Street, offers a full range of educational and other services—including prenatal education, early childhood education, charter schools, and other K–12 supports—and serves as the model for the Obama administration's Promise Neighborhoods. In Boston, the Codman Square Health Center in the Dorchester neighborhood centers community development through health; Codman is a major medical facility focused on the physical and social well-being of the community and, in addition to medical care, includes an array of adult and youth education programs and other services. Similarly, the Annie E. Casey Foundation's Rebuilding Communities Initiative, Enterprise Community Partners' Neighborhood Transformation Initiative, the Ford Foundation's Neighborhood and Family Initiative, Living Cities' Integration Initiative, and LISC's Building Sustainable Communities Initiative are among a number of foundations and community development intermediaries promoting holistic efforts to address the needs of poor communities and their residents. Even though these initiatives have been successful in garnering philanthropic support, it is harder for them to attract the kind of commercial capital that flows to physical assets.

47. The Affordable Care Act, by insuring substantially more people (many in low-income communities), has created the need for more health centers, particularly in underserved neighborhoods. See, for example, Eric S. Belsky and Jennifer Fauth, "Crossing Over to an Improved Era of Community Development," in Federal Reserve Bank of San Francisco and Low Income Investment Fund, *Investing in What Works for American Communities* San Francisco: Low Income Investment Fund 2012), 72. Belsky and Fauth estimate that investments totaling as much as $16 billion will be needed for new community health centers.

48. Half of all Bay Area households spend more than 30 percent of their income on housing costs, a proportion substantially higher than the national average. To afford housing, Bay Area residents must travel farther to get to work, as many jobs have moved away from city centers. The number of Bay Area commuters traveling more than 45 minutes to work is the second highest in the nation. The dual burden of housing and transit is even heavier for lower-income families. Bay Area households earning $20,000–$50,000 spend 63 percent of their household budgets on the combined costs of housing and transportation, the highest percentage in the country. See, for example, http://bayareatod.com.

49. Ben Hecht, "From Community to Prosperity," in Federal Reserve Bank of California and Low Income Investment Fund, *Investing in What Works for America's Communities: Essays on People, Place and Purpose* (San Francisco: Low Income Investment Fund, 2012), 194.

50. Amy Chung and Jed Emerson, "From Grants to Groundbreaking: Unlocking Impact Investments," ImpactAssets and Living Cities, December 2014, https://www .livingcities.org/blog/198-aligning-grants-with-impact-investments-can-help-catalyze-the-growing-impact-investing-field.

## Conclusion

1. Gordon Woo, "Fighting Emerging Pandemics With Catastrophe Bonds," RMS blog January 28th 2015. http://www.rms.com/blog/2015/01/28/fighting-emerging -pandemics-with-catastrophe-bonds/.

2. "Drought Triggers ARC Insurance Payout in Sahel Ahead of Humanitarian Aid," PR Newswire, January 22, 2015, http://www.prnewswire.com/news-releases/drought -triggers-insurance-payout-in-sahel-ahead-of-humanitarian-aid-300024479.html.

3. Fifty percent of the vaccinations IFFIm funds take place in Islamic countries. Recall that a *sukuk* is an Islamic equivalent of a bond that is consistent with Sharia principles, which technically prohibit the charging or payment of interest. Unlike a conventional bond, which confers ownership of debt, a sukuk technically grants the investor a share of the asset, along with the commensurate cash flows and risks. This IFFIm sukuk was coordinated by Standard Chartered Bank, working with Barwa Bank, CIMB, the National Bank of Abu Dhabi, and NCB Capital Company.

## Epilogue

1. In the developing world, evidence shows that one year of primary schooling boosts wages by 5–15 percent and that each year of secondary education increases wages by up to 15 percent. Nicholas Burnett and Desmond Bermingham, "Innovative Financing for Education" (working paper, No. 5, Open Society Institute, Education Support Program, New York, 2010). In the United States, investments in early childhood education for low-income children have an estimated return of $7 to $1. The net present value of one high school graduate yields a public benefit of $209,000. Henry Levin et al., *The Costs and Benefits of an Excellent Education for All of America's Children* (New York: Teachers College, Columbia University, 2006).

2. D. Capital Partners, "Impact Investing in Education: An Overview of the Current Landscape" (working paper, No. 59, Open Society Institute, Education Support Program, New York, 2013). See also Burnett and Bermingham, "Innovative Financing for Education"; and "Data Indicators," World Bank, http://data.worldbank.org/indicator.

3. Innovative Finance Foundation, "Innovative Financing for Global Education" (working paper, No. 58, Open Society Institute, Education Support Program, New York, 2013).

4. Martin Igoe, "Wanted: the 'Bill Gates for Education,'" Devex 23 June 2015. https:// www.devex.com/news/wanted-the-bill-gates-for-education-86397.

5. Douglas Belkin, "More College Students Selling Stock in Themselves," *Wall Street Journal*, August 5, 2015, http://www.wsj.com/articles/more-college-students-selling -stockin-themselves-1438791977.

6. Rosabeth Moss Kanter, "Why Can't We Move?" *Harvard Magazine*, July–August 2015, 43; and *Move: Putting America's Infrastructure Back in the Lead* (New York: Norton, 2015).

7. Richard Dobbs at al., *Infrastructure Productivity: How to Save $1 Trillion a Year* (New York: McKinsey Global Institute, 2013).

8. See, for example, Tyler Duvall, Alastair Green, and Mike Kerlin, "Making the Most of a Wealth of Infrastructure Finance," McKinsey and Company, June 2015, http://www.mckinsey.com/insights/infrastructure/making_the_most_of_a_wealth _of_infrastructure_finance.

9. From text of Schwartz's presentation at the Rockefeller Foundation Conference, "Investor and Policy Lab on Private Finance for Development: Connecting Supply to Demand," May 2015.

10. Barbara Samuels, in text of a presentation: "Connecting Demand and Supply: Building Local Infrastructure Marketplaces for Sustainable Development Results," Global Clearinghouse for Development Finance. Investor and Policy Lab on Private Finance for Development: Connecting Supply to Demand. Rockefeller Foundation, May 18, 2015.

# INDEX